THE SOCIALIST AGENDA

The
Socialist Agenda
Crosland's Legacy

Edited by David Lipsey
and Dick Leonard

JONATHAN CAPE
THIRTY BEDFORD SQUARE LONDON

First published 1981
Copyright © 1981 David Lipsey and Dick Leonard
Jonathan Cape, 30 Bedford Square, London WC1

British Library Cataloguing in Publication Data
The socialist agenda.
1. Crosland, Anthony
2. Political science—Great Britain—History
—20th century
3. Socialism in Great Britain
I. Lipsey, David   II. Leonard, Dick
320'.01   JC257.C/
ISBN 0-224-01886-8

Printed in Great Britain by
Butler & Tanner Ltd, Frome and London

Contents

Introduction

by David Lipsey and Dick Leonard

This book is dedicated to the memory of Anthony Crosland, socialist thinker and Labour Cabinet Minister, who died in 1977 at the age of fifty-eight. But not only to his memory, for the common thread that links the authors, besides their attachment to the man himself, is a belief that the political philosophy of which Anthony Crosland was the leading post-war exponent deserves to live on. Like all political faiths, it needs to be adapted to new times, new times which in this case are also more difficult times. It is a tragedy for millions besides his friends that he himself is no longer alive to carry on the constant process of revision and reassessment that took up so much of his life.

That tragedy is reflected in the present eclipse of much of what he stood for. But the fundamentals of Croslandism are robust enough to withstand the quirks of political fashion. His brand of radical humanitarianism, his creed of equality with liberty, still contain the seeds of a rich harvest. If this book helps some of them to germinate, it will have fulfilled its purpose.

The authors write as individuals; no attempt has been made to achieve a consensus amongst them, for we wish to reopen and not to close a debate. The book falls into four parts. In part 1, to set the scene, we reproduce two contemporary tributes to Crosland – Dick Leonard's piece from *The Economist*, and Lord Donaldson's address at the Westminster Abbey Memorial Service, delivered by him but prepared in collaboration with his wife, Frances.

In part 2, David Lipsey attempts a synoptic view, summarising where Crosland himself stood and discussing some of the main criticisms which have been levelled against his position. He argues that revisionism has not failed; it has never been tried.

Dick Leonard concentrates on a question about which Crosland was himself much concerned: namely what the Labour party's attitude should be towards the electors on whose support it depends. He argues that the party has consistently taken too little account of the known views and prejudices of the bulk of actual and potential Labour voters. This cavalier attitude, he suggests, has seriously reduced the opportunities for securing the election of Labour governments able, if they so choose, to put Croslandite philosophy into practice.

Part 3 addresses the central economic question: can Crosland's belief that non-inflationary growth is not only desirable but attainable still stand in the post-OPEC circumstances of modern Britain? In particular, can it be made compatible with the facts of modern trade union power? Here, there is a conflict between those who (like I. M. D. Little) believe that a precondition of success is an end to that power; those who (with Professor James Meade) take the view that the power of the trade unions must be radically redirected to quite different objectives; and those who (like Giles Radice and William McCarthy) advocate reforms which lie within the established 'social contract' approach.

Part 4 considers the relevance in modern conditions of certain aspects of Croslandism. Thus, Professor Raymond Plant discusses the present state of the case made out in *The Future of Socialism* for equality; Colin Crouch, the debate on public spending; Professor Maurice Peston, the challenge from the Right to Crosland's thesis that democratic socialism and liberty are natural bedfellows; and Tyrrell Burgess contributes a modern perspective in the crucial field of education.

The authors wish to thank the executive of the Fabian Society (to which the proceeds from this book will go) for their help and encouragement; to the staff of the Society for work beyond the call of duty on the mundane tasks associated with producing a book of this character; to the Society's readers, Brian Abel-Smith, Stephen Brooks and Sandra Melville, for their comments; and in particular to Dianne Hayter, the Society's General Secretary, for her patient tolerance as well as her help. Others to whom the authors owe a debt, either individually or collectively, include Susan Crosland, Philip Williams (David Lipsey) and David Heald, Tom Richardson and Joan Crouch (Colin Crouch). As will be evident to the reader, the biggest debt of all is to Anthony Crosland himself.

Just as the chapters are the author's own, so is the blame for their shortcomings. For the shortcomings of the book as a whole, the buck stops with the editors.

October 1980

Anthony Crosland:
A Chronology

1918   Born 29 August, in St Leonard's-on-Sea, son of Joseph Beardsel Crosland, civil servant, and Jessie Crosland, university lecturer in French

1929–37   Attended Highgate School

1937–40   Scholar of Trinity College, Oxford

1940–45   Service in Royal Welch Fusiliers and Parachute Regiment, rising from fusilier to captain. Served in North Africa, Italy, France and Austria.

1946   Returned to Oxford. First class degree in Philosophy, Politics and Economics. Chairman, Oxford University Democratic Socialist Club; President, Oxford Union.

1947–50   Fellow and lecturer in Economics, Trinity College, Oxford

1950–55   MP for South Gloucestershire

1952   First marriage, to Hilary Anne Sarson (dissolved 1957)

1953   *Britain's Economic Problem*

1956   *The Future of Socialism*

1956–58   Secretary of Independent Commission of Inquiry into the Co-operative Movement

1959–77   MP for Grimsby

1961–62   Chairman of Fabian Society

1962   *The Conservative Enemy*

1964   Second marriage, to Susan Barnes

1964–65   Minister of State for Economic Affairs

1965–67   Secretary of State for Education and Science

1967–69   President of the Board of Trade

1969–70   Secretary of State for Local Government and Regional Planning

1970–74   Shadow Environment Secretary

1972   Contested deputy leadership of Labour Party

1974–76   Secretary of State for the Environment

1974   *Socialism Now and other essays*

1976   Contested Labour Party leadership

1976–77   Secretary of State for Foreign and Commonwealth Affairs

1977   Died, at Oxford, 19 February

A Crosland Bibliography

Books by Anthony Crosland

1953 *Britain's Economic Problem*
1956 *The Future of Socialism*
1962 *The Conservative Enemy*
1974 *Socialism Now and other essays*

Books to which he was a substantial contributor

1952 *New Fabian Essays*
1958 *Co-operative Independent Commission Report*
1971 *The Politics of Education*, with Maurice Kogan and Edward Boyle

Fabian pamphlets

1960 *Can Labour Win?*
1971 *A Social Democratic Britain*
1971 *Towards a Labour Housing Policy*
1975 *Social Democracy in Europe*

Part 1

I

In Memoriam: I

by Dick Leonard

This tribute first appeared in *The Economist*, 19 February 1977.

Like his close personal friend and political mentor, Hugh Gaitskell, Anthony Crosland was struck down at a time when, in conventional terms, his personal political prospects had never seemed brighter. Foreign Secretary, the probability of becoming Chancellor within six months, and with it the serious possibility, if he made a success of the job, of eventually succeeding James Callaghan as Labour's leader and prime minister.

Now all that is might-have-been. The solid achievements of almost nine years of ministerial office, in six different posts, would suffice to assure him an honoured place in the upper – if not the top – ranks of Labour politicians. But it is almost certainly as a thinker and writer that Crosland will be most remembered. Already in his lifetime he had the rare satisfaction of reading the judgment of Professor Anthony King that he was the greatest British socialist thinker of all time – greater than Robert Owen, William Morris and R. H. Tawney. He blushed at the tribute, but few things would have made him happier than to see it confirmed by history.

It is difficult to recall the impact which his major work, *The Future of Socialism*, made when it first appeared in 1956. To a shaming extent, the Labour party (or at least its moderate wing) has been living off the intellectual capital of *The Future of Socialism* ever since, and many of its concepts have become such common coinage that few of those who trade in them are aware of thier origin.

The most striking – and to left wing socialists the most
shocking – conclusion of *The Future of Socialism* was the un-
importance of the ownership of industry. Large scale industrial
undertakings, Crosland argued with a wealth of detail, were
controlled not by their owners but by their managers. There was
no point, therefore, in nationalising industries just in order to
obtain control: the state, which was much the most powerful
force in all industrial societies, could get all the control it
needed, with less disruption, by other means.

This did not mean that Crosland was opposed in principle to
public ownership: indeed he advocated nationalisation of land
twenty years before the Community Land Act was placed on
the statute book. But he argued with passion that each specific
proposal for public ownership must be justified by the contribution which it made to socialist objectives, which he consistently defined as being more readily obtainable in a pluralist
than in a wholly state owned economy.

The socialist aim about which, like Gaitskell, Crosland
felt most strongly was equality. This he defined in practice, not
in any mechanical way, but simply by the assumption that the
things which he himself liked and enjoyed should be available to
everybody – including, specifically, to his working class constituents in Grimsby – rather than be restricted to the few. In a
famous passage, he wrote:

> We need not only higher exports and old-age pensions,
> but more open-air cafés, brighter and gayer streets at
> night, later closing-hours for public houses, more local
> repertory theatres, better and more hospitable hoteliers
> and restaurateurs, brighter and cleaner eating-houses,
> more riverside cafés, more pleasure-gardens on the
> Battersea model, more murals and pictures in public
> places, better designs in furniture and pottery and
> women's clothes, statues in the centre of new housing-
> estates, better-designed street-lamps and telephone-
> kiosks, and so on *ad infinitum*.[1]

Crosland did not invent the phrase 'quality of life', but
it summed up his feeling that only the best was good enough
for his Grimsby constituents. This belief in equality lay behind his consistent but not uncritical support for economic

growth and a high level of public expenditure, over which he fought three stubborn battles within the cabinet in his last year. Redistribution, Crosland argued, was easier and less painful with a large and growing national cake than with a small one. He also felt deeply that socialists should not seek special privileges for themselves – and he was privately sharply critical of Labour colleagues whose children attended fee paying schools.

This emphasis on equality was part of the family tradition which Crosland inherited. Both his father and his uncle, who were senior civil servants, turned down knighthoods. Though Tony rejected the Plymouth Brethren beliefs of his parents, something of their puritanism lingered on in his attitude to work (he had a bad conscience when he wasn't doing any) and to time, which he regarded as a precious commodity. He was the only person I have met who personally measured his time in periods of less than a quarter of an hour. 'Drop in at about ten to seven' he would say – and mean it.

But his family's religious extremism was perhaps most clearly reflected in his absolute devotion to high intellectual standards. He repeatedly revised everything he himself wrote through successive drafts, and – almost uniquely among senior ministers – insisted on writing major state papers himself. One of the more notable examples was the consultation paper on transport policy, launched in April 1976 by his successor, Peter Shore, a few days after he ceased to be Environment Secretary.

Had Crosland remained in the academic world, which he graced for three years as a lecturer in economics at Trinity College, Oxford, few doubt that he would have had a career of exceptional distinction. Instead, he was claimed for politics by Hugh Dalton, and kept there, after he lost his seat in 1955 and was uncertain whether he wanted to go back, by Hugh Gaitskell. Thereafter he had no doubts that this was what he wanted to do – and despite some financial worries he never again had any other job outside politics. In the 1970–74 period, for example, he was one of very few Labour shadow ministers who were full time MPs, and characteristically he devoted himself to mastering the many complex problems which he would have to face at the Environment Department, when he finally took over in March 1974. There can be few cases of ministers better prepared – and more readily able to argue on equal terms with their civil servants – than the new Environment Secretary in 1974.

Inherent in this commitment to politics was an unshakeable devotion to the Labour party. As an Oxford undergraduate, he had been on the brink of joining the Communist party in 1939, but thereafter he never had any doubt about which party to support. He fought hard alongside Gaitskell to prevent a left wing takeover in 1960–61, but he never again thought this a serious possibility, though he was worried by the electoral effects of the recent antics of Labour's National Executive Committee (NEC). On the other hand, he did take seriously the threat of the party being split in two – and the prospect of the more right wing half being realigned with the Liberals had absolutely no appeal to him.

It was this concern for holding the party together – rather than disagreement over the merits of the European common market of which he remained a lukewarm supporter – which led to the estrangement between Crosland and many more fervent Labour pro-Europeans in 1971. He believed that they were recklessly putting the future of the party at risk by voting in favour. His own abstention was taken more hardly by many of the pro-marketeers than the votes against British membership which were cast by Sir Harold Wilson and Denis Healey. They retaliated by refusing to vote for Crosland when he ran for the Labour deputy leadership in 1972, with the result that Edward Short was elected instead. Crosland was deeply hurt by the prevalent belief among the pro-marketeers that he had trimmed his position for personal advancement. When he had made up his mind on an issue it was difficult to shift him, but his skin was wafer thin and he was intensely sensitive to any questioning of his motives.

It was not only his thin skin which marked Crosland out as an improbable politician. He lacked many of the traditional political skills – he was a hopeless gladhander, and at an early age had acquired a reputation for being sensationally rude. He mellowed – and was always considerate to those who could not be considered his intellectual equals – but the damage was done, and multitudes of people remained unnecessarily in awe of him. He was an intensely private man, surprisingly shy for somebody who had revelled in an extrovert reputation. His charm, his infectious gaiety, his loyalty and concern for his friends was known only to a relative few: his public reputation was of a formidable but not particularly warm personality. What did communicate to a wider circle was the exceptional nature of his marriage to Susan Barnes. She has been the ideal wife for him and the source of much of his inner strength.

His high standing in intellectual circles – which extended to America, Japan and Western Europe – had not spread widely among the British general public. When Labour elected a new leader, in 1976, opinion polls showed that he was the least known by far of the six contenders. This was sensed by MPs, and was one reason for his poor showing – he came bottom of the poll with seventeen votes.

He was relatively unknown because he had never held one of the senior government offices – and he only began to be a household name during his last months as Foreign Secretary. His failure to be promoted to this level until April 1976, when Callaghan preferred him to Roy Jenkins, was at least partly due to bad luck. Gaitskell, who probably saw Crosland as his ultimate successor, would most likely have appointed him Chancellor had he lived. Wilson's long tenure of the leadership substantially blighted Crosland's prospects – he gave him good jobs but never the top ones. In 1967 the resigning Chancellor, Callaghan, recommended Crosland for the post, but Crosland's longstanding friend but fierce rival, Roy Jenkins, was appointed instead. It was only when Callaghan himself reached the top table that a place at his right hand was found for Crosland.

Crosland's ministerial achievements compare well with those of any recent minister. As Education Secretary, he gave the movement towards comprehensive education an irreversible momentum (proceeding by persuasion rather than legislation, though he recognised that it would later be necessary to deal with an irreconcilable rump), and he initiated a large expansion of teacher training and other forms of non-university higher education. He stopped a monstrous proposal for one un-necessary third London airport – at Stansted – in 1968, and another – at Maplin – in 1974. He drew up the blueprint for the Environment Department, for which Peter Walker was wrongly given most of the credit, and he bequeathed to his successors far ranging reviews of housing and local government finance. His major legislative achievement was the 1975 Community Land Act.

At the Foreign Office, he promptly wound up the cod war with Iceland (a brave decision for a Grimsby MP), convened the Geneva conference on Rhodesia and showed himself a more positive European than his predecessor, Jim Callaghan. But he had too little time to make a lasting impact.

Although widely admired for the logical force of his speeches, Crosland was never regarded as a great parliamentarian. Yet I vividly remember his performance in the standing committee on the 1972 Housing Finance Act, which first convinced many of his friends that here was a potential leader of the Labour party. Virtually single handed, he triumphed over a battery of Tory ministers and civil service advisers, and established a complete intellectual superiority in discussing the details of a highly complex and technical piece of legislation. The two senior ministers responsible for the Bill were promptly reshuffled into other jobs, and when the Tories later went into opposition they made no serious attempt to impede the repeal of what they had earlier heralded as a major reform. It was, perhaps, a unique parliamentary achievement, but it was witnessed only by the thirty-seven MPs who were closeted for fifty-five long sessions in committee room thirteen.

In due course, a successor will emerge for James Callaghan. But Crosland leaves a gap which nobody else can fill – not least the huge bump of irreverence which I always found his most endearing characteristic. Let him write his own epitaph, again from *The Future of Socialism*:[2]

> Now the time has come for a greater emphasis on private life, on freedom and dissent, on culture, beauty, leisure, and even frivolity. Total abstinence and a good filing-system are not now the right sign-posts to the socialist Utopia: or at least, if they are, some of us will fall by the wayside.

2

In Memoriam: II

---

by Lord Donaldson of Kingsbridge

This Address was given by Lord Donaldson at the Memorial Service for
Anthony Crosland at Westminster Abbey, 7 March 1977.

Many tributes have been paid to Tony Crosland as a politician
and as a thinker. I am not going to add to these but to speak
personally of him as he seemed to his friends.

Tony did not at all like fulsome praise, and it is difficult to
praise him without becoming sententious in a way he could not
abide. So I shall say too little rather than too much.

I first met him in 1949 when I was at the selection meeting
which chose him as prospective Labour candidate for South
Gloucestershire. After the meeting I told him that we had a
house near by and would be glad if he stayed with us when he was
in the constituency. Soon after, he turned up, driving an open
car and wearing a beret. After that he stayed with us whenever
he was in the constituency, and then four or five times a year
for the next twenty years, until we gave up having a country
house.

My whole family looked forward to these visits for weeks
beforehand, but the flatness after he had gone was relieved by
the knowledge that he would come again. This was not merely
because his presence was very stimulating but because he was so
much fun. He was never an easy guest. He was always determined to put off meals until he felt sufficiently relaxed to enjoy
them, and he used to deploy his considerable armoury in
delaying tactics until sometimes we had lunch an hour or more
late. He closed all conversations which did not interest him, and
he never refrained from complaining of any lapse in the

standards of comfort of the house. My wife kept up a running battle with him for twenty-eight years, but almost invariably gave in, gracefully. He made no concessions to my children, then in their teens, and did nothing to ingratiate himself with them. Yet he did ingratiate himself with them. I think they were proud of him as we all were.

I do not want to give the impression that he was not appreciative. He was enormously appreciative by nature but he had his own way of showing it. He was intensely loyal to all his old friends and took great trouble, for example, to visit Hugh and Ruth Dalton when they were old and out of the swim. Indeed he used to bully other people to go too. He was always very solitary. He loved the country and he loved walking but he preferred to walk alone, just as, I think, to the end of his life he took an annual holiday alone.

There are two things I would particularly like to say about him. The first is that he had an unusually high moral sense, a secular one, certainly, but it should not be forgotten that he was brought up in a deeply religious atmosphere. He had a happy childhood and was brought up by parents of distinguished intellect and culture, and he never lost touch with his two sisters. His philosophy, his politics and all his views were based on his feeling for man as an individual, and he cared passionately not only for such issues as greater equality, but also to create a society in which men could enjoy life. These qualities were not always understood because he was essentially pragmatic and had no time for sociological ambitions which do not recognise the inherent contradictions in human nature and society which ensure that no progress can be made without pain. He was a passionate searcher for the truth and in all his written work he can be seen visibly struggling for it. He was more genuinely socialist in temperament than almost anyone I ever met.

Secondly, it is wrong to suppose that he was a largely cerebral being. He was in some ways highly emotional. He believed with passion in everything he believed in, and never troubled to conceal an almost irrational distaste for everything else. He was extremely exclusive and he cared only for serious issues. He could not bear small talk or social gossip. I do not mean to suggest that he was always serious in behaviour because, as I have already said, he had a great sense of fun as well as wit. We shared a love of music, both classical and jazz, of low level, country house tennis, of the open air, of sightseeing, where he was far better informed than we were, and of the novels of Rex Stout. He was greatly interested in pictures and he and his wife had begun a modest collection.

If he sometimes seemed hostile or arrogant in the social world, the people who worked with him were genuinely devoted to him. In Westminster Abbey at this memorial service, there are people who have travelled from Grimsby to honour him but there are also people who have travelled from South Gloucestershire who have not seen him for more than twenty years.

For myself, I can only say that I can name four or five people who have strongly influenced my life and, although Tony was years younger than me, he was certainly one of them. I think Hugh Gaitskell would have said the same. It is well known that Hugh, who died at about the same age, surrounded himself with a group of brilliant young men, even now called the Gaitskellites, but I think no one who knew them would deny that Tony was the closest of these. Hugh had a strong and sometimes obstinate mind and was, in Tony's own words, 'head and shoulders above us all'. He would not have been easily influenced. But no one could associate closely with a mind of Tony's quality and originality without being influenced by him.

He developed slowly and not fully until after his marriage. When he was young he seemed a little reckless and one sometimes wondered whether, in spite of his exceptional talents, he would succeed as a politician. In a curious way he seemed to be insufficiently calculating.

He was always a tremendously hard worker. When he was writing *The Future of Socialism*, he worked for twelve or fourteen hours a day and it was almost impossible to lure him out of his flat even for a meal. For this reason he probably was happiest at a hard slogging ministry like the Department of the Environment. He said once to my wife that, in politics, it could be a mistake to make one's run too soon. Just as he was getting into his stride his run was cut short.

But the thing which perhaps no one understood or allowed for was his capacity to love. Those of us who knew him well were not surprised when he found someone with whom he could settle down and mature – although we had begun to wonder

17

about that. No, what surprised us was the ease and simplicity with which he slipped into the roles of husband, of stepfather, and of head of the family. If he had not met Susan Barnes all this might never have been revealed and he might never have fulfilled his potential. But it was a marriage of two equals and he gave to it as much as he received.

Part 2

3

Crosland's Socialism

by David Lipsey

I

Is revisionism – the political philosophy of which Anthony Crosland was undoubtedly the post-war High Priest – dead?

Certainly it is out of fashion. Obituaries for revisionism have been pronounced by its opponents whether on the Right (see, for example, Colin Welch)[1] or Left (Tony Benn, himself a revisionist who repented).[2] But more disturbing has been a growing *trahison des clercs*, the desertion of revisionism by those, of whom David Marquand is a striking example,[3] who claim that it was once their creed.

It is not my intention to attempt any point by point rebuttal of these critics. Often, the best refutation lies in reading Crosland himself, for the critics are flailing at straw men. Marquand in particular attributes to Crosland centralist and statist ideas which belong rather to the Webbs.

For such cruel distortions there can be no excuse, for there is nothing inaccessible about Crosland's own writings. Only a certain over optimism – of which Crosland later repented – mars *The Future of Socialism*.[4] Even so, the combination of its intellectual rigour with its passionate moral conviction makes it still an exhilarating book to read. The essays and articles collected in *The Conservative Enemy*,[5] the Fabian tract *A Social Democratic Britain* and the introductory essay to *Socialism Now*[6] all have a force which transcends the current disappointments of political life.

Consistency is not a virtue with which politicians are widely associated, so the consistency of the underlying thought which runs through all Crosland's writings is all the more impressive. Of course, over more than twenty years of writing, there are changes of emphasis; occasionally, changes of mind; even (though very rarely) straight contradictions. Of course, Crosland had to deal with new problems which came to the centre of the political stage, whether the politics of the environment, or of participation; of the backlash against public spending, or of new threats to social cohesion posed by vandalism, violence and racial division. But broadly it is true that Crosland never abandoned the basic revisionist argument advanced in *The Future of Socialism*. 'There is no need for revisionists to revise our definition of socialism';[7] 'I see no reason to abandon the revisionist analysis of socialism in favour of a refurbished Marxism'[8] — thus in his last substantial work, the introduction to *Socialism Now*, Crosland reasserts his fundamental faith. In *The Future of Socialism*, Crosland had erected a towering castle. The rest of his life was devoted to defending it against all comers.

II

Why, in the Britain of the 1980s, do the comers against Crosland's castle seem so numerous, and the defenders so dispirited? In large measure, the reasons are historical.

For eleven of the last seventeen years, we have had a Labour government, a Labour government most of whose leading members regarded themselves as broadly revisionist. At the end of it, Britain's rate of economic growth has gone from being slow to being virtually non-existent; unemployment is (by post-war standards) high; inflation is still menacing and the balance of payments is only supportable because of the contribution of North Sea oil and gas. Our national wealth is not only static; it remains unequally distributed, with the minority of super rich standing in stark contrast to the disquieting number of still poor. The scars of social inequality remain deep etched into the national landscape. Politically, we enter the 1980s under not a Labour, but a right wing Conservative government which is securely established, with a majority to see it through a five year term of office. In other words, so the critics argue, Crosland's philosophy has been refuted in practice – economically, socially, politically.

Yes, but is it true that in the 1960s and 1970s we had Croslandite Labour governments?

We tread here on dangerous ground. Crosland was a loyal member of both the 1964–70 and the 1974–79 Labour governments. In *Socialism Now*, he criticises those who write off 1964–70 as 'a total disaster, or at least … exhibit a selective amnesia in which the successes are forgotten and only the failures remembered'[9] and he would today be similarly contemptuous of those whose amnesia seems to stretch even to the fact they were *in* the government from 1974 to 1979. In that period, many measures were taken which furthered Croslandite objectives, whether equality at work under the Employment Protection Act, 1975, and the implementation of the Equal Pay Act, the 20 per cent rise in the real value of the old age pension, the further spread of comprehensive education until in 1978 it embraced over 83 per cent of secondary pupils, or the low pay provisions of successive incomes policies. In the department where he had major responsibility for social reform, the Department of the Environment, many Croslandite measures were realised – security of tenure for furnished tenants, the Community Land Act, abolition of the agricultural tied cottage, a fundamental realignment of transport policy towards public transport for the less well off, and proposals to enhance the status and rights of council tenants. In other words, Labour governments have been nowhere near the total failure in social policy that the critics claim.

Yet, in *Socialism Now*, Crosland admitted of the 1964–70 Labour government that 'nobody disputes the central failure of economic policy' where 'growth was consistently sacrificed to the balance of payments'. 'This central failure bedevilled all the efforts and good intentions of the Labour government. It constrained public expenditure, antagonised the trade unions, alienated large groups of workers … and frustrated policies for improving the industrial structure'.[10]

He would have said much the same thing in 1981. It is ironic that Tony Benn should brand the Labour cabinet's submission to the deflation imposed by the IMF in 1976 as the death knell of revisionism for, on that occasion, Crosland, revisionism's leading intellectual, unsuccessfully urged his more orthodox colleagues to stand firm against the Fund's intolerable demands. Crosland, the prophet, had in 1953 warned of the IMF which 'played no useful or constructive role, confining itself to giving petulant and unconstructive advice at ill chosen moments'.[11] In 1976, he saw nothing that escaped him earlier: nothing in revisionism which persuaded him that submission to the demands of the international bankers was the right way to defend the interests of the British working class.

Crosland was increasingly shocked by the surrender of the Right of the Labour party in the face of the resurgence of a right wing monetarist ideology in Britain and elsewhere in the 1970s. To distinguish himself from them, he adopted the habit of styling himself a democratic socialist, and them social democrats.

Certainly, he remained an opponent of the Left of the Labour party, but not because they were too radical. Rather, for his taste, they were not radical enough. He rejected their views on the means to socialist ends. Clause IV of the Labour party constitution of 1918 and the massive extension of public ownership were to him now largely irrelevant to the achievement of socialist objectives. But he did not throw the baby out with the bathwater, left wing ends with left wing means. In *The Conservative Enemy*, he hit at the Right of the Labour movement before the Left: for the traditional Right he wrote, 'lacks a truly radical appeal, and often seems insular, class orientated, conservative and middle aged'.[12] For Crosland, politics were a means to achieve political, not personal, goals and if 'ideals were not always fully attainable', they should 'at least determine the directions of policy'.[13] He grew increasingly out of sorts both with what he saw as the conservative pragmatism of the post-Gaitskell Labour leadership and the fluffy liberalism of other colleagues, who saw rights for homosexuals and membership of the EEC as a sufficient dose of radicalism to last a decade or two.

Membership of the EEC – would that one could avoid the subject; for if discussing the record of Labour governments is dangerous ground, this is the quicksand.

Crosland's own position on the EEC modulated over the years between a greater and a lesser enthusiasm. He was not primarily a pro-European because of the putative economic benefits of membership – after a painstaking assessment of the

arguments he came to the conclusion that entry was economically a 'non-event'. But he was impressed by the potential political benefits of entry, in healing the scars of a Europe twice
divided by war in this century, and in creating a new more
powerful European voice in international affairs. At times of
maximum conviction, Europe even made his famous shortlists
of numbered priorities for a Labour government.

But in the 1970s, when I knew him, he regarded it more and
more as an issue of relatively modest importance below such
social policy issues as housing and education, and not in the
same league as the major macro-economic issues of growth,
employment and inflation.

So when, in 1971, the pro-Europeans under Roy Jenkins voted
with the Tory government and in defiance of the Labour Whip
in favour of entry, Crosland deliberately abstained, rather than
split with his party on an issue he believed to be secondary.

Even now, the scars have not healed. The pro-Europeans
were outraged at what they took to be Crosland's lack of courage. Given the attacks they themselves suffered for their stand
from the Left, that was psychologically understandable; and I
have no wish to impugn their motives in the way that some of
them so freely impugned Crosland's. But from the standpoint of
1981, three things are clear about this dispute.

Firstly, the more extreme pro-Europeans wildly exaggerated
both the importance of Europe and its merits. Few now talk
the heady language of those crusading days a decade ago. Now,
it's all 'reform the CAP', 'justice on the Brussels Budget', 'cheap
food' – the bread-and-butter matters that the pro-Europeans
scorned then to discuss. In other words – whisper it who dares!
– events have proved Crosland more right on Europe than his
detractors on Labour's Right.

Secondly, the pro-Europeans' stand put them out of line,
both with the solid centre of the PLP, and with the centre of the
trade union movement. This hideously damaged the party in
general, and the non-Left within it in particular. Marquand
trenchantly lashes 'anti-intellectual' attitudes in the party in his
Encounter article; but those attitudes stem from the self-satisfied
behaviour of those at the time who, in Jack Jones's words,
looked at Europe through 'wine spattered spectacles'.

Thirdly, having split with the mainstream of the party on
this one issue, a few amongst the pro-Europeans got carried

away by their own bravado. They were all in a negative sense revisionists; that is, they shared Crosland's views on the irrelevance of the traditional Labour commitment to public ownership of the means of production, distribution and exchange. But this minority amongst them included some who lacked a corresponding commitment to the positive side of revisionism, its insistence that socialism was about equality. They knew what they were against; but what were they for? The answer became that they were 'for' Europe. Buoyed up by this faith – as well as the encouragement they received from new found admirers in the Conservative press – they were soon cheerfully denying other elements of the Labour faith, whether a belief in social expenditure, or the need to work with the trade union movement, or the need to set social limits to the operation of crude market forces, or even equality itself. They thus went to the edge, or beyond, of Labour's broad church.

Enough! Much damage has been done already by this dispute to the prospect of a democratic socialist Britain. It remains only to hope that the experience of the Thatcherian reaction will be enough to lure these fair-weather socialists back to the fundamentals of the revisionist faith – and that no potential recruit to Croslandism will be put off by its popular, misconceived association with the renegades amongst the Labour pro-market Right.

III

The history of Labour's last sixteen years helps explain how it is that Croslandism has become so unfashionable. What it does not explain is why so many who are by instinct Croslandites seem so dispirited in defence of the philosophy he taught.

The answer lies in the problem of growth. It is not just a matter of the past record. As I have argued above, many of the shortcomings of our growth performance must be attributed to an insufficient commitment to that objective even by Labour governments. It is not that revisionism has failed; it has not been tried. But more fundamentally, the prospects for the future do not look much better. Crosland's socialism, so the argument goes, was a socialism for good times. But these are not good times, nor are they likely to become so. Growth has stopped; the democratic socialist prescription offers no very good way of getting it going again; and, without growth, its prescriptions for a relatively pain-free redistribution of income and wealth evaporate.

Certainly, for Crosland, growth was a necessary condition for achieving the socialist objective of greater equality.

It was so, firstly, because an increase in the general level of real income was itself equalising. It increased access to goods such as motor cars which gave to their owners the freedom which had previously been the privilege of the better off. He was delighted when 'the first miners' car rally was recently held in Yorkshire. Half the population now leave home for at least a week's annual holiday'.[14] As incomes rise, the better-off find it increasingly difficult to discover more outlets for extra expenditure, and so the visible gap between rich and poor narrows.

Secondly, growth plays a further indispensable role in 'achieving equality without intolerable social stress and a probable curtailment of liberty', namely, it enables 'the better-off to accept with reasonable equanimity a decline in their *relative* standard of living because growth has enabled them (almost) to maintain their *absolute* standard of living despite redistribution'.[15]

Thirdly, unless there is growth, there will be a continued and savage restraint on public expenditure. For, without growth, increasing public spending logically entails increasing rates of taxation. That presents economic problems, as people attempt to make up the shortfall in their take home pay by increasing their wage rates, so causing (in a zero growth environment) inflation. Politically it brings any government rapidly against the taxpayers' revolt, in Britain as well as California, and to the nemesis of electoral defeat.

So growth was needed. How fast? Crosland's views varied. At the time he wrote *The Future of Socialism*, productivity had risen since 1948 at a rate of $2\frac{1}{4}$ per cent a year. Crosland believed that this rate of growth might be 'almost sufficient for all reasonable purposes' since it would 'double the standard of living in 25 years'.[16] As the real world fell short of achieving this and unemployment rose, Crosland became ambitious for more: in *Socialism Now* he called for 'planned and controlled growth up to the limit of our productive potential – say, 4 per cent per annum'.[17]

Whatever the precise *rate* of growth, the *need* was unquestionable. Thus, Crosland vigorously opposed philosophies which attacked growth – he clashed sharply with J. K. Galbraith's attacks ('private affluence and public squalor' – when last did we hear that?) on the 'acquisitive society' of the 1950s. And he resisted equally firmly the zero growth extremists amongst the environmentalist movement of the 1970s.

The proponents of growth argued that the deteriorating quality of life resulting from pollution and other 'disbenefits' of growth meant that economic growth *should* stop and in any case that the combination of exponential economic and population growth, set against a static quantity of real resources, meant that, willy-nilly, it *would* stop.

Now, Crosland was an instinctive environmentalist in the senes that he wanted better homes and parks, and fewer office blocks. What infuriated him was the 'elitist, protectionist and anti-growth view of the environment' expressed by middle and upper class champions who 'want to kick the ladder down behind them'.[18]

Against them he argued that growth was needed to pay for the homes and the parks that he, like the environmentalists, wanted.[19] Similarly, growth (as the Japanese were discovering) could provide the resources to pay for the control of pollution. The way to stop world population rising was greater prosperity, since higher income per head was closely correlated with smaller family size. As for resources, as they become short, their price would rise; this would make it profitable to produce acceptable substitutes.

With the exception of this last, where the issues of energy and of nuclear policy remain unresolved, these arguments have generally stood the test of time. In any case, our experience of life without growth has hardly been such as to reconcile us with equanimity to the prospect of doing without it. Today, a more modest and attractive environmentalism has, in Britain at least, superseded the earlier enthusiasms of the eco-doomsters.

IV

So we want growth. How do we get it? Crosland's second and more controversial proposition was that, properly managed by a government truly committed to growth, broadly the existing order of the economy could provide it – and could provide it without in the process generating unacceptable levels of inflation. This optimism remained with him from those early days to the more difficult 1970s under the shadow of OPEC.

By 'existing order of the economy', Crosland meant the following. Firstly, a substantial market sector where prices, and not administrative fiat, governed what was produced. Secondly, a privately owned (if in practice managerially run) productive sector working alongside a state sector, and responding to broadly existing levels of profit and incentives in its production and investment decisions. Thirdly, a Keynesian state, committed to using the controls at its disposal, whether regulatory, fiscal or monetary, to sustain growth and secure full employment. Fourthly, a free trade union movement which pursued its objectives in a way compatible with the survival of such an economic structure.

For Britain, at least, many now believe that these four pillars of the mixed economy can no longer remain untouched. I distinguish four broad critiques.

Firstly, the Labour Left attack the first and second pillars. That is to say, they believe that the role of the market should be greatly diminished in favour of a greater (if ill defined) measure of planning, and that a huge expansion of public ownership, spiced with workers' control, is the only way in which growth and full employment can be revived.

Secondly, the Thatcherite Right attacks the second and third pillars. It denies the capacity of state action to sustain growth, and emphasises the need instead for increased private production and consumption, and renewed personal incentives. Such a shift must take place within the framework of a strict monetarist policy, designed to contain inflation and preserve British competitiveness.

Thirdly, the Labour pragmatists, whose all embracing scepticism has in common with Thatcherism strong reservations about the potential for state action, while (unlike her) remaining agnostic about the likely rejuvenating effects of incentives. Theirs is a philosophy of 'hanging on', in the hope either of a revival in the world economy or of some domestic spiritual miracle whereby political exhortation to try harder will be transubstantiated into an industrial renaissance.

Fourthly, the emerging school of 'new social democrats' – represented in this book by Ian Little and Professor James Meade – place the main blame for the collapse of the revisionist order on inflation, caused by the rapacious behaviour of organised labour. The solutions they advance are designed to allow the market sector of the economy to prosper free of crippling industrial warfare.

To deal properly with each of these critiques would require not an introductory essay, but a book; and the man who would now be busily writing that book is dead. We can be certain that Crosland would have rejected the Left's view now, as he rejected it throughout his active political life. Firstly, he would have rejected it because of its logical inconsistencies. The Left advocate more planning, but reject the planning of incomes. They emphasise the need for stronger state direction and control of the economy, yet adopt a neo-anarchist belief in the productive capacity of a liberated shop floor. Crosland would have had little time for a theory of socialism which depended on a suspension of the laws of logic.

Secondly, he would have remained sceptical of the importance of 'planning and industrial policy, which are rather marginal influences on economic performance'.[20] He had no faith that civil servants at the Department of Industry would make a better job of running British industry than existing managers and, in support of this view, he would have pointed to the deepening problems of Eastern Europe in sustaining production of high quality, technologically advanced products. He never saw anything in the performance of the existing public sector which encouraged him to favour any major extension of it; indeed, competition offered a far greater chance of economic success than the spawning of yet more state monopolies. Nor did the existing public sector, characterised as it was by 'managerial bureaucracies', offer much comfort to those who believed that extending public ownership could in any meaningful way extend democratic control.

Thirdly, he would have rejected the Left's views from a conviction that for Labour to adopt them would condemn the party to permanent opposition. In chapter 10 of *The Conservative Enemy*, he adopted Max Weber's distinction between 'two ethics which may govern public conduct: the ethic of ultimate ends, and the ethic of responsibility. He who follows the former has no interest in political power". And the same would apply to a left wing Labour party, committed to policies such as massive nationalisation, a great extension of welfare spending, extreme liberal policies on immigration and the police and a free-for-all on wages – policies which every public opinion poll has shown to be deeply and consistently unpopular with the electorate. The adoption of these policies would in practice mean that Labour would be, in Nye Bevan's words, 'pure ... at the price of impotency',[21] reduced to mere protest as the Tories went ruthlessly on their way.

For Thatcherite Toryism, Crosland felt wholehearted disgust. Economically, it would not work. There is no real evidence that increased incentives make any major difference to output (though Crosland himself was opposed to much higher taxation of earned *income* – as opposed to higher taxation of high *wealth* – in order to preserve existing incentives). The tight monetarism that lies at the centre of the Thatcherite philosophy would still further squeeze demand for home production, undermining profits, reducing investment and generally making for stagnation or worse. After all, Thatcherism had been tried (by Heath, Mark 1); and it failed. The notion that a cure for Britain's ills lay in stronger doses of a medicine that had already been proved to poison the patient would have struck Crosland as more than mildly puzzling.

Beyond economics, though, Crosland would have loathed the politics of Thatcherism – its single-minded concentration on the bourgeois virtues, its celebration of inequality, its embrace of a dog-eats-dog society where the top dog gets all the gravy, and its accompanying attitudes of intolerance, whether of blacks, 'scroungers' or trade unionists.

Towards the Labour pragmatists, he would have displayed more sympathy. He would agree with them that economic growth is a strange and not altogether understood process, dependent on complex social as well as economic forces. He would have agreed also that there was no way in which Britain could be wholly isolated from world economic recession, or the effects of rising prices and short supplies of oil. His instincts would have chimed with theirs – that the best policy is sometimes 'Don't just do something; stand there'. We are, as it were, on top of a mountain. It may be cold in the wind, but a large movement in either direction will send us tumbling down the sides. We should do better to seek more shelter where we are. So we should forget all notions of a grand, global reconstruction of our economic system; and concentrate instead on making sure that all the smaller steps we do take are steps in the right direction.

Thus far, he would have gone with them – but no further. For Crosland would have been distressed by the way in which the pragmatists, short on a positive strategy of their own, have been seduced into adopting elements of the strategy of the Right. He would have disapproved of Labour's adoption of over rigid targets for the money supply (not, incidentally, as is widely believed, a condition of the IMF loan of 1976, but a damaging addition to those conditions of the Labour government's own making). He would have been shocked by the degree to which Labour ministers turned against public spending, and towards lower taxes as an appropriate goal for a democratic socialist party. And, to take one particular controversial point, I do not believe that he would have been prepared to sit back while British growth and British industry was wiped out by a flood of foreign imports. In 1965, he wrote, 'the right policy for a balance of payments deficit [is] to operate directly on the balance of payments, whether by import restriction or export promotion, thus giving time for longer term policies to increase efficiency to take effect'.[22] At the time of the IMF negotiations, he argued that it would be better to impose import controls than accept the prescribed deflation. By 1980, I have little doubt that he (with his old friend and mentor, Wilfred Beckerman) would have announced his conversion to a system of across-the-board import controls to protect a growing British economy from an unsupportable balance of payments deficit. On the basis of such a policy of import controls, he would have believed it possible to negotiate with the trade unions an agreement on incomes sufficient to keep inflation within manageable bounds.

The trade unions – what answer would he have given to those who attack this fourth pillar of the mixed economy? His political temperament would have made him instinctively hostile to the anti-union social democrats. In 1968, he joined with Jim Callaghan, in opposition to Barbara Castle's proposals for legal reform of the unions, *In Place of Strife*. He remained a supporter of the trade union–Labour party alliance.

He was reinforced in this view by what he called the 'McGovern débâcle' in the 1972 American Presidential election which 'dramatized the appalling danger to a left-wing Party of neglecting its traditional working-class supporters in the interests of a largely middle-class "New Politics".'[23]

At the same time, the events of the winter of 1978–79 – the uncollected rubbish in the streets, the unburied dead and, perhaps above all, the exultant vengefulness of the tone of some of the shop floor union leadership would have hurt him, as indeed it hurt the whole leadership of his party. His advocacy of conciliation, understanding and co-operation might have continued, but perhaps – who knows? – a shade more wearily, and with a little less of his usual boundless optimism than before.

V

The uncertain prospect for growth lies at the heart of many present criticisms of the Croslandite position. But it is not the only one. Another, which has greatly grown in strength in recent years, is a critical reaction against Crosland's espousal of the desirability of rising levels of public expenditure (for a discussion, see Colin Crouch's essay, chapter 10). This line was, of course, native to the Conservative party, but it spread also to the Right of the Labour party and the Labour government. Public expenditure cuts began as a device to achieve a traditional deflation to cope with inflation and the weak balance of payments. They became intrinsic to a massively publicised economic strategy, propagated by Messrs Bacon and Eltis, to the effect that it was the growth of the public sector that was holding Britain's economy back.[24] Eventually some members of the government (for example William Rodgers) were to argue that public spending was intrinsically wasteful.[25] Socialists should instead concentrate on extending the practical freedoms of our people by increasing the real value of the take home pay they had to spend for themselves.

Despite this assault, Crosland never turned from his belief in the importance of public spending. *Pace* Marquand, he never believed in what that writer describes as 'the old Croslandite

33

assumption that the central purpose of social democracy is to increase the social wage as fast as possible'; for him, social welfare spending was a means to the end of greater equality. Only in so far as it served that end was it justified.

As time went on, Crosland did come to believe that public spending was proving a less effective means to his egalitarian ends than he had once thought. His advocacy of public expenditure became more qualified. He realised that 'the vastly increased sums going out in social provision have produced a disproportionately small improvement in the net flow accruing to those in need; so poverty and inequality persist despite a major rise in public expenditure'.[26] He accepted the need to watch out for waste lest public spending be absorbed into 'self-sustaining bureaucracies'.[27] And he recognised the need to contain public expenditure so that it did not lead to ever increasing rates of taxation which frustrated the wholly appropriate demands of working people for increased personal consumption.

But in none of this did he go so far as his more critical colleagues in turning against public spending. He was not convinced by the Bacon and Eltis thesis that public spending was absorbing too high a proportion of the nation's resources, at least in the context of the 1970s. The unemployment figures were clear evidence that there were unused resources in the British economy. Public spending could bring these men back to work, without depriving private employers of their workforce.

He recognised too that some public spending itself contributed directly to growth. It seemed a peculiar sort of logic that cut the investment programme of, say, the Post Office in the hope that somehow that would persuade private industry to increase *its* investment. The argument that lower public spending would mean lower taxes and thus greater incentives had little appeal for him, since, as we have seen, he was by no means convinced that incentives would do much for growth. He showed that, contrary to the alarmist figures quoted in some quarters, British public expenditure absorbed a proportion of the GNP not wildly out of line with that in other (often, more prosperous) industrial countries – this despite the fact that the British share was inflated by our need to pay benefits to our untypically high number of unemployed.

Finally, fundamentally, whatever the disappointments, he was never one to underestimate the improvements that higher public spending had brought in its train. A revolution in housing vastly improved and expanded educational facilities, the Health Service, an enormous improvement in the living standards of the elderly and the jobless – these were real victories for socialism. And 'If people were asked "Do you think it more important to devote resources to developing electric hair brushes, or to providing sheltered housing for the elderly?", they would want to help the elderly. It is Labour's job to give them the choice'.[28]

Beyond this Labour mainstream criticism of public expenditure lies another, more fundamental, which sees as a central feature of a new socialism an opposition to bureaucracies, and a greater emphasis on individual liberty, deregulation, a smaller scale for industrial production and an increase generally in self-management.

On Labour's Right, Evan Luard calls his recent book *Socialism without the State*,[29] Giles Radice writes on *Community Socialism*,[30] and David Marquand wants a 'libertarian, de-centralist social democracy'.[31] On the Left, a stream of popular pamphlets and speeches pour out, attacking the bureaucratic state and its managers, the police and security forces in particular, and calling for their control by means of 'open government' and 'democratic accountability'. In the productive sector, they call for a massive extension of worker control (indeed, most of them call for it in the public services as well, blissfully unaware, it seems, of how that might clash with the responsibilities of accountable and elected politicians).

This is not a wholly new philosophy. Bukharin and Marx; syndicalism and Webbite Fabianism – the two strands of socialist thinking have long run together. And indeed the current revival in the libertarian wing is not the first of recent years; in the false dawn of 1968, too, there was a shortlived vogue for participation, direct democracy and generally a revolt against authority.

Crosland was an early participant in this debate. For example, he dedicated chapter 14 of *The Conservative Enemy* (written almost a decade before 1968) to 'Industrial Democracy and Workers' Control'. He there concluded, as he did every time he considered this subject, that 'the problem [of dehumanisation of industry] is basically one of "democratic participation" – not, however, the mass participation of all workers in the higher management of the enterprise, but the participation of the primary work-group in deciding how its work should be divided, organised and remunerated.'[32]

For other aspects of the movement, again, he had great enthusiasm – for example, for neighbourhood councils, tenants' rights in housing, and pressure groups like the Consumer Council and the Civic Trust.

But with his characteristic unwillingness to ride the tides of political fashion, and his preference for the common sense priorities of his Grimsby constituents to the current formulations of the NW3 trendies, he would never have become an unconditional supporter of the new movement. He was, for one thing, by instinct suspicious of any creed that seemed to involve a 'busy, bustling society ... herding us all into participatory groups'.[33] He feared that participation would tend to act not as a levelling force but, perversely, to increase further the effective power of the articulate middle classes. He was also, perhaps, conscious of the danger of the immobilism that could result when too much power was too widely diffused, so that positive action would be crippled by countervailing power. As the US seems in recent times to have demonstrated, too many democratic veto groups can mean too little action. The Fabian baby was not to be thrown out with the Fabian bathwater ... 'there is no substitute for institutions, with their bureaucracy, rules, clerks and computers. Of course one must reform or replace them if they become ossified, but one cannot simply abolish them; they are the only instruments of social reform'.[34]

VI

What did Crosland see as the aim of his kind of socialism? His objective was to create a more equal society.

The Labour party embraced twelve different socialist traditions, all described in chapter 4 of *The Future of Socialism*. Marxism was of course one; but so were (for example) Christian socialism and William Morris's anti-commercialism and Owenist co-operation. All these traditions had made their contribution;

and no one of them had any historical right now to claim exclusive possession of the Ark of the Covenant. From these traditions, Crosland extracted five chief elements.[35]

Firstly, a revolt against the inefficiencies of capitalism. Secondly, the socialist detestation of poverty and discrimination. Thirdly, a belief in the concept of fraternity and the co-operative ideal. Fourthly, a broad support for measures designed to promote the welfare of society as a collectivity, with which went support for a high level of public expenditure and public provision generally. Fifthly, greater equality and the creation of a more classless society.

The first goal Crosland considered now of less importance. For, he argued, what we have is no longer capitalism, in the sense of a system dominated by those who own the means of production, distribution and exchange. More important still, it is no longer inefficient, combining more successfully than any alternative system growth, freedom of choice and full employment. These arguments I have already discussed; though they will re-echo through many of the contributions which follow.

As for poverty, he concluded that, as growth continues, so benefits filter down to the least well off. The statistical evidence for the absolute improvement in the condition of the poor is overwhelming. So, ending poverty, though a top priority, will come about almost as a natural process.

To the modern reader, as it did to Crosland later in his life, this seems a naïve view. By the time he wrote *Socialism Now*, he was exercised by the 'stubborn residue of poverty'. He had read the arguments of Townsend and others that deprivation is to be judged by the size of the gap between the average living standard and that of the poor. To improve the absolute living standard of the poor is not enough if still they are 'relatively deprived' by comparison with their contemporaries. One generation worries about food poverty and hunger; the next about fuel poverty; the next – who knows? – about transport poverty and mobility.

At the same time, Crosland never lost his belief that the absolute standard of the poor mattered too; that the common sense view of the immense reduction in the misery caused by poverty since the war was right. He did not go the whole way with the extreme view of the 'poverty lobby' that, without greater equality, nothing has been done to alleviate poverty, that a family on Supplementary Benefit today – provided for in a pinched sort of a way – suffers as much as the shoeless, foodless of the 1930s.

So Crosland ends up with a compromise. By 1974, his objective had become the more complex one of raising the means of the poorest 20 per cent relative to that of the remaining 80 per cent and, at the same time, 'so markedly increase their *absolute* incomes that any person of compassionate good sense would agree that poverty had diminished'.[36]

On fraternity, Crosland is agnostic: 'not because I think its content less important, but simply because I find it impossible to reach a definite conclusion about its relevance in contemporary conditions'.[37] The unrestrained competition of Victorian times with its sweatshops and child labour has gone and, with it, the mainspring of the original impulse towards greater fraternity. There is a danger that further restraint on aggressive competition will lead not to co-operation, but to 'social ossification and the denial of individual rights'. Nor is the co-operative spirit a necessary, let alone a sufficient, condition of greater industrial efficiency. Indeed, concern for the social weal has proved notably ineffective in this regard where industries like the railways and the coal mines have been taken into public ownership. So it is by no means clear that the gains from greater co-operation exceed the losses – less freedom, and the danger to efficiency – as a cosy *bonhomie* blunts the sharp edge of our industrial management. Even if it were clear, it is not easy to see what institutions would be needed to bring about greater fraternity in practice.

Crosland was to spend the late 1950s as Secretary to the Independent Commission into the Co-operative Movement chaired by Hugh Gaitskell. Perhaps partly in consequence, he became later in life more sympathetic towards the co-operative ideal (though not, I fear, as a result of his experience then, any less fearful of its potentially adverse effects on efficiency). 'We retain,' he says in *Socialism Now*, 'an amazing sense of class and little sense of community. Company chairmen pay themselves huge salary increases at a time of wage restraint; trade union leaders and local councillors debate whether to defy the law; both are a tiny minority, yet they each symbolize the lack of respect for community decisions'.[38] His earlier scepticism towards incomes policy – a policy originally associated with the Left of the Labour party – turned to passionate support for it as a way of subordinating excessive individual claims to those of the community as a whole. Yet this shift went only so far, for Crosland never lost his concern lest an excess of community spirit led to busybodying invasions of privacy and personal freedom.

So Crosland was left with two outstanding values, social welfare and equality. As he wrote more, the former became more and more a means to the latter. He favoured a universal National Health Service partly because of a moral conviction that the activity of health care was inappropriate to the market but mainly, I think, because he was convinced that only through a universal system would the proportion of health care resources going to the rich be reduced and those going to the poor be increased. This preoccupation with the distribution of the fruits of public expenditure meant that in later life he looked with a jaundiced eye on those forms of public expenditure – on the universities or the arts or on railway subsidies – which disproportionately favoured the better off, and favoured those forms – improved housing, pensions and aid to the disabled – which did most for needy groups.

'The belief in social equality ... still remains the most characteristic feature of socialist thought today'[39] – and the one which Crosland wholeheartedly embraced (see Professor Raymond Plant's essay, chapter 9). In *Socialism Now*, he explained that 'by equality, [revisionists] meant more than a meritocratic society of equal opportunities, in which the greatest rewards would go to those with the most fortunate genetic endowment and family background ... we also meant more than a simple (not that it has proved simple in practice) redistribution of income. We wanted a wider social equality embracing also the distribution of property, the educational system, social-class relationships, power and privilege in industry – indeed all that was enshrined in the age-old socialist dream of a more "classless society".'[40]

The phrase in parenthesis is significant. Crosland, unlike some of his colleagues, was never converted to the view that we had enough or too much equality. The battery of arguments deployed over 182 pages of *The Future of Socialism* in favour of greater equality still seemed to him unassailable. What worried him was the slowness of progress towards greater equality. He tended, I think, to underestimate the ability of the haves to use their skills as well as their power to hang on to their advantages. He relied on democracy to increase equality – everyone using their one vote to bring about increased equality. But over time the attitude of the average man to equality has become more critical as he stands by his differentials and seeks opportunities for his children to rise out of their class rather than with it. To-day, there will be no greater equality unless there is also greater fraternity – a willing giving, not a grabbing.

Until that conversion is made, an evident difficulty will remain in seeking to base a political party on an ideal which is not (at any rate, yet) shared or rated highly by those to whom it is supposed to appeal. In a conservative country, that is the difficulty which increasingly dominates the life of a socialist party seeking to win office and to practise, as well as preach, change.

VII

Equality was then, for Crosland, the essential socialist goal. But it was not the *only* goal. Of at least equal importance was a belief in liberty and the values of a pluralistic democracy. Totalitarianism of either colour was anathema to Crosland, even if that totalitarianism was being advocated as a means to achieve other goals (such as equality) in which he fervently believed. Unlike some on the Left of the Labour party, he was devoted to democratic institutions, and his hatred of Communism was unquenchable. The difference between 'us and them' he declared to be an 'unbridgeable gulf'.[41] He never accepted that Communism created a more economically successful society.

But his attack was more fundamentally an attack on dialectical materialism itself. For he rejected its mechanistic assumption of the primacy of economic factors. To him, the western tradition of liberal democracy was enormously more valuable than 1 per cent on or off the rate of economic growth. He protested against the Left's 'eternal failure to comprehend the significance of democracy'.[42] He harboured no illusions as to the determination of the minority of the 'hard Left' to make use of the susceptibilities of a minority of the 'soft Left' to push democracy to one side (a point discussed by Maurice Peston in chapter 11). His trips to Russia and to China, together with his reading of the 'dissident' Eastern European literature, meant that this aspect of his thinking became more rather than less important, even when the hottest phase of the Cold War seemed no more than a historical nightmare.

This commitment to liberal democracy was backed by a complete commitment to the rule of law. In 1968 his instinctive sympathy with some of the demands of the radical students' movement stopped dead when it became 'intolerant ... authoritarian ... and espoused a violence ... never justified unless it is the sole method of establishing democracy'.[43] By 1974 he is appalled when 'the rule of law is challenged by some Labour councillors and trade unionists [since] ... historically – and let no socialist ever forget this – the law has been the means by which the weak obtained redress against the strong'.[44] (Ironically, he himself suffered his most unpleasant experiences as a minister in trying to legislate for an amnesty for those Labour councillors who ignored his warning to them to stay within the law in their opposition to the Conservatives' Housing Finance Act.)

This attachment to the institutions of liberal democracy was born of a deeper attachment to a liberal society. Indeed in one sense Crosland's whole purpose was to show that the socialist goal (as he saw it) of greater equality was wholly compatible with – indeed would actually enhance – the workings of a free society. In *The Future of Socialism* he wrote, 'As ... society becomes more social-democratic with the passing of the old collective grievances and injustices ... we shall turn our attention increasingly to other, and in the long run more important, spheres – of personal freedom, happiness, and cultural endeavour: the cultivation of leisure, beauty, grace, gaiety, excitement, and of all the proper pursuits, whether elevated, vulgar, or eccentric, which contribute to the varied fabric of a full private and family life'.[45] And because these were the goals, certain means to socialism favoured on the Left were rejected. Rationing sat ill with the gaiety Crosland preferred to the Puritan austerity of some old style socialists, and so the continued existence of a market in consumer goods remained central to his thought. The dedicated politicisation of life which comes naturally to the far Left had little appeal to Crosland:

'The majority prefer to lead a full family life and cultivate their gardens. And a good thing too ... we do not ... want a busy, bustling society in which everyone is politically active, and fussing around in an interfering and responsible manner'.[46]

Just as he repudiated the Left's insistence on the predominance of politics, so also he refused to exaggerate the gap between the two main political parties. I do not wish to be misunderstood. The gap between Labour and Conservative was to him unbridgeable and he had the deepest distrust for the advocates of a new centre party.

But 'there must inevitably be *some* common ground between a statement of socialist and one of progressive conservative beliefs. The area of common ground, moreover, is likely to be greater today than in the past'.[47] The notion of a class war without truces had gone out of his intellectual window with Marx.

VIII

In *The Conservative Enemy*, Crosland himself wrote: 'A dogged resistance to change now blankets every segment of our national life. A middle-aged conservatism, parochial and complacent, has settled over the country; and it is hard to find a single sphere in which Britain is pre-eminently in the forefront.'[48]

Now, two decades later, the picture is infinitely more bleak, and plagues the right wing radicals of the Thatcher government as it plagued the left wing radical who served, until his death, its predecessor. Only the complacency has gone to be replaced, even worse, by a growing and literally anti-social pursuit of individual or small group salvation. In the Britain of 1980, *sauve qui peut*.

In this climate the very attractiveness of revisionism as a faith is in danger of becoming its weakness. For it is essentially an optimistic philosophy. It promises liberty *as well as* equality, prosperity *and* fairness; individual freedom *together* with a sense of one community. Such optimism is out of fashion. Revisionism's insistence on the possibility of purposive, practical political action runs counter to the deepening defeatism of the traditional political élite. Though the revisionists won all the arguments at the logical level – certainly while Crosland was alive – they were less successful at the emotional level. They failed to generate an *élan* amongst a whole generation which preferred the excitement of assertion, the naked clash of power, the 'demo' to the intellectual demonstration. Those on the Left who should have been preaching a relevant message to the country as a whole were taken up with debating irrelevancies with each other. And while Labour split its ideological hairs, the right wing ideology of the free market, skilfully deployed by the Institute of Economic Affairs and given a phoney credibility by Britain's national weaknesses, established itself first among the élite, then, through a process of osmosis, amongst the public at large.

And yet, as Crosland must surely have insisted, there is hope. In 'Radical Reform and the Left', Crosland recalls those who predicted the 'inevitable victory of Nazi Germany'; and quotes Orwell: 'power-worship blurs political judgment because it leads, almost unavoidably, to the belief that present trends will continue. Whoever is winning at the moment will always seem invincible. If the Japanese have conquered South Asia, they will keep South Asia for ever; if the Germans have captured Tobruk, they will infallibly capture Cairo'.[49]

But as tides ebb, so also do they flow. If, as I expect, the Thatcher experiment fails; if (as anyone with confidence in the power of human reason must expect) the jejune blend of *dirigiste* planning and workers' control beloved of the Left is exposed in its barrenness, may not then the fruitless, silly search for final solutions come to an end? May not then the humane and flexible vision of the democratic socialists, idealistic, yes, but tempered with due practical scepticism, may not that philosophy rise again from the ashes as the guide by which we conduct our affairs? And may we not yet see that (in the famous passage from *The Future of Socialism* quoted by Dick Leonard in his tribute, above) 'the time has come ... for a greater emphasis on private life, on freedom and dissent, on culture, beauty, leisure, and even frivolity. Total abstinence and a good filing-system are not now the right sign-posts to a socialist Utopia.'[50]

At any rate, I hope so, and perhaps the chapters in this book contain some of those new sign-posts of which our turbulent society stands in need.

4

Labour and the Voters

by Dick Leonard

The study of voting behaviour and political attitudes – that is, political sociology – is a proper study for the politician. There is a tendency in some quarters to despise, or even morally condemn, such studies. This tendency is based on a confusion. Most people would rightly think it despicable simply to ask the voters what they wanted most, and then to promise it regardless of party principle or previous policy. But this is not the object of a study such as this. Its object is to discover, first, what deeper factors, other than short-term party programmes, determine voting behaviour; secondly, to see how the British political parties stand in relation to these factors; thirdly, to consider how the Labour Party might put itself into a better rapport *with them.*[1]

Crosland himself retained a consistent interest in the attitudes and behaviour of voters. He read and mastered, as *Can Labour Win?* made clear, all the earlier literature on the subject and he took a lively interest in opinion poll data at all times – not just when an election was pending.

Yet the Labour party at large, and especially many members of the National Executive Committee, have to a substantial degree retained the hostile attitude against which Crosland warned twenty or so years ago. The consequence has been that Labour's use of survey research material has been spasmodic and, often, ill directed; the benefits derived from the money actually spent have been a great deal less than they might have been, and there has been a singular failure to draw long term valid conclusions from the mass of relevant data available both in published polls and voting studies and in the private polls commissioned by the party.

At best, Harold Wilson and James Callaghan may have been able to improve their electoral tactics as a result of their access to poll material, most effectively, perhaps, in the February 1974 election. Yet, even in the immediate context of election campaigns, Labour has tended to derive far less benefit from the polls than its Tory opponents. An informed comment from the 1970 general election campaign is, unfortunately, typical of the party's attitudes over much of the past two decades:

> There is no evidence that these surveys had any impact on Labour strategy. The party in fact seemed to lack the skill to commission polls that would be of much real use to it, still less to digest or give effect to their findings. The absence of expertise or rigorous thought about what polls could offer and the absence of trust over the dissemination and analysis of the reports that were received greatly diminished any return on the party's efforts in this field.[2]

This incompetence – due to wilful ignorance and an élitist contempt of the need to take pains to discover what ordinary people are thinking – is a major contributory factor to the failure of the Labour party to establish itself as what Wilson was fond of calling the 'natural party of government'. By this, he no doubt meant achieving a predominance among the voters comparable to that of the Democrat party in the United States – which has failed to gain a majority in either the Senate or the House of Representatives in only two out of the last twenty-four congressional elections (in the 80th congress, 1947–49, and the 83rd, 1953–55).

The relative success of the Republican party in electing presidents (four times in the past twelve elections) has obscured the extent to which the Democrats have established a commanding lead over the Republicans in terms of party identification. The most thorough study of the survey and other data available, undertaken by Kristi Andersen of the University of Chicago, reveals that the Democrats increased their lead almost continuously over a period of more than fifty years, being a mere 4 per cent ahead in 1920 and a whopping 24 per cent in 1974.[3]

The collapse of the Republicans has been to the direct

advantage of the growing army of 'independent' voters rather than to the Democrats – which is why the result of presidential elections, in particular, still remains in doubt; but the relative gain of the Democrats has been immense.

It was the great Depression, and particularly the impact of the presidency of Franklin Roosevelt, which provided the Democrats with the opportunity of breaking, and indeed reversing, the historical predominance of the Republican party. And evidence is not lacking that the Labour party was presented with comparable opportunities by the same depression, the experience of the Second World War and the impact of the great 1945 Labour victory, but the party has singularly failed to capitalise on this advantage.

This evidence was marshalled by David Butler and Donald Stokes in their ground breaking volume, *Political Change in Britain*.[4] Their research, based on five rounds of interviews with a panel of some 2,000 voters between 1963 and 1970, showed that Labour had a lead of 15 per cent over the Tories, in terms of long term party identification, among electors who first cast their votes in the 1945 election, and that this lead was maintained among the successive cohorts of voters who entered the electorate during the succeeding two to three decades. As these voters became a larger and larger proportion of the electorate as older more pro-Tory electors died off, the Labour share of the total vote should have risen consistently.

Instead, Labour's electoral fortunes have fluctuated violently and, though Labour governments were elected to office in 1964, 1966 and in two 1974 general elections, in none of these elections – even in 1966 – did Labour do as well as its lead over the Tories in long term party identification should have ensured. The concept of party identification as opposed to current voting intention is clearly weaker in Britain than in America: most British voters change one when they change the other, whereas American voters, who are much more accustomed to the concept of cross-voting, cling more tenaciously to home base when making temporary forays.[5] Nevertheless, a sufficient proportion of British voters behave in the same way for a meaningful distinction to be made between actual election results and 'normal' results, meaning what would have happened if every voter had voted according to his long term party self-identification. It is possible to construct such 'normal' election results from data collected by Professor Ivor Crewe and his colleagues in the British Election Study, at Essex University, who have, since 1974, continued the work pioneered by Messrs Butler and Stokes.[6] Their findings show that in every one of the six general elections held since 1964 the Tories did better, and the Labour party worse, than a 'normal' result would have suggested. Instead of the Labour party winning four elections and the Tories two, a series of 'normal' results would have produced six Labour victories, each of them by a more handsome margin than those actually achieved.

Part of the reason for Labour polling worse than its 'normal' poll can undoubtedly be attributed to the economic difficulties which have beset Labour governments during this period and the failures of Labour ministers in dealing with them. But Tory governments, too, have encountered such difficulties and failures among Tory policies have certainly not been lacking, so the *consistent* under-polling by Labour, even when it has been in opposition, cannot be entirely explained by this factor.

Some of the explanation can certainly be attributed to the superior level of Tory organisation and the larger material resources which the Tories have been able to deploy. This has been well documented, particularly the extent to which they have benefited from the postal vote.[7] But, tempting though it may be to put the entire blame on organisational defects, to do so would be to fly in the face of a convincing mass of survey and opinion poll data. This leaves no room at all for genuine doubt that the reason for Labour's cumulative failure to achieve its full voting potential is that a large number of would-be Labour voters are repelled by Labour policies, Labour attitudes and, in some cases, by Labour personalities.

Yet again the most persuasive evidence has been collected by Professor Crewe and his team. This has shown a marked falling off in support for principles and policies traditionally associated with the Labour party. The decline in support measured over a ten year period, both for Labour identifiers generally and for 'core' Labour identifiers (defined as 'working class trade unionists with a very or fairly strong Labour identification'), is shown in table 1. Six attitudes traditionally associated with Labour support were subscribed to on average by only 40 per cent of Labour identifiers in February 1974, compared with 55 per cent ten years earlier.

Table 1: Falling support for Labour principles

	All Labour identifiers			'Core' Labour identifiers		
	1964 %	Feb 1974 %	Change Feb 1964– Feb'74 %	1964 %	Feb 1974 %	Change Feb 1964– Feb'74 %
In favour of nationalising more industries	57	50	−7	64	50	−14
In favour of spending more on social services	89	61	−28	92	57	−35
In favour of retaining close ties between trade unions and the Labour party	38	29	−9	50	34	−16
Whose sympathies are generally for strikers	37	23	−14	33	25	−8
Who do not believe that the trade unions have 'too much power'	59	44	−15	74	52	−22
Perceiving 'a great deal' of difference between the parties	49	33	−16	62	41	−21
Average (mean)	55	40	−15	63	43	−20

Source: The Economist, 11 March 1978

The Essex team comments: 'Among Labour identifiers ... there occurred in the 1960s a major haemorrhaging of support for the party's main tenets. The gap between official party policy and the views of identifiers was already wider in the Labour party than in the Conservative party in 1964. Between 1964 and 1970 the gap grew wider still'.[8]

By 1979 it had apparently grown to a gaping chasm. Identical questions were put to a large sample of Labour identifiers immediately after the May 1979 election and a further falling away of support was recorded for each of the propositions listed in the table.[9]

While Labour identifiers have been progressively abandoning attitudes and policies associated with their own party, many of them have come to accept, instead, policies adopted by the Tories. The second table was published in the *Observer* on 22 April 1979, during the course of the general election campaign, and it was based on a survey of some 1,200 voters carried out during the previous week by Research Services Ltd. Table 2 summarises the replies of *Labour* voters only: it shows them giving majority approval, sometimes by a very wide margin, for the major campaign objectives put forward by Mrs Thatcher and her team. Commenting on this table, Professor Anthony King, who presented the survey findings in the *Observer*, wrote: 'Seldom can a major party have penetrated so deeply into the political thinking of the other side's staunchest supporters.'[10]

Table 2: Labour voters on Tory aims

	Should the next government attempt to achieve these objectives?		
	Should %	Should not %	Don't know %
Reduce violent crime and vandalism	95	3	2
Reduce Supplementary Benefit for strikers, on assumption that they are getting strike pay from their unions	63	30	7
End secondary picketing by strikers	78	14	8
Reduce income tax, especially for the higher paid	52	45	3
Give council house tenants the right to buy their homes, with discounts for people who have lived in them for three years or more	75	20	5
Reduce the number of civil servants	70	22	8
Sell off parts of some state owned companies	40	49	11

Source: the *Observer*, 22 April 1979

In the light of these findings, and of a great deal of other opinion poll material, it is little wonder that Labour has fallen so far behind its voting potential; rather is it remarkable that so many Labour voters have supported the party so long and so

49

faithfully when so large a gap existed between their personal aspirations and the professed aim of the party.

To a large extent the issues probed in the *Observer* survey reflected the particular concerns of May 1979 and the themes which the Tories sought to project during the election campaign. It might be wrong to attach too much long term importance to them. But there are three particular areas of concern which have made a sharp impact over a long period, which have brought deep unpopularity to the Labour party and over which, though there has been a history of misrepresentation and sheer mendacity by the Tory press, it is impossible to escape the conclusion that a great deal of the damage has been self-inflicted. Those issues are nationalisation, Labour–trade union relations and personal freedom.

It should by now be a truism that virtually any nationalisation proposal is likely to be a net vote loser for Labour. There have been polls with biased questions and others carried out in suspicious circumstances. Questions referring to 'public ownership' also regularly produce a somewhat more positive response than those referring to 'nationalisation'. But when every allowance is made, the repeated findings of a mass of reputable surveys conducted over the years is crystal clear – that only a relatively small minority of the population is favourable to proposals for further nationalisation. This does not mean, *pace* Mrs Thatcher, that a majority is convinced that measures of denationalisation are practicable or desirable. It does mean, however, that much the most popular view is that 'enough is enough'. A fairly typical response was that reported by Butler and Stokes who, in 1970, found that 19 per cent favoured more nationalisation, 40 per cent believed that there should be no more nationalisation, but no denationalisation either, and 29 per cent wanted at least some denationalisation (12 per cent 'don't knows'). Butler and Stokes found, through their panel surveys, that individual responses to nationalisation questions varied considerably over time, but that there was little variation in the overall figures other than a tendency for the pro-nationalisation minority to diminish over time.

In the face of this mass of evidence, the broad thrust of which, if not the detail, has been familiar to every newspaper reader for at least two decades, one would have anticipated that the Labour party would have handled the issue with some

circumspection. This has certainly been true of Labour governments, which cannot fairly be accused of pursuing doctrinaire
pro-nationalisation policies during the recent past. In so far as
the Wilson and Callaghan governments sought to extend the
boundaries of nationalisation, for example by nationalising the
steel industry in 1966 and the shipbuilding and aerospace
industries in 1976–77, the arguments which ministers advanced
in favour of their policies were based far more on the parlous
state in which the industries found themselves, and the seeming
inability of the private owners to effect a viable restructuring of
them, than on any suggestion that nationalisation was inherently
superior to private ownership. The Wilson-Callaghan governments' main instrument for channelling public money into
manufacturing industry – the National Enterprise Board – was
specifically designed to avoid many of the disadvantages of
traditional nationalisation, with an emphasis on sustaining the
mixed economy and on flexible rather than fixed boundaries
between the public and private sectors.

Little of this circumspection has characterised the approach
of the National Executive Committee, which has repeatedly
supported sweeping proposals for further nationalisation,
couched in the most doctrinaire terms. Two episodes stand out.
The first was the adoption of the purely arbitrary figure of the
twenty-five largest companies as candidates for nationalisation
in May 1973 – a commitment from which Harold Wilson
succeeded in disengaging the party only with great difficulty.
The second was the proposal to nationalise the banks and
insurance companies adopted by the Labour party conference
in 1976, after being commended by the NEC spokesman, Ian
Mikardo, in spite of the opposition of the newly elected Labour
leader, James Callaghan. This proposal was junked with rather
less difficulty, largely because it rapidly became clear that the
workers and the unions in the industries concerned were not in
favour of the proposal, itself a comment on the frivolity of the
NEC's approach to the subject and in sharp contrast to the
situation prevailing in every industry previously brought into
public ownership by a Labour government.[11]

Yet though the NEC did not get its way in these cases, its
attitude and the controversies which they provoked yielded a
large harvest of publicity and gave fresh currency to Labour's
image as a doctrinaire party of unreconstructed nationalisers.

On occasions democratic parties knowingly choose to put forward highly unpopular proposals – and quite justifiably if they are convinced these are the best or only means of achieving vital objectives. Yet the extraordinary thing about the national-isation proposals which the NEC has so blithely supported over the past decade or so is that no attempt has been made to relate them to the fundamental purposes for which the party exists. No arguments are advanced or evidence adduced to demon-strate that the sum of human liberty will be enlarged as a result of more public ownership – or equality or fraternity either, for that matter. Or that greater efficiency, greater productivity, faster growth or reduced inflation will be the likely outcome of such changes. All is justified on the grounds of increasing the control which the state (or, to be fair, the 'democratically elected representatives of the people') can exercise over the economy, or important sub-sections thereof.

If it could be shown that an enlarged public stake in the economy produced beneficial economic effects this would, perhaps, be a sufficient justification for the NEC's approach. But, on the contrary, the evidence is beginning to accumulate that a large public – or publicly directed – sector is a positive drag on economic growth and is thus against the economic interests of the mass of industrial workers. Too much should not be inferred from the dismal economic performance of the Communist directed countries, particularly the Soviet Union, over the past two decades. It is impossible to separate out the effect of monopoly state ownership and control of all large and medium scale economic undertakings from the stifling influence on enterprise and innovation that is more generally charac-teristic of a closed totalitarian political system, as Popper demonstrated so clearly in *The Open Society and its Enemies*. More relevant is the evidence from Western countries where, on the whole, the fastest growth has occurred in those where the state has intervened least in the direction of industry and commerce.[12] And, if one examines the record of those countries where demo-cratic socialists have been heavily involved in government, the more successful economic achievements have occurred in countries – such as Sweden, Germany and Holland – where the extension of public ownership has not been a major objective of party policy. It is true that some such countries, for example, Norway and Austria, have had quite big public sectors – for the largely fortuitous reason that German owned undertakings were expropriated at the end of the Second World War. But, typically, such undertakings have been left to operate in a commercial manner and have not been subjected to detailed political control.

Of course, it is not a black and white picture, and numerous examples could be cited of the relative success of public enterprise and public interference and of the relative failure of private undertakings and of *laissez faire* government policies. Yet the broad message is, I believe, now irrefutable. It is that more often than not the man from Whitehall does not know best, and that governments are better advised – in most circumstances – to restrict themselves to macro-economic and fiscal management rather than to attempt to shoulder the burdens of entrepreneurship.

This does not mean that Labour should become a doctrinaire anti-nationalisation party. There will be occasions, as Edward Heath so painfully discovered over Rolls-Royce, when public ownership is the only – and therefore the proper – course open in an otherwise impossible situation. Yet the time is overdue for the Labour party to make it clear, in the most conspicuous possible way, that it no longer regards public ownership as a totem, that it will never propose it for its own sake and that what remains significant to it as a party are the *ends* which socialists traditionally hoped would be furthered by nationalisation rather than the *means*, which all too often have been seen to be inadequate.

The German Social Democratic party made such a declaration at Bad Godesberg in 1959 and was much criticised for it at the time, not least within the British Labour party. Yet it would be a bold person who would claim, looking back over the past two decades, that the Labour party has achieved more than the SPD for its followers in this period or that it has remained closer to the aspirations of the mass of the voters.

When Hugh Gaitskell attempted something along the same lines in 1959–60, with his proposed amendment of Clause IV of the Labour party's constitution, he got his fingers badly burned. Although his maladroit tactics were largely to blame, this unfortunate precedent is likely to continue to deter his successors, though arguably the need for such a symbolic gesture is far greater today than it was in 1959.

If nationalisation has been an albatross round Labour's neck, the party's association with the trade unions has acted as something less than a dependable lifejacket. Yet here the problem is rather more complex. It is undeniable that the party has benefited enormously from the trade union connection, without which it could not have existed in its present form. The trade union movement acted as midwife to the party and has sustained it in good times and in bad with its voting strength, its political funds, its organisational knowhow and, not least, its large fund of common sense.

If anything, the unions have been over solicitous of the party's health, like a possessive mum reluctant to see a growing son stand on his own two feet, and this has stunted the party's development in a number of ways. For example, if the unions' political funds were not there to be called on in time of need, it is scarcely conceivable that the party would not have developed more effective fund raising schemes of its own or at least have worked effectively to ensure the provision of adequate state funding of political activities. Similarly, the dominance of trade union block votes at Labour's annual conference has acted as a road block against the development of more democratic procedures within the party and has been a continuous disincentive to attempts to recruit a genuine mass party membership. (It is extraordinary that in Sweden, with one seventh of our population, and in Austria, with one eighth, the socialist parties should each have twice as many individual members as the Labour party.)

It is also clear that the Labour party suffers greatly from the increasingly unpopular image of the trade unions, with which it is understandably widely associated in the public mind. And here I am not thinking, primarily, of the events of the winter of 1978–79 which were, at the very least, a major contributory factor to Margaret Thatcher's election victory on 3 May 1979. Poll after poll over the years has shown growing majorities of voters who think that the trade unions have too much power[13] and that they should not have close ties with the Labour party.[14]

I am not proposing that this, in itself, is a sufficient reason for breaking such ties. It is, however, ample justification for examining them critically and in particular for asking ourselves whether a somewhat looser connection, such as exists between trade unions and democratic socialist parties in many other countries, would not be more beneficial – both to the party and the unions.

For the unions too have suffered from the over-close relationship of the past. Suffered in particular because the Labour party and Labour governments have felt too inhibited to make constructive criticisms of trade union practices which have become unpopular and, therefore, largely self-defeating. The trade unions have been given no sense by the party that their legal privileges and exemptions, for all or most of which a good case can in fact be made, need to be earned and re-earned over time, rather than being taken for granted. The worst example was, perhaps, the party's unconditional promise in 1972 to repeal the Tory Industrial Relations Act, without receiving in return any worthwhile undertakings either of a reform of trade union practices or of willingness to co-operate with a government sponsored incomes policy. Such *quid pro quo*s must certainly be sought before there should be any question of undertaking to repeal James Prior's trade union Act.

The third area where Labour has acquired a damaging public image is in the whole field of personal freedom and liberty. As Maurice Peston points out elsewhere in this book (see chapter 11), it is the Tories' credentials in this area which really are open to question, and the late Dingle Foot once wrote a notable article in which he explained why he, a former Liberal, chose to join the Labour party precisely because its members showed a greater concern for personal freedom than did its opponents. Foot's conclusion, written in September 1974, was that 'During the past quarter of a century, the Labour party have increasingly become the champions of human rights', and he spelled out impressive chapter and verse in support of this claim.[15]

Yet though a discerning observer like Dingle Foot was able, by scrutinising the actions of Labour governments, to conclude that the Labour party was essentially a libertarian party, this is not the impression which has been conveyed to the mass of voters. Here there is rather less survey data available but virtually all that exists points to the conclusion that it is the Conservative party which is more commonly seen as the party of freedom while Labour tends to be regarded as the party of restriction and control. Compare the answers to two questions put by the Gallup Poll in April 1979 (see table 3).[16]

Table 3: Freedom or Control?

If the Labour party [the Conservatives] won the next general election do you think there would be more personal freedom [government control over people's lives] or less ... or wouldn't things change?

Personal Freedom

	Labour %	Tory* %
More	8	31
Less	25	12
No change	53	42
Don't know	14	14

Government control over people's lives

	Labour %	Tory %
More	36	17
Less	6	32
No change	45	35
Don't know	13	17

Source: Gallup Political Index, May 1979

* Figures do not add to 100 per cent because they are rounded up or down to the nearest whole number.

Because of its continuing emphasis on social responsibility and the need for public authorities to ameliorate or counteract the pressures of the market place, a democratic socialist party is always liable to be branded as a party of bureaucrats. The Swedish Social Democratic party, despite its outstanding achievements during forty-four years of office, seems to have owed its defeat in 1976 partly at least to this factor. Hans Zetterberg, director of the Swedish opinion poll organisation, SIFO, was able to measure a significant increase in the extent to which the party became tarred with a bureaucratic image during the three preceding years (see table 4).[17]

Table 4: Swedes and the Social Democratic party

Do you regard our Swedish Social Democrats mainly as bosses, bureaucrats and top dogs, or mainly as socialists, reformers and friends of the poor and oppressed?

	1973 %	1976 %
Bosses, bureaucrats, top dogs	36	41
Socialists, reformers, friends of poor and oppressed	39	36
Doubtful, don't know	25	23

Source: Hans L. Zetterberg, *The Swedish Election 1976*

If, as seems likely, the Labour party is also widely seen as the instrument of an unfeeling bureaucracy it is particularly unjust, as it was the Tories, through their Health Service and local government reorganisations in the early 1970s, who have given the biggest, sharpest twist to the bureaucratic spiral in recent years. Yet, once again, it would be sanguine to put all the blame on the misrepresentation of our opponents. Many Labour councillors, in particular, by their attitudes, their pronouncements and sometimes by their actions lend support to the stereotype of a party more interested in petty controls than in extending freedom.

The most striking recent example concerns the proposed sale of council houses to sitting tenants, which polls have repeatedly shown to be highly popular, despite the manifold practical difficulties which are undoubtedly passed over much too lightly by Tory advocates of a property owning democracy. The attitude taken by the Labour party nationally is a perfectly defensible one in terms of principle, despite its lack of appeal to the majority of voters. This is that, though Labour is not in principle opposed to such sales, it cannot support them in areas where there is a shortage of housing for rent as they would diminish the ability of local authorities to help those with the greatest housing need. Yet many Labour councillors, and more local Labour parties, have taken a far harder line and have opposed sales even in areas where no shortage existed, taking the sea green incorruptible line that any disposal of public assets was impermissible. This is putting party doctrine before the wishes of the voters with a vengeance – and judging, for example, by the above average swings recorded against Labour in new town seats in May 1979, quite a few voters were prepared to give practical effect to their resentment.

The party leadership's own recent record on the proper balance to be struck between freedom and controls is certainly not above criticism. Despite a firm manifesto commitment, the Callaghan government refused to introduce a freedom of information Bill, and even declined to lend a helping hand to Clement Freud's private member's Bill in March 1979 when such support could well have provided a lifeline to its own sinking fortunes. Jim Callaghan and his colleagues need urgently to re-examine their own attitudes and also to give much firmer guidance to Labour councillors and constituency party officials. They should make it quite clear to them that restrictions on liberty *always* need to be justified, and that when there is any doubt at all where the balance of advantage lies, the benefit must be given to the advocates of freedom.

This chapter has not been, except incidentally, about Labour party policies: it has been more concerned with attitudes and presentation. Above all, it has been concerned about what attitude the Labour party should adopt towards the voters. On this Crosland, though he constantly referred to the topic in a jocular vein, had no doubt at all what the proper attitude should be: one of profound respect. He consistently mocked those who were concerned with public opinion in certain intellectually smart and media-conscious London postal districts – SW1, EC4 or NW3 (this was sometimes amended to NW1, where I must plead guilty to living). The reported views of the denizens of these areas were constantly weighed – to their disadvantage – against those of the working class voters of Grimsby, whom Crosland took to be far more representative of British public opinion.

In his later years, he became increasingly concerned that the Labour party was becoming alienated from the aspirations of such voters. He never believed that Labour should adopt a purely 'populist' approach. As he argued in 1971, that 'would mean the restoration of hanging and flogging, a Powellite policy on race, vast reductions in income tax, the withdrawal of family allowances, and an end to student grants and overseas aid ... I state flatly that such policies are unacceptable to any Social Democrat'.[18] Yet he felt strongly that Labour should not gratuitously offend voters' susceptibilities by adopting policies for which there was not an overwhelming case either on grounds of principle or of practical necessity, which flew in the face of majority sentiment. There is nothing craven about such a view, which is surely a profoundly democratic one.

And, by ignoring it, as this chapter has argued that the Labour party has tended to do over these highly sensitive issues, the party has saddled itself with an enormous handicap. Nor is it open to us, as Bertolt Brecht wrote with savage irony of the East German regime in June 1953, to elect a new people because the existing one has failed to come up to our expectations.

Part 3

5

Social Democracy and the International Economy

by I. M. D. Little

For me, social democracy is what Tony Crosland defined it to be in *The Future of Socialism*. It is a reformist movement towards a society of greater economic and social equality in which class distinctions will be greatly reduced (especially in the UK) and poverty eliminated to the extent which is possible by means of social action. A high degree of liberty of the subject (in the 'liberal' sense of non-coercion) is also an end, which precludes the predominant state ownership of the means of production.[1] The mixed economy is a *sine qua non* of social democracy. Socialism is about equality, not ownership, he claimed. There is no Utopian blue-print, and the ends are deliberately fuzzy because the trade-offs between liberty, equality and efficiency are not explored to the point of defining desirable degrees of inequality and private ownership. This was not necessary, for he clearly believed that one could go a long way towards greater economic and social equality without any marked increase in collective ownership, or any marked effect resulting from a decrease in incentives and hence efficiency. Some individual liberties and rights would, of course, have to be constrained (as in any society) in the interest of social or economic equality – such as the right to educate one's children as one would like. But this would hardly go beyond the limitations on personal freedom which have come to be very widely accepted as desirable. The trade-offs were thus not yet very interesting. In the course of time he would have played it by ear as events unfolded.

So much for the socialist element in social democracy. Many of those to the left of Tony Crosland might say that this was at best merely capitalism with a human face. But many sympathisers could call themselves socialists while continuing to believe that private enterprise for private gain working within a developed market system is valuable in itself, and both has done and will do more for humankind than any other way of organising economic and social life. Unfortunately, I do not think that his definition of socialism has taken root. Most people associate the word with public, or anyway collective, ownership.

Political democracy was also, of course, a *sine qua non* for the defence of freedom. Governments must be elected, and they may be more or less socialist in their emphasis on equality and individual rights. This has certain implications. A country in which social democracy is to make progress cannot from time to time elect a government which is too extremist and undoes all the reforms. Nor, more pointedly, can it elect a government which will put an end to elections. A considerable degree of consensus is presupposed. Any developments which undermine that consensus constitute a threat. Although he did not put it that way, and wrote of *The Conservative Enemy*, I think he believed that reformist social democracy would create its own consensus, and that alternative governments were therefore not likely to be very extreme. I do not know whether he kept to this belief to the end.

Besides consensus, there is, I think, another precondition for the success of social democracy. This is that a social democratic government should be in sufficient control, and be constrained only by the democratic political process. It must, of course, listen to and be influenced by interest groups but not be dominated or threatened by them. Tony Crosland turned Laski upside down and wrote '... whatever the modes of economic production, economic power will, in fact, belong to the owners of political power. And these today are certainly not the pristine class of capitalists'.[2] He had in mind, of course, the essential tameness of the capitalists and their lackeys. Laski and the Marxists were so far wrong that it has turned out to be organised employees[3] who succeed in preventing governments from fulfilling some of the aims of democratic socialism. Tony Crosland had not then foreseen, nor had anyone, that governments might not be strong enough to take the measures required to assure reasonably full employment.

Let me now turn to the question whether the economic developments of the 1970s constitute a threat to social democracy. Almost all the OECD economies are suffering from high rates of inflation, which have been only slowly reduced from the peaks of 1974 (or 1975 in the UK). Recovery from the 1974–75 recession has been very slow. Unemployment is very high as compared with the 1950s and 1960s. This is especially true of Europe. In the USA, recovery has been faster; unemployment is not historically high, but inflation is. The threat that inflation will again escalate is very real for both Europe and North America.

Many developing countries, even oil importers, have done better than the developed. A few have even succeeded both in bringing inflation almost to a halt and in resuming rapid growth. The non-oil developing world has achieved this by borrowing heavily, thereby assuming much of the total deficit which is the counterpart of the surpluses of oil exporters.

This may all seem to add up to a world economic crisis, or anyway an OECD crisis. But I do not think this is correct. To my mind, to describe something as a world or an international economic crisis presupposes that either the cause of the trouble lies in international economic relations or events, or that the remedy necessitates concerted economic action.

Of course, the recession was no doubt partly caused by the huge oil price rise of December 1973. This represented a large potential increase in world savings which could not immediately be matched by investment. On balance, non-oil exporters would have to reduce their own savings to counteract this, and run deficits. This was quickly realised by financial authorities in the OECD countries; but it was not done. The OECD was back in overall trade balance in 1975, leaving it to the non-oil developing countries to carry the trade deficits, the resultant borrowing helping them to weather the storm much better than the OECD.[4] Why was it not done? For few countries was there a problem in financing the required deficits. International money was not scarce. In so far as one could speak of a world monetary system, it did not crack – and indeed most observers have been surprised at the smoothness with which 'petro-dollars' were recycled to the developing countries. Nor did OECD governments lack power to stimulate demand. The reason why it was not done, and is still not being done to a sufficient degree for the OECD countries to have recovered adequately from the recession, is to a very large degree the fear of inflation.

Of course, the total OECD balance has included some large deficits and surpluses and there has been some consequent railing at the surplus countries. For these surplus countries, it clearly cannot be balance of payments fears which are inhibiting growth. It can only be the fear of inflation. Even where traditionally conservative monetary or fiscal policies seem to be the inhibiting factor, it must be remembered that such conservatism is itself rooted in the fear of inflation. It also seems probable that many of the deficit countries would have stimulated demand further if it had not been for inflation, and the fear of accelerating it. Most of the countries could have borrowed more, emulating some developing countries such as Brazil and South Korea.[5] The USA has also borrowed heavily and has recovered better than most from the recession. Today, despite her huge deficit, it seems that it is primarily the fear of accelerating inflation which is resulting in restraint.

It can be argued that the UK has been the country most inhibited by balance of payments considerations. It seems that fear of another sterling crisis may have been one of the most important considerations in recent years and such a crisis would necessitate meeting creditors' conditions which might themselves preclude a more rapid expansion of demand. Nevertheless, I believe that the reason why a greater stimulus of demand has not been forthcoming is basically inflation. If the UK had had as little inflation as, say, Germany, there would have been no question of a sterling crisis.

It is being argued that the UK, despite a now reasonably healthy balance of payments, would again have a serious deficit if demand were adequate for full employment. No doubt this is true, at present exchange rates. It is further argued that any given fall in the pound would do little good, because it would result in wage increases which would soon wipe out the inducements to export, and import-substitute, which the price changes bring about. An improvement in the foreign trade position would require an ever falling pound. Consequently, the Cambridge group advocates protection against imported manufactures, which, it is claimed, would have less effect on wage demands than a devaluation, with the result that a given improvement in the balance of payments would be achieved with much less inflation than would result from devaluation. There is no need here to enter again into this controversy. I have argued elsewhere that I believe that protection would be very misguided, and very harmful in the long run.[6] The only point to be made here is that this argument for protection is wholly based on the prevalence of a wage-push inflation which makes it impossible to reduce (or even to moderate rises in) real wages when the need arises. Real earnings can be contained within the needed macro-economic bounds only by reduced employment.

Thus it seems that one cannot blame the long drawn out recession on the now seven year old oil price rise, nor on any breakdown in international payments mechanisms, nor much indeed on a lack of co-operation or good neighbourliness on the part of OECD governments. Even the much feared heavy increase in indebtedness on the part of a small number of developing countries has produced no global disaster, though it could be very serious if continued recession and increased protectionism by the developed countries prevent their exports from rising sufficiently to make the debt service tolerable.

But is not inflation itself an international problem? Of course it is, in the sense of being pervasive. But I doubt whether it is in the sense of requiring international remedies or co-operation. It is more like cancer than the plague. This has become clearer with the demise of Bretton Woods. Under a fixed par value system it was almost impossible not to 'import' a world inflation. But the system had vanished effectively in August 1971, and finally in 1973, with the widespread adoption of floating rates. Since then a country which does not have the seeds of inflation in its own garden is able rather easily to fence itself off from a general rise in world prices by letting the value of its currency rise.

Of course, the oil price rise itself, which could hardly be countered by revaluation, caused some generalised increases in prices as it worked its way through the system. But this in itself was negligible compared to the price rises since 1973–74. This is not to deny that the resulting fall in real income was not also a causative factor in inflation – but, in this guise, the price rise becomes but one of a great many factors which can cause wage demands. This is discussed further below.

It can still be argued that the present high rates of inflation are a hangover from the boom of 1972–73, which for the first time since 1951 was coincidental in all countries, and that the boom was itself of an epidemic nature, caused in some degree by the heavy US deficit which flooded the world with liquidity, resulting in an unprecedented rise in reserves in the period 1970–72. This latter factor in turn can be ascribed to a failure of the world monetary mechanism as it developed after Bretton Woods. So perhaps, after all, the present inflation and hence the still continuing recession is the result of a world crisis in the proper sense.

There was widespread excess demand in 1973, both for commodities and, to a lesser extent, for labour. But this was a fairly short lived demand boom between two periods of stagflation. Inflation had been definitely accelerating for several years prior to 1973, when demand was not strong. Naturally the boom was a contributory cause of the further acceleration that took place. It is much less clear that the increase in world reserves was a predominant cause rather than a permissive element in the great boom. There is no need to enter into this monetarist controversy here.[7] Even if some element of a monetary epidemic was then present, stagflation has been with us in the UK for a decade. In several other OECD countries a slowdown of growth from 1968–70 was also accompanied by an increase in inflation.

Thus, it is abundantly clear not only that cost-push inflation is the rule but also that claims that inflation is imported have a very hollow ring. It might also seem surprising in these circumstances that monetary explanations have retained the credence they gained in the late 1960s and early 1970s. If, as it has been claimed, money can act only through demand, then money is no explanation of a cost inflation. And the corollary is that monetary restriction can act only through the creation of unemployment. It is, however, conceivable that organised labour watches the money supply, and bids higher the greater the increase in the amount of money. In other words, the amount of money acts directly on expectations, including above all those of union leaders. Is this a fantasy? If it is, it will probably not remain one for long. There is no doubt that money acts directly on *some* expectations. Recently, Stock Exchange prices have tended to fall as the money supply increases, in defiance of simple Keynesian theory. Both Wall Street and the City have watched monetary expansion with an eagle eye. In recent years an expectation of increased inflation has been taken as bearish, since real profits have fallen with inflation in both the UK and USA. All this may mean that Professor Milton Friedman is creating the conditions which validate his analysis, an heroic effort! However, even this sophisticated and possibly fantastic justification of monetarism leaves money as only one of many determinants of cost-inflation. If the actors in this anti-social game are strong enough, the possible causes of accelerated demands are many: an increase in the quantity of money; a temporary rise in food prices; the oil price rise; increased taxation; slower growth than people have come to expect; and even bad weather for the holidays. One may vote against the government, or vote for inflation, or both.

Even if it is accepted that collective bargaining is the basic cause of inflation in the developed countries, it can still be argued that the seriousness of the stagflation is causally related to the 1972–73 boom. This may be the case but it is really saying no more than that when high rates of inflation once set in, they are very hard to bring down – a proposition which implicitly accepts the cost-push view of inflation. The actors gear their expectations to existing high rates of inflation. Even if they are acting only defensively, they perpetuate the inflation. They may indeed accelerate it, if between them they are demanding in real terms more than the economy can deliver. For they then inevitably find that their monetary demands fail to secure what they want, inflation becoming faster than was expected. So next time they increase their monetary demands. Indeed, all inflations have accelerated, and some with a *falling* ratio of money to national income,[8] until the situation became so bad that the authorities, or some new authorities, have enforced a major crackdown usually involving both recession and also wage and price controls. This kind of acceleration is consistent with demand induced inflation if the government itself is among the demanding actors. It may be the government that is the prime cause, by using excessive and ever increasing budget deficits instead of taxation to try to satisfy its own demands. This kind of accelerating inflation has been typical of some Latin American countries, though in some (such as Argentina and Chile) the trade unions have played their part too.

In Europe it has not generally been governments which have caused inflation through deficit finance, despite the very high level of government expenditure which is a hall-mark of social democracy. However, high government expenditure can exacerbate cost-push inflation if it so constrains personal incomes, especially wage incomes, that demands for more personal disposable income are magnified. This, however, presumes that the conditions for cost inflation exist, that is, that the competing actors are strong enough to force the pace.

Among the remaining actors, it is possible that monopolistic capitalist enterprises could be the prime movers in the inflationary process, each trying, but failing, to increase its profit margins in the belief that others were doing the same, with labour acting no more than defensively. But in view of the fact that profit rates fell rather generally, and especially heavily in the UK, as inflation accelerated, this is not plausible. It seems that business was too competitive or too constrained by the government (and the taxation of unreal stock profits) even to succeed in defending itself. There is no possible doubt that the determination of wages by competitive collective bargaining on the part of organised labour is the heart of the problem. Organised labour finds it difficult to see this, especially when, as recently, prices have risen faster than wages. If, as a result of some event such as the massive oil price rise, the country becomes poorer, profits cannot always take the whole shock — if the shock is big, profits are too small a part of national income to do so, without disastrous effects on investment and employment. The only other way out is borrowing but, as we have seen, borrowing can itself be inhibited by inflation. If real wages have to fall, then even mere defensive action by organised labour is necessarily inflationary. In the UK, real wages were maintained in the early phase of the recession. Their later fall has been a delayed but essential adjustment. An economic system which cannot survive a shock without the massive inflation experienced by the UK is scarcely viable. Nor is it at all sure that collective bargaining will not now lead to unacceptable rates of inflation even in fair weather.

If strong labour organisation and collective bargaining is to be regarded as part of social democracy, then there is a contradiction in the movement. In *The Future of Socialism*, Tony Crosland did not accept this. Thus in the mid-1950s he could correctly argue that in periods when there was little or no excess demand, wages rose only moderately and prices very little. He concluded that 'the case for a national wages policy is not definitely made out on the grounds that full employment must *ipso facto* induce an autonomous wage-inflation'.[9] He argued that it was 'not the responsibility of the Unions to determine whether or not we have a price-inflation. This is the responsibility of the government, which should create, by its fiscal and monetary policy, those economic conditions in which the action of Unions and employers will lead (broadly) to the price-level which it desires.'[10] Tony Crosland further argued that if the unions were to become responsible for wage restraint, and be overly concerned with national economic policy, this could only deprive them of the confidence and loyalty of their members, who would no doubt turn to the Communist party instead.[11]

All this was very reasonable in those days, and I believed much the same myself. Alas, there has been a sea-change between then and now. Now we can see that the economic conditions in which the action of unions and employers would lead (broadly) to the price level desired would be appalling. Tony Crosland did, of course, wisely shift his views. In 1973 he wrote, 'In democratic countries some inflation is clearly endemic' and 'it is the purest wishful thinking to suppose that in an increasingly planned economy (especially when a growing part of the population is employed in the public sector) governments can adopt a *dirigiste* attitude to the control of prices, but a *laissez-faire* attitude to the determination of incomes; the more so since this would involve abandoning one possible means of achieving a greater equality of income.'[12]

In 1975 he wrote, 'Administered in co-operation with the trade unions, such [prices and incomes] policies have the further advantage of transforming wage bargaining from mere power bargaining to an exercise in the social determination of relative incomes. Some of the most encouraging experiences in this field have been in Scandinavia where, with the full consent of the trade union movements, centralised bargaining procedures in which the government is directly represented have been accepted as the normal means of determining incomes.'[13]

The tension between these views (that it might be disastrous for democracy if the unions were jointly responsible for incomes policy, and disastrous if they were not)[14] is clear. Neither view is outmoded, although it could be argued that rapid inflation has made it more likely that the rank and file would remain loyal to a leadership which assumed a responsible quasi-governmental role. Finally, we should further now note that the Swedish harmony, which he so much admired, seems also to have broken down.

The problem goes beyond inflation. It can be asked whether widespread strong organised unions and professional associations are compatible with social democracy at all. It seems to me that in practice the pursuit of their particular interests inevitably works against the attainment of greater equality and full employment; and against expenditures required for defence and the high standards of free education and health, and the maintenance of a safety net against poverty, which seem to be the hall marks of social democracy. Even the reality of political democracy is threatened if governments are weak in relation to such interest groups. The country can become ungovernable – at least as ungovernable as some Latin American countries – unless the most powerful interest group, or groups, determine legislation outside the parliamentary process.

Some will argue, of course, that it is business interests which are unduly powerful *vis à vis* government. I think that Tony Crosland himself answered this latter case, to my mind convincingly, at least for the UK. That he did not, as a working politician, face the former (except obliquely)[15] is not surprising, and it is in itself evidence of the power of such organisations.

The question may be asked whether wage-push inflation has not, after all, improved the distribution of income and wealth – one of the major ends of social democracy. The answer is that it recently has, as a result of a profit squeeze which was inconsistent with sufficient investment, not merely for adequate growth but even for reasonably full employment. Real wages can get too high in relation to the capital endowment of a country. This is a problem which is endemic to developing countries, but it seems that it is spreading to Europe. Too high industrial wages do not merely result in underemployment of the capital stock. They also cause a low level of investment,

which is also excessively labour-saving (given that low level).
This implies that industry (and any other sector where real
wages can be pushed up) employs fewer people than is desirable.
Other sectors get lower wages or, if a minimum wage is in
operation, unemployment results. (The situation may be partly
relieved by the development of secondary labour markets where
wages are freely determined. This has become a feature of the
Italian economy, to which the dualism previously associated
with developing countries has clearly spread.) This situation is,
of course, the more likely to develop the lower is the rate of
investment. Thus while a profit squeeze improves the distribution of income of organised workers as against dividend
receivers, it worsens the distribution of earned income, as well as
slowing growth or even bringing it to a halt. In a mixed
economy, squeezing profits through inflationary wage increases
is not a sound road towards equality. Redistribution of wealth
(including pension funds) is the right road, so that private
profits are more equally spread.

Having argued that the threat to social democracy is in no
significant measure external, let me turn finally and very
briefly to the external responsibilities of social democracy. To
argue that socialism is about equality, but only equality in one
country, is neither morally nor intellectually very appealing –
certainly not to someone such as myself who has been almost
wholly concerned with the problems of developing countries for
the past twenty years. Tony Crosland fully recognised this,
although he was not personally much or for long concerned
with their affairs, and indeed protested that I spent most of my
time on them. Thus he resoundingly stated in the preface to *The
Future of Socialism*, 'It goes without saying (or, rather, it usually
goes with saying, but without doing) that socialism now has
more application to Britain's relations with other, poorer
countries, than to internal class relations within Britain.
Viewed on a world scale, the British worker belongs to a
privileged upper class; and he should concede, as well as
demand, greater equality.'[16] Also the chapter 'Towards a
Welfare World' in *The Conservative Enemy* is devoted to the
problem of aid, and the need greatly to increase it. But 'saying
without doing' has continued to apply, and aid as a proportion
of GNP has fallen as fast as the flow of promises to increase
it.

Worse than this hypocrisy is the cynicism of the new protection. Britain was in the van of the EEC battle to get textile agreements really sewn up tight, so that a few jobs would be maintained at home at the cost of eliminating many more in the developing countries;[17] and those many more jobs would be held by far poorer people with no welfare state to fall back on. This action is a bitter blow to those of us who believe that exports of labour-intensive manufactures are one of the most promising ways in which growth with greater equality can be promoted in the developing countries. What a contribution to the New International Economic Order! It is not just the immediate harm. The developing countries, already suspicious of trade with the old imperialists, will be driven back to a capital-intensive industrialisation which promotes inequality as a result of its low and selective demand for workers. Those who argued that the Western powers would soon put on restrictions if they relied on trade are being proved right. So, I fear, social democracy in the UK is in practice concerned neither with inequality between nations, nor with the cause of greater equality within them – except verbally, of course. This is to some extent true of all social democracies, but it should be added that quite a number of the smaller continental countries have demonstrated greater concern than the UK.

I have argued that inflation, with its concomitants in any democracy of more unemployment than need be, slow growth and general uncertainty, is, apart from the Communist parties of Portugal, France and maybe Italy, the major threat to social democracy in Western Europe. This inflation is not the result of inter-relationships between countries or of any breakdown in them. There is no World Economic Crisis. The threat is indigenous to social democracies in which people can so organise themselves as to make demands on the economy which cannot be met and to seriously hamper its workings if they are not met. Inflation is primarily the result of a growth of nodules of power outside democratic government. This is the contradiction that has somehow to be eliminated, or at least contained. This same contradiction results in the Western democracies exhibiting ever less concern for the poor in other countries.

6

The Fixing of Money Rates of Pay

by Professor James Meade

I The Nature of the Problem

As Anthony Crosland frequently pointed out, incomes policy in the 1950s was the policy of Labour's Left, not the Right. After nearly thirteen years of Labour government since 1964, most of them devoted to one attempt after another to find an effective way of keeping money wages and productivity in line, by one of those strange transformations of public and party life, it is so no longer. But with inflation ever more clearly the constraint on our ability to achieve full employment, the need for some form of incomes policy ought to be the first thing on which everybody in the Labour party could agree. For recent experiences of industrial turmoil with lost production, unemployment and inflation – to say nothing of closed schools and hospitals – suggest that our arrangements for the fixing of money rates of pay need rather radical reform if our type of free, compassionate democratic society is to survive. Let me start by outlining the nature of the problem, as I see it.

For many years after the Second World War, there was a general view that on Keynesian grounds monetary and fiscal policies should be so designed as to maintain full employment. There were strong pressures to observe this principle with little regard to what was happening to money rates of pay. On this principle, however rapidly money pay was being pushed up, demand management policies were to be sufficiently expansionary for the whole output of goods and services to find purchasers even though their money costs and prices might be much inflated. Policies with this effect have been promoted not only on the general or 'macro' level of monetary and budgetary strategy but also in particular on 'micro' cases of lame ducks, such as British Leyland, where from time to time government funds have been provided to maintain output and employment somewhat independently of the level at which rates of pay might be set.

Combined with this expectation that full employment would be maintained with little regard to the level of money pay, there have been many developments which have increased the bargaining powers of trade unions and have encouraged the use of such powers.

1 Legislation by the last Labour government concerning trade unions and conditions of employment increased the monopolistic powers of labour organisations.

2 Developments of modern technology have enabled small compact groups of workers to hold up large ranges of economic activity: a few computer operatives to put a stop to large governmental processes, a limited number of producers of a vital component to halt important assembly lines, a few air traffic controllers to close a major international airport, a limited number of electrical engineers to cripple industry, and so on, with the result that at a very small cost in strike pay for a small number of strikers a very large amount of economic loss can be inflicted.

3 At the same time, markets for the products of individual manufacturing concerns have become more differentiated with the result that individual productive concerns face less perfectly competitive markets for their products. Each individual enterprise is *pro tanto* less averse to granting a pay rise and to covering the consequential rise in its cost by an offsetting rise in the price charged for its product. The resistance of the employing enterprise to a pay claim is thus reduced.[1]

4 The very marked rises in real rates of pay and standards of living which have taken place since the bad old days of the 1930s have meant that employees have more capital resources behind them and thus a greater staying power if they do decide to strike or take other industrial action which will cause a temporary decline in their incomes.

5   Rates of Unemployment and Supplementary Benefit have
also improved since the bad old days of the 1930s. This development, which is greatly to be welcomed, has probably had the
incidental effect of reducing somewhat the pressure on unemployed workers to find jobs even at low rates of pay.

As the years have passed and one group after another has
exercised its muscle power, the message has spread. Group after
group has come to realise that it has latent monopolistic
bargaining powers, the extent of which it had not previously
appreciated; and group after group has come to be willing to
use such powers with less and less regard for their unfortunate
effects upon the community.

This presents a difficult moral issue in the case of groups of
workers in particularly sensitive sectors of the economy. Should
they be less free than others to exercise their muscle power? All
praise to those who have refrained from doing so. Consider the
case of the hospital nurses or the police who have so far refused
to take industrial action, though their latent bargaining power
may well be as great as, or even greater than, that of, for
example, the coal miners. With a three day week in industry
and a certain amount of shivering at home, the community can
sit out quite a lengthy coal strike. But how long could it hold out
if all hospitals and police services were completely closed down?

Before one is free with one's condemnations of any such group
which has not refrained from action, one needs to consider
carefully the pressures on a group which sees all other groups
receiving large increases of pay by the exercise of monopolistic
bargaining power and which is asked to deny itself a similar rise
in pay by refraining on humanitarian grounds from exercising
its own even greater bargaining power. School workers, hospital
workers and social workers cannot, like miners and lorry drivers,
merely confine their activities to crippling industry and causing
widespread unemployment; they have the stark choice between
hurting the children, the sick and the deprived or doing
nothing.

Or consider the case of such trade union leaders as Tom
Jackson of the Communication Workers or Sidney Weighell of
the Railway Workers who at the Trades Union Congress in 1978
opposed the return to free collective bargaining – or what I
prefer to call uncontrolled monopoly bargaining – and who
with other union leaders has argued for an alternative Better

77

Way for fixing money wage rates at fair and uninflated levels. When later they in turn put forward claims for large percentage pay increases on behalf of their own members, backed by the implied threat of industrial action, they are accused of humbug and hypocrisy, of talking big about moderation in general and then putting in excessive claims for their own members. But such accusations are grossly unfair. There is nothing at all hypocritical or inconsistent in arguing for an alternative method to be applied simultaneously to all groups for the attainment of fair but moderate pay settlements, and at the same time making sure that, if there is to be a continuation of uncontrolled monopoly bargaining, then in the consequential free-for-all their own members – in the immortal words of Frank Cousins – are going to be part of the all. A statesman who argues for an international disarmament treaty is not a hypocrite because, in the absence of such a treaty, he maintains the armed power of his own country.

The free-for-all 'devil take the hindmost' that results from the present methods of settlements of pay through uncontrolled monopoly bargaining inflicts severe moral damage on society. The spread of the ideas that each group should be free to form a powerful independent monopoly, should be judge in its own cause as to what its pay ought to be, should be given special legal privileges to enable it more effectively to inflict damage on others until its aims are achieved, and, if it is to compete successfully in its claims *vis-à-vis* other monopolistic groups, must be ready to become less and less compassionate, scrupulous and conscience stricken in the means which it chooses to employ – all this encourages the present increasing disregard of the rule of law and thus helps to undermine an essential foundation for a decent society. This damage to the fabric of society may well be the most important aspect of the matter; but I am an economist and in this chapter will concentrate on the economic issues. However, as a citizen I do so with the thought constantly at the back of my mind that to have one's rate of pay determined by impartial award rather than by causing discomfort and distress to one's fellow citizens would be to respect the rule of law in preference to the methods of unarmed guerrilla warfare.

The distress and discomfort which is caused when one group of workers takes industrial action is no longer confined to the employers of those workers. Indeed it falls nowadays primarily upon other groups of wage earners.

In the bad old days of the early nineteenth century, the strike was the only weapon available to a group of workers. It was aimed at an employer or a limited group of employers whose profits were to be hit by the discontinuance of production and who might, therefore, stand to lose less by accepting the strikers' demands than by the continuation of the strike. Workers could make real gains at the expense of the excess profits of a group of employers who were in open or tacit combination to hold wages down.

This is no longer the typical situation. It is manifestly not so in the case of a nationalised industry or of public employment. If the miners obtain a higher wage, then either the government's budget revenue suffers through the reduced profits or increased losses of the National Coal Board – in which case it is the general taxpayer or those whose welfare depends upon government expenditure who suffer – or else the price of coal is raised and the miners gain at the expense of the general consumers of coal. Similarly, if school workers and hospital workers receive higher wages, there is no Gradgrind unscrupulous employer at the expense of whose excess profits they can be paid. In fact, the increase in their wage will be at the expense of the ratepayers or taxpayers or, if increased wage costs lead to some reduction of service, at the expense of the school children or the hospital patients.

Even in the private sector of the economy, any gains in real earnings to be achieved in today's conditions from a further general squeeze in profits are very limited. Of the net national income no less than 90 per cent now goes to earned incomes,[2] leaving only 10 per cent for incomes from property of all kinds. Thus a 30 per cent cut in total incomes from property would be needed to obtain a once-for-all increase of 3 per cent in earned incomes, a rise which could be continually obtained year after year by a normal increase in productivity. The figures just quoted are for incomes before tax; the distribution of incomes after tax is even more heavily weighted in favour of earned incomes. Moreover a substantial part of company profits and other forms of incomes from property accrue to pension funds and thus to the support of retired workers. Indeed no less than 50 per cent of the securities quoted on the Stock Exchange are now held by pension funds and other similar institutions. And some level of profits is in any case necessary to maintain incentives in industry and in particular to promote investment and capital development. The level of real earnings today is dependent above all on the size of the national cake rather than on its distribution, on output per worker rather than on any reduction of excess profits.

This means that, if any one group does succeed in obtaining an exceptionally large increase in pay, any resulting real rise in its standards in excess of the general increase in productivity in the country as a whole is likely to be achieved primarily at the expense of other earners. It will result in the inflation of the prices of its products which are charged to other earners, the extent to which it can be financed by a further squeeze on profits being very limited.

I am not suggesting that we should be unconcerned about the distribution of income and property. On the contrary, there is much that can be done. Thus excess monopoly profits should be restrained by the promotion of competition through the free import of competing products and through measures against restrictive business practices and the improper use of monopoly powers. Where substantial monopoly is inevitable, selling prices should be subject to control or the operations should be nationalised. Impediments to the movement of persons from low paid to high paid jobs should be removed. Tax measures should be taken to mitigate inequalities in post-tax incomes and to promote a wider dispersal of the ownership of property. Social benefits and welfare services should be developed. With our present legislature, elected by adult franchise, all these measures have been applied. To what extent they could be better and more effectively applied is an important matter which I cannot discuss in this chapter. I wish only to make two points: first, that conditions at present are already such that there does not exist any large untapped reservoir of excess profits from which any really substantial increases in the general level of real earnings can be financed; and second, that whether, and if so how, policies for the redistribution of income and wealth should be reformulated, improved or strengthened is a matter to be determined by the action of our democratically elected parliament and government rather than through the uncontrolled industrial action of independent monopolistic groups enabling those in the strong bargaining positions to gain at the expense of the weak.

Political as well as economic developments have transformed the functions of the trade unions and the strike weapon as instruments for the distribution of incomes. In the early days of the nineteenth century, the worker was the underdog politically as well as economically. Parliament was the preserve of the masters; legislation and its administration were heavily biased against servants and workers; the idea of achieving any decent settlement of wages through impartial arbitration based on principles acceptable to the workers or of obtaining a redistribution of income other than through industrial action could be dismissed as a Utopian nonsense. But all this is different now. With adult suffrage the worker is no longer, thank goodness, politically an underdog. Through parliament, the trade unions under the Labour government obtained legislation which much increased their bargaining strength. Parliament could similarly be used by popular vote to introduce alternative, acceptable methods of fixing rates of pay and to take other measures for the redistribution of income and property.

Apart from any undesirable effects on the distribution of real pay between different groups, our present methods of fixing rates of pay inflict serious economic loss on the community. The loss of output or of desirable public services during a strike, go slow or similar industrial action is the most obvious cause of such loss to the community as a whole. But it is by no means the most important loss. Much greater and continuing reductions of output and earnings are due to the persistence of a stagflating economy with its undesirably high levels of unemployment.

This unhappy state of affairs comes about in the following way. The process of uncontrolled monopoly bargaining in the conditions which I have described leads to a general set of demands for rises in real pay which outstrip the underlying available increase in productivity and real output. The result is the threat of an explosive inflation of money costs and prices.

Attempts to get a quart out of a pint pot will, of course, always be frustrated; but the process can have some very unfortunate side effects. It leads to an increasingly serious problem of runaway inflation. Sooner or later the authorities will have to take restrictive monetary and fiscal measures to restrain the rising level of money expenditures in attempts to restrain the explosive monetary inflation. The result will be serious unemployment as rapidly rising labour costs can no longer be covered by equally rapidly rising money demand for the products of industry. The Chancellor of the Exchequer is nowadays continually faced with this tragic dilemma. Should he expand demand to provide employment or should he restrain money expenditures in order to fight inflation? We end up with a situation of stagflation, a combination of an unhappily rapid rate of inflation and an unhappily high level of unemployment.

This Quart-out-of-a-Pint-pot syndrome can arise either because our thirst expands from a pint to a quart or because the capacity of the pot shrinks from a quart to a pint. Our present severe attack of stagflation was triggered off by the shrinkage of the capacity of the pot which occurred as a result of the fourfold increase in the price of oil in the mid-1970s.

From a Keynesian full employment point of view, this led to a deficiency of total effective demand; the oil producers refrained from spending and saved much of the abrupt increase in their incomes; the consumers paid more for oil and so had much less to spend on their own outputs of goods and services; the maintenance of full employment called for a Keynesian stimulation of demand.

On the other hand, from a cost-price-inflation point of view, the situation called for anti-inflationary policies. The change was equivalent to a reduction of real output per head in the oil importing countries, since each unit of their manufactures would exchange for less imported oil. For full employment, this called for some reduction in the real wage rate. The cost of living rose because of the rise in the price of oil; and to maintain employment without any additional inflation of money costs and prices it would have been necessary to resist increases in rates of pay in spite of the increase in the cost of living. But there was a natural attempt to maintain previous rates of increase in real pay and to push up pay increases sufficiently to take into account the increased cost of living due to the increased price of imported oil. People were trying to continue to get, say, 3 per cent per annum real increases when the deterioration in the terms of international trade had reduced their net productivity increase to, say, $1\frac{1}{2}$ per cent.

The result was a sudden intensification of the dilemma of

stagflation as the capacity of the pot suddenly shrunk from a quart to a pint.

In addition to the Quart-out-of-a-Pint-pot syndrome, there is another kind of explosive mechanism, which we may call the 'Keeping-ahead-of-the-Jones' syndrome. People are very concerned with wage differentials. Smith feels badly used not simply because his pay is low but also because he has lost out in comparison with Jones. Suppose that candlestick makers consider that they should be paid 5 per cent more than butchers and bakers and that at the same time butchers and bakers consider they should be paid at least as much as candlestick makers. Starting from the same wage the candlestick makers demand a 5 per cent rise. The butchers and bakers respond quickly with a demand for a similar 5 per cent rise in order to keep in line with the candlestick makers. The candlestick makers then respond with another 5 per cent demand in order to get ahead once more, to which the butchers and bakers respond with another 5 per cent demand in order to catch up once more. And so on. In vain attempts to escape from the frustration of this leap-frogging process, each group may put forward its claims more and more rapidly and may put forward on each occasion larger and larger claims in an attempt to offset in advance the anticipated counter-claims of the other group. In these conditions the rate of wage inflation will quickly explode.

In its idealistic political mood, the trade union movement as a whole presses for improvements for the low paid. In their realistic down-to-earth bargaining mood, the particular unions which represent the better paid press for a restoration of their differentials. These leap frogging movements intensify the problem of stagflation. Just as it is impossible for Smith to drink a Quart out of a Pint pot, so it is equally impossible for Smith to drink more than Jones and for Jones simultaneously to drink one pint more than Smith. The outcome of any such attempt is bound to be an unhappy one.

The basic loss to the community from a stagflating economy is the unemployment and the reduced real output of goods and services, and so of real standards of living, which inevitably must result sooner or later from the restrictive monetary and fiscal measures taken to avert the threat of a real runaway explosive inflation.

II Macro-Economic Strategy

I suggest that escape from the dilemma of stagflation can best be achieved by a combination of two fundamental changes.

Firstly, we need to impose some form of financial-monetary restraint in our society and to rid ourselves of the idea that, whatever may happen to the rate of rise of money wage rates, spenders will always be supplied with sufficient confetti money to cover the resulting cost of production, however rapidly the inflation may be developing. I shall proceed with the rest of my chapter on this assumption, namely, that by the use of monetary and budgetary policies the total demand for goods and services is being controlled so as to lead to a moderate but steady rate of growth – let us say, by way of example, a rate of growth of 5 per cent per annum – in the total demand for labour to produce those goods and services.

Secondly, against the background of this steady 5 per cent per annum growth in the total money demand for labour, it would be necessary to have some method for fixing rates of pay which ensured the attainment and preservation of full employment.

The purpose of this chapter is to consider specific problems connected with the fixing of rates of pay. But before doing so a rapid survey of some of the implications of the proposed financial policy will be useful.

What I am proposing is neither pure Keynesianism nor pure monetarism. I suppose that the pure Keynesian doctrine would be to use monetary and fiscal policies to expand total money expenditure whenever there was any general unemployment and to contract such expenditure when there was a general excess demand for labour. In this case the fixing of money rates of pay becomes the instrument not for maintaining full employment but for preventing wage-cost price inflation. I am in this respect standing Keynesianism on its head. I am suggesting that demand management should be used to control monetary inflation and deflation and that, against that background, the rate of pay should be used to achieve and maintain full employment. In that respect I am in line with the monetarists. But I do not believe with them that demand management should be confined to monetary policy conducted simply with a view to ensuring that the total stock of money increases at a steady rate. On the contrary, I advocate the use of monetary and, above all, of fiscal policies for a management of demand, as finely tuned as possible, to ensure a steady rate of growth in the total money demand for labour. The controllers should watch total wage earnings rather than the stock of money.

Moreover, unlike many monetarists, I believe that one necessary condition for the feasibility of any such rule for monetary and fiscal policies is that it should be accompanied by a suitable reform of arrangements for fixing rates of pay. If money rates of pay were allowed to go up by 15 per cent in any year, total money earnings could be restricted to a rise of 5 per cent in that year only by a devastating deflation of the total demand for the products of industry sufficient to reduce by 10 per cent the number of persons in employment over whom the restricted total of money earnings was to be spread or, in other words, to add a net figure of some two million to the number of unemployed. My two suggestions – that financial policies should be designed to maintain a steady 5 per cent per annum growth in the total money demand for labour, and that, against this background of a steady growth in the total demand for labour, rates of pay should be set so as to maintain full employment – make up a single package. The financial policy is not to be attempted without suitable reform of arrangements for settling rates of pay.

This means that any set of financial policies to restrain the rate of growth of total money earnings to a steady 5 per cent per annum could not be suddenly applied overnight. It would have to be introduced by a series of gradual reductions in the rate of growth of total money expenditures spread over a period of, say, three or four years.

III Decentralised Settlements of Rates of Pay as Instruments for the Maintenance of Full Employment

Let me turn then to the problems involved in fixing money rates of pay in such a way as to promote employment against the background of monetary and fiscal policies which are so designed as to maintain a steady rate of growth of, say, 5 per cent per annum in the total money demand for labour.

85

An obvious decentralised way to achieve this result would be to ensure that in each occupation, industry or region of the country the rate of pay was set in such a way as to promote employment. In any particular sector in which there was a scarcity of labour, the money rate of pay would be raised to the extent needed to equate supply and demand, the higher rate of pay helping not only to reduce the demand for labour in that sector but also to attract a greater number of workers so that employment could be expanded there. In any sector in which there existed a surplus of unemployed labour, there would be no call for any absolute reduction in money rates of pay, but increases in such rates would be restrained or altogether avoided; this would help both to maintain the demand for labour there and also to make rates of pay in the other expanding sectors of the economy still more attractive. If such principles for the setting of rates of pay were applied in each sector of the economy against the background of a general 5 per cent per annum expansion in the total money demand for labour, the overall result should be a general rise in the level of employment and, when full employment was reached, a continuing rise in the average money rate of pay which maintained employment without any excessive or explosive price inflation and with real rates of pay rising at the underlying rate of increase in real output per head.

Such a principle for the fixing of money rates of pay would, however, involve important modifications of present practice. There is much evidence of a widespread tendency throughout the industrially developed countries of the free enterprise world to set rates of pay for various jobs through trade union and other institutions at levels which bear a rather stable customary relationship to each other with little or no regard to the extent to which there is a relative excess demand for or supply of labour in any particular sector of the economy.[3] Nevertheless, there have in fact been very considerable changes in the relative sizes of the labour force in the various sectors of the economy. But the flow of labour from one sector to another does not seem to have been due in any substantial degree to high rates of pay in expanding sectors and low rates of pay in contracting sectors; the main motive force seems rather to have been good job opportunities in expanding sectors and bad ones in the contracting sectors. Labour has moved to where work is available.

The evidence that relative rates of pay have not in fact been a main motive force for the redeployment of labour rests upon the fact that there have not been any very marked changes in relative rates of pay. But this does not in itself imply that changes in relative rates of pay would not have exerted a powerful influence if they had in fact occurred on any appreciable scale; and there is some evidence that choice of occupations has indeed been highly sensitive to the limited variations in rates of pay which have in fact occurred.[4]

A decentralised adjustment of particular money rates of pay to particular conditions of supply and demand would in any case be an effective way of ensuring that the average rate of pay for the economy as a whole moved in such a way as to achieve and maintain full employment against the background of a steady 5 per cent per annum growth in the total money demand for labour. Moreover, it would also help to promote the desired movement of labour from contracting to expanding sectors. Changes in job opportunities can be combined very effectively with appropriate changes in relative rates of pay. But to rely wholly on job opportunities for the redeployment of labour is wasteful and unkind. It means in fact that unemployment, that is to say, the non-availability of a job in one's present occupation, must be a main driving force. And it may well be the less mobile workers who are made redundant in contracting sectors. A restraint of wage increases in such sectors will help to maintain employment in those sectors for workers to whom the cost of movement is high and will give an incentive to move to the better paid occupations on the part of those workers (the young unmarried workers, in particular) for whom the cost of movement is not so high. As a result both the total level of unemployment and also the real cost of movement of a given amount of labour from one sector to another will be reduced.

Finally, if we reject the decentralised solution of adjusting particular wage rates in each sector of the economy so as to promote employment in each sector separately, the avoidance of excessive wage-cost inflation for the economy as a whole demands some alternative, more centralised mechanism for determining the absolute level of money pay. In my opinion the difficulties in the way of the more centralised methods which I will consider later constitute the decisive argument in favour of the more decentralised principle outlined in this section.

IV Other Criteria for Fixing Rates of Pay

I am suggesting that, against the background of other measures for affecting the distribution of incomes and property and against the background of monetary and budgetary measures to ensure a steady rate of expansion in the total demand for labour, the overriding criterion for fixing the rate of pay in any sector should be the promotion of employment in that sector. How far does this criterion conflict with the other criteria which are often considered for this purpose? Three criteria are often proposed, namely: 1 comparability with the rates of pay of other workers; 2 the linking of rates of pay with improved productivity; and 3 the special improvement of conditions for low paid workers.

1 Comparability
In the UK it has been fashionable to consider the fixing of wage rates in particular sectors of the economy by the institution of special independent commissions to make comparability studies with the pay of similar workers in other sectors. But in an economy with free and costless movement and freedom from any unnecessary restrictions on entry into alternative occupations, industries and regions, the institutionalisation of this principle would be unnecessary. The primary basic comparability could be left to the individual worker to vote with his or her feet. In other words, to set wage rates and conditions of employment in the various sectors of the economy which will recruit sufficient workers to meet the demand for labour in that sector – the basic principle which I have been advocating – is the same thing as setting wage rates and conditions which compare adequately with wage rates and conditions in the other sectors which compete for similar workers. All one need do is to let the individual workers do their own comparability studies and let wages and conditions of work then be set at levels sufficient to man up or to woman up the various competing sectors of the economy.

If movement from one job to another were in fact easy and costless, that, I think, would be all that one need say on the subject of comparability. Let the individual workers compare and choose for themselves. But movement is not completely free and costless and, as a result, is slow and sluggish. As I shall argue later, this makes it desirable to pay regard not only to the immediate situation but also to probable future developments in employment to judge whether a wage is appropriate to maintain a balance between supply and demand over a reasonable period of time. Judgments of this kind should properly rest on comparability studies in the sense that it is necessary to judge whether a given wage level in one sector of the economy when compared with the wages and conditions likely to be available for similar workers in other sectors of the economy would be appropriate over the longer run to attract and retain the labour force which would be needed to maintain a balance between supply and demand in the sector concerned.

Whether or not a present wage offer needs to be improved in order to avoid a future deficiency of labour is, of course, a matter on which opinions can differ and which inevitably rests upon hypothetical judgments. It is just the sort of question which calls for an impartial assessment of the kind which I shall discuss later. To this extent, the principle of comparability is needed in order to set wage rates which will balance supply and demand in the various sectors of the economy. But to press the principle of comparability beyond that is to embark on a mysterious metaphysical exercise. How is one to balance job security and pension rights against high immediate pay, or balance a quiet life at a routine job against a tiring but exciting job with longer holidays? Individuals differ in their valuation of the characteristics of different jobs. One can do no more than try to assess whether at given relative rates of pay sufficient individuals prefer one job to another.

This distrust of what may be called administrative comparability has some rather far reaching implications, which can perhaps best be illustrated by reviewing it in its most extreme form. Consider then a system of national job evaluation which, by giving marks to every relevant aspect of every job (such as responsibility, unpleasantness, degree of skill, dexterity), produced a national rate of pay for every job or rather a national scale of relativities of pay between all the jobs in the community. Jobs could be compared on this evaluation scale and it would be clear which were to be regarded as meriting the same rates of pay and which were not.

But how would one fix the absolute level of money rates of pay? There would have to be, I suppose, some national body to fix the level of some particular rate of pay, which, since the relativities would be settled by the job evaluation scale, would peg all the rates of pay. In other words, there would be a complete, centrally determined wages policy. Less extensive systems of administered comparability would not lead to this extreme result. But the problem remains. The more extensive the system of administered comparability between a large range of occupations, the more important and the more difficult becomes the problem of deciding how and by whom the absolute level of any given group of comparable jobs is to be settled.

2 Productivity

It would, of course, be most undesirable to introduce any system of wage fixing which prohibited any group of employers and workers from a voluntary agreement that the workers should receive some increase in pay in return for undertaking additional duties or changing their methods or conditions of work in such a way as to increase their output. But it is quite a different matter to introduce, as was recently the case in the UK, the principle that workers can receive an increase in wages above some stated norm (for example, a 5 per cent annual increase) only in so far as they increase their output per head in such a way as to cover the additional wage cost. As anything more than a very temporary emergency measure, any such rule would be grossly unfair and grossly inefficient. There are many industrial processes where technological conditions make increases in output per head relatively easy; in other cases increased productivity may be impossible or, even if possible, may be incapable of measurement. Any long run application of the principle that wage increases should be tied to increases in measured productivity would thus be grossly unfair.

It would also be grossly inefficient. Increased productivity in one industry by cutting costs may lead to a very great increase in the demand for the industry's product and so in the demand for labour in that industry; in such a case there is need for a rise in relative rates of pay to attract more labour. But in another industry, for whose product the demand is inelastic, an increase in output per head and so a reduction in costs and prices will lead to little increase in demand and thus to a need for a smaller labour force to produce the required output; in such a case efficiency requires a fall in relative rates of pay in order to reduce the attractiveness of the occupation. Thus increased productivity may cause an excess supply or an excess demand for labour in the jobs concerned. There is thus no analytical need on special grounds of productivity to modify the general rule that rates of pay should be set so as to help to balance supply and demand in each sector of the economy.

Nevertheless, changes in productivity do introduce very real complications and difficulties which may require modification of the general rule.

In order to give an incentive to introduce new and more efficient methods of production, it may be desirable to offer increases in pay and to allow increases in profitability where productivity is increased. In some industries there will then be a conflict between the need to offer rewards for greater productivity and the need to contract the total labour force which is still needed in the industry. Is it possible in such cases to allow for some increases in pay as an incentive for those who are already employed in the industry but to offer less attractive terms to new entrants to discourage them from entering an industry in which the need for labour has contracted? This is one of the most intractable of economic problems. But it remains of crucial importance that, in the longer run, reduced costs should lead to reduced prices to the consumer and that the consumer's response should then be allowed to determine the ultimate expansion or contraction of the labour force in the industry.

3 Low pay

The basic cure for low pay is to make it easy for the workers concerned to move from the low paid to the higher paid occupations, by increasing their knowledge of the possibilities of employment in the better paid occupations, industries and regions, by increasing the opportunities for training for the better paid jobs, by removing obstacles to movement from one region to another (such as the present difficulty for a worker with security of tenure in a rented house in one district to find alternative accommodation elsewhere) and by removing artificial monopolistic restrictions against entry into other sectors of the economy. In spite of policies of this kind, there may, of course, remain some pockets of sweated labour where, through ignorance and apathy, freedom to take voluntary trade union action has not been effective in preventing exploitation and unnecessarily low and unacceptable levels of pay. In the limited range of such unacceptable cases, it is the right and duty of the state to intervene by the operation of compulsory Wage Councils or otherwise to ensure that adequate wages are paid.

Moreover, the suggestion that the primary function of wage fixing in each sector of the economy should be to promote employment in that sector by taking account of the conditions of supply and demand for labour in that sector does not mean that one should not be concerned about the distribution of income and wealth. But it does mean that for this purpose the main reliance must be placed on governmental policies of the kind which I have already enumerated rather than on a general squeezing of profits through an inflationary upward pressure of wages with the consequent risk of unemployment.

V Institutional Arrangements for the Fixing of Rates of Pay

1 Competition in the labour market

If the primary function of the fixing of rates of pay is to be to maintain a balance between the supply and demand for labour in each sector of the economy against a general restrained non-inflationary financial background, is there not a simple solution? Bash the trade unions and restore competition in the labour market. Let the competition of workers for jobs bid down the wage rate where labour is plentiful and let the competition of entrepreneurs for workers bid up the wage rate where labour is scarce. There are, however, some compelling reasons for not relying upon this simple text book remedy.

In the first place, a full return to competitive conditions in the labour market would have to involve very ungenerous treatment of the unemployed in order to ensure that the competition of the unemployed in search of work resulted in no increases, indeed in reductions, of wage rates wherever the supply of labour exceeded the demand. But in a humane, compassionate society one does not want to have to rely on the threat of starvation of those who are unfortunate enough to lose their jobs in a contracting sector of the economy as the means of ensuring moderation in the wage rates set in such occupations. One needs to find some alternative method which applies supply-demand criteria for the fixing of wage rates for those in employment without inflicting needless hardship and anxiety on those particular individuals who are inevitably adversely affected by economic change. Of course one must not remove all incentives to seek work. But there are in fact some policies – in particular the proper development of the payment of unconditional child benefits – by means of which the treatment of the unemployed and incentives to seek work could both be simultaneously improved.

There is a second compelling reason for rejecting simple unadulterated trade union bashing. Man is a social animal; and the whole of history illustrates a basic need for people to form organised associations as workers in the same occupation or place of work just as they do in the other political or leisure aspects of their lives. Indeed in the work community, as in every other community, quite apart from rates of pay, there are common conditions and concerns which call for collective discussion and representation.

Thirdly, economies of large scale production mean that in many cases the employers of labour will be very few relative to the number of employees and will inevitably be able to exert downward monopsonistic pressures on rates of pay. Unfair bargaining positions would be created and labour would be exploited if workers could not be organised into monopolistic bargaining groups to meet monopsonistic employers. This is indeed the basic economic justification for monopolistic labour organisations.

There is a fourth reason why a simple return to competition in fixing rates of pay is unacceptable. The competitive mechanism might work with relatively little hardship if workers could move readily from those occupations, trades, industries or regions in which pay and employment prospects were poor to those in which they were good. There are many things which can and should be done to make movement between sectors of the economy easier than it is; and I will refer to some of these later. But whatever is done, movement will never be free and costless. Quite apart from any monetary costs, most people feel a disturbing loss at having to leave the friends, relations, neighbourhood and working conditions to which they have become accustomed; and where, as is increasingly the case, both husband and wife have jobs, acceptable movement may well involve both partners simultaneously finding satisfactory jobs in a new locality. As a result, movement of labour from one sector to another will often be a rather slow process.

This sluggishness in labour movements has an important implication for fixing rates of pay.

Consider the following extreme example. Suppose there to be an industry for which the demand is high and expanding but in which there is a severe bottleneck of some form of needed capital equipment. In such an industry there may be serious unemployment simultaneous with a high demand for the industry's product. There could, for example, be many unemployed weavers together with a high demand for cloth, simply because there were not enough looms. If the redundant weavers could not move readily out of the industry for the time being and then move readily back again when additional looms had been installed, there would be a temporary period of severe unemployment in the industry. Text book competition between the workers would drive pay down to starvation levels, without conferring any substantial benefits in the form of an expanded volume of employment so long as the supply of looms remained inadequate to employ all the available workers. It is true that the very low wage costs combined with the very high demand for cloth would lead to exceptional profits on the existing looms and thus to an exceptionally strong incentive to invest in additional looms. The reduction in the rate of pay might therefore help to speed up the expansion of capacity in the industry. This would inevitably take some time, possibly a long time. But as it occurred labour would in due course become scarce and, as new looms were continually installed to meet the expanding demand for cloth, the wage rate would be bid up from its starvation level to the high level needed to attract the required additional workers.

How far should the initial slump in the rate of pay be encouraged in order to speed up the investment in new looms? Or how far should it be resisted in order to stabilise the incomes of the workers concerned, particularly in view of the fact that a low rate of pay would have little or no immediate effect on the volume of employment? Such a situation would call for a difficult assessment of the possible effects of restrained wage rates not so much in providing jobs now as in speeding up the process of providing jobs at good wages in the future.

The example which I have just given is one in which labour immobility threatens to lead to a temporary slump in a given wage rate. The opposite situation is, of course, equally possible. If it had been the weavers and not the looms that were in temporary short supply, the danger would have lain in an excessive temporary boom in the wage rate which could not be maintained without unemployment when the balance of the labour force had been restored.

For reasons which I have just outlined, I do not believe that a simple return to individual competition in the labour market is the answer to the problem of fixing rates of pay. Freedom of association of workers to formulate claims for, and to stabilise, rates of pay and other conditions of work is a basic requirement of our system. But while a simple return to complete individual competition is not the answer, there is in my opinion one basic respect in which the present monopoly powers of the trade unions should be reduced.

To operate a pre-entry closed shop should be unlawful. Freedom for a group of workers to associate in order to press jointly a claim to a given rate of pay is one thing. Freedom for that group of workers to insist that no other workers shall be employed in that occupation without their permission is a totally different and objectionable privilege. It means that a tight monopoly of a limited number of workers can preserve an exceptionally high rate of pay, preventing other, less well paid workers from entering the occupation with the result, first, that unnecessary inequalities of earnings are preserved, the poor outsiders being disallowed from joining the rich insiders, and, second, that the supplies to the consumers of the services of the privileged group are unnecessarily restricted and charged at unnecessarily high prices.

2 Labour co-operatives

It has been suggested that the way to deal with the wage fixing problem is to get rid of wages. Let our business concerns be turned into labour owned, labour managed co-operatives in which the workers hire at fixed interest or rent the necessary capital and land needed for production, sell the produce, pay the interest and rent, and distribute the remainder among the working members. The state can have a monetary-fiscal policy of the kind which I have outlined, whereby the general level of total money demand for the products of industry grows at a steady rate. The labour co-operative's earnings rise steadily as a result; but the workers have no power and no inducement to cause stagflation by an excessive upward pressure on wage costs. They simply take what they can get.

Alas, I do not think that this provides a general solution. I believe that labour managed, labour owned concerns can be expected to work well only when three conditions are fulfilled, namely: (i) that small scale production is economic; (ii) that the technology is not too capital intensive; and (iii) that the entry of new concerns into the industry is easy. I must confine myself in this chapter to very brief, intuitive explanations for each of these conditions.

(i) Large scale production is liable to lead to monopolistic conditions. The objective of a capitalist entrepreneurial concern may well be to maximise total monopoly profit. The corresponding objective of a labour co-operative would be to maximise monopoly profit per head, a maximisation which is achieved by reducing the number of heads as well as by increasing the total profit. A large scale labour co-operative is thus likely to be even more restrictive than a large scale capitalist entrepreneurial concern. The need for price control or similar anti-monopoly policies would, therefore, be even more marked than at present. But as soon as the authorities impose such controls, conflict with the official controllers of the business is likely to take the place of conflict with the owners of the business. Strikes against employers might well be replaced by strikes against price controllers. Moreover, with large scale enterprises, there would be great dilution, if not complete disappearance, of the sentiment that the actual workers were in fact managing and running the business; divorce between managers and workers, between them and us, would inevitably reappear and the basic attraction of labour co-operatives would be eroded.

(ii) Let me turn to my seond condition. Labour co-operatives in highly capital intensive concerns would be imperilled because of the risk of disaster. Consider a concern in which 90 per cent of the value added must go to paying the fixed interest or rents for the hire of capital and land, leaving only 10 per cent for the workers. A 5 per cent fall in the net price of the product would halve the workers' incomes, whereas in a concern in which 90 per cent of the value added went to the workers it would need a 45 per cent fall in the net price of the product to halve their incomes. There is indeed a very real basic reason why capital should bear as much of the risk as possible. Broadly speaking, a man can at any one time work only at one job – or at least at a very limited number of jobs – whereas he can invest his total capital in small sums in various shares in many different concerns. With his work, all his eggs are already inevitably in one basket; with his capital, he can have one egg in each basket. Workers in any case run the risk of losing their jobs if things go badly with the business; but in a capitalist entrepreneurial business the risk is shared with the capitalists who stand to lose profits. In a pure labour co-operative in which all capital is raised at fixed interest, the whole of the risk is borne by the workers. The other advantages of labour co-operatives may outweigh the disadvantage of this risk factor in labour intensive activities. But it becomes a decisive disadvantage in the case of highly capital intensive activities.

(iii) I come to the third condition, namely that there should be ease of entry of new labour co-operatives into the industry concerned. Consider an economy at any one time composed of a number of independent productive concerns each with its given equipment of fixed capital and land. Suppose it to be faced by a given level of total money expenditure on the products of the economy, a level which is growing at a steady rate as a result of the monetary and fiscal policies described above. Each concern is charging a certain price for its product, is producing a certain output and is employing a certain number of workers. But there may well remain a substantial volume of unemployed labour.

Suppose first of all that these concerns are all run on capitalist entrepreneurial principles. At the given wage rate, each concern will have an incentive to take on more labour as the demand for its products expands.

Suppose, however, that the concerns are all run as labour co-operatives. The incentive for any one co-operative to take on more members does not depend in any way upon a wage which is demanded by new members. In expanding the membership there are two advantages and two disadvantages: income per head will be raised in so far as the expansion of output brings any increasing returns to pure scale and in so far as the fixed debt on the fixed capital can be spread over more members;

income per head will be reduced in so far as there are diminishing returns to the application of more labour to a given amount of fixed capital and in so far as increased output in conditions of imperfect competition leads to a reduction in selling price. But once the optimum size of partnership is attained by the balance of these factors there is no outside wage mechanism available to mop up any remaining unemployment. Indeed, an increase in the demand for a co-operative's products is likely actually to reduce the incentive to increase its membership: the increased demand will enable it to raise its selling prices; as a result the fixed interest on its debt will become less significant; and there will be less incentive to seek new members to share the debt burden.

In the labour co-operative economy unemployment could be reduced only by the low income unemployed setting up new co-operatives to compete with the high income employed. But the setting up of new concerns requires investment in new fixed capital. It will take time even if the problems of finance of the capital on fixed interest terms by new inexperienced concerns can be overcome. With the capitalist entrepreneurial system the restraint of money wage rates can be equally effective in promoting the establishment of new concerns. But it will above all have an immediate and direct effect in promoting the expansion of existing concerns. In the case of labour co-operatives, this incentive could exist only if such co-operatives were prepared either to hire labour at fixed rates of pay in addition to the employment of the profit sharing members at a higher income per head, or to admit new members on profit sharing terms which were less advantageous to the newly admitted members than to the existing members. But in both these cases there would be a reversion towards a distinction between the privileged 'them' of the original owners and the unprivileged 'us' of either (a) the new wage hands or (b) the new second class member. The unadulterated egalitarian labour co-operative economy has no such incentive to employ unemployed workers; unlike the capitalist entrepreneurial system, it must rely for its expansion on ease of entry for new competing co-operatives; and this is its basic weakness as a proposed universal remedy for the disease of stagflation.

Where the necessary conditions are satisfied, labour co-operatives are to be encouraged and promoted. Moreover, there

are many possible forms of participation by labour in the outcome of the capitalist entrepreneurial concerns, ranging from
simple profit sharing schemes to schemes in which the whole or
part of the value added of a concern is to be divided between
owners, managers and workers. Participation is most desirable;
and the possibilities of schemes in which workers and owners of
capital participate both in the management of the concern and
also in the net income earned by the business call for much
greater attention by economists than they have received up to
the present. But I must confine myself in this chapter to the
observation that for the foreseeable future there does not seem
to be any complete solution of the problem of fixing rates of pay
along the lines of simple labour managed, labour owned
co-operatives.

3 The corporate solution

A number of proposals have been made for the organisation of
an annual joint review of the economic situation by the CBI and
the TUC – and, some would add, the government – with the
object of deciding what would be the possibilities for, and the
implications for employment of, given rates of wage increases. It
is hoped that such a joint review might lead to a moderation of
those pay claims which are out of line with the available increases in the national product; and indeed it might be a very
useful first step, particularly if it were undertaken against the
background of a firm governmental commitment to adopt
monetary and budgetary policies which ensured a 5 per cent
growth in the total money earnings, no more and no less. Thus
the unemployment situation might be judged to call for a 1 per
cent increase in the volume of employment. In this case only
4 per cent of the 5 per cent increase in the total national money
earnings would be available for increasing average earnings per
head – a fact which a CBI–TUC review could emphasise. Any
such review could thus be useful in influencing expectations and
in forming a background to any decisions on particular claims.

But the mere existence of such an annual review, while it
might be useful, would alone be inadequate. The TUC has no
power to determine the action of the individual independent
trade unions. Suppose, for example, the review suggested that
a 4 per cent increase in average earnings would be appropriate.
If 4 per cent is to be an average and if some are to receive more

than 4 per cent, others must receive less than 4 per cent. But a 4 per cent norm is liable to be treated as a minimum and many powerful unions may not hesitate to use their extensive monopoly powers to demand considerably more than 4 per cent. If the CBI–TUC combined effort was to be effective, it would have to be extended in such a way as to enable the joint review body to distribute the 4 per cent between the various claimants, deciding which should get more and which less. But this is to embark on a detailed incomes policy; and if there is to be such a policy it should not in my opinion be administered by the CBI and the TUC, but by some body, such as the old National Board for Prices and Incomes, set up by and subject to the decisions of Parliament and the government. It is not a matter which should be determined by the most powerful monopolistic organisations of employers and workers.

4 A centralised incomes policy

There are in any case very strong disadvantages in a detailed, centralised, official policy which sets restrictions on individual rates of pay. A comprehensive incomes policy requires that limits of some sort should be set on the rates which can be paid to any worker or group of workers. The fact that the employer is perfectly willing to pay a higher rate must not be allowed to grant exemption from the restriction; all wage settlements must be covered by the regulations. This involves one of two possible types of arrangement. Either some simple norm like a 5 per cent increase must be laid down to cover all cases with a very limited number of precise and carefully defined special exceptions (but a simple general system of this kind makes it impossible to relate particular wage rates to particular conditions of supply and demand in each sector); or there must be extended bureaucratic intervention to settle the appropriate rate for each sector of the economy. In a modern highly developed economy with so many industrial, occupational and regional differences, with so many different wage structures and methods of payment, and with so many types of worker, skilled and unskilled, full time and part time, a simple universal norm applied with very limited exceptions is bound to lead quickly to many anomalies; but on the other hand, the application to each specific sector of a detailed set of criteria is bound to involve an unbearable extension of bureaucratic intervention.

5 Arbitration

Trade unions are monopolistic bodies. Monopolistic bodies should either be dissolved (a solution which, for the reasons already given, is not appropriate in this case) or should be constrained in the social interest by some outside impartial consideration of the prices which they charge. In my opinion much the most hopeful, civilised approach to the setting of rates of pay is to continue with the existing system of bargaining between workers and employers but to replace the ultimate appeal to the strike weapon with an ultimate appeal to some external impartial arbitral body.[5]

The following is a brief sketch of three forms which such a system might take. With all three forms any agreement freely entered into between employer and employed would be legitimate; and all three forms require the institution of some form of Pay Commission, so constituted as to ensure confidence both in its expertise in labour market problems and in its impartiality, and to which unsolved disputes could be referred.

Form I In this case the trade unions would in general preserve all their existing monopolistic powers for wage bargaining, which might indeed even be reinforced in certain ways. The government would, however, set an annual 'norm' for the rate of increase in pay of, say, 4 or 5 per cent. Any employer who wished to resist a pay claim which he considered to exceed this norm could refer the claim to the Pay Commission whose sole job would be to determine whether or not the claim was in excess of the norm. If it were judged to be in excess, the employees would be invited to scale down their claim appropriately. Industrial action to support their original claim would not, however, be unlawful; but in this case it would carry with it a serious curtailment of their legal bargaining powers, which would remain undiminished in the case of any claim which had not been judged to be in excess of the norm. I discuss later the sort of curtailment of bargaining power which might be operative in the case of industrial action in support of a claim which had been judged to be in excess of the norm.

Form II In this case also the trade unions would in general enjoy a full panoply of monopolistic powers for wage bargaining. The government would, however, set no norm for increases in pay. But any disputed claim, however large or small, could be referred by employers, by employed or by the government to the Pay Commission, whose duty in this case would be to judge whether over the foreseeable future the claimed rate of pay would or would not impede the promotion of employment in that sector of the economy. In accordance with this judgment, the Pay Commission would make an award in favour either of the employers or of the employed, subject to the rule that no award would be made in favour of the employers if it implied an actual reduction in money rates of pay. An award in favour of the employed would be enforced by treating its terms as if they constituted part of the individual contracts of employment between employer and employee. An award in favour of the employers would entail a serious curtailment of the legal bargaining powers of the employees if they refused to accept the award and took industrial action in pursuit of their original claim.

Form III In this case there would in general be severe restrictions of the legal bargaining powers of the trade unions, restrictions which on the lines outlined later might well go much further than the Employment Act of 1980. But the employees and their trade union could take any claim which was resisted by the employers to the Pay Commission, whose duty would be to judge whether the claim was either (1) simply a resistance to an actual reduction in money rates of pay, or (2) one which would not impede the promotion of employment in that sector of the economy over the foreseeable future. If either of these conditions was satisfied, the Pay Commission would give an award in favour of the claim which would be enforced by treating its terms as being part of the individual contracts of employment between employer and employee.

All these forms would be operating against a background of fiscal and monetary policies which were ensuring a steady rate of expansion in the total demand for labour and also against the background of a battery of social security, social welfare, tax, anti-monopoly, price control and nationalisation measures to ensure an equitable distribution of income and wealth. Against this background the market mechanism could be operative, and no agreed bargain between employers and employed would be ruled out. In any expanding sector in which employers agreed that a wage increase was desirable to attract labour, there would be no limit to an agreed rise. In any contracting sector in which the employees agreed that the wage rate should

be restrained in order to preserve jobs, there would be no
obstacle to any agreed solution, though in all cases, if they so
desired, the employees could effectively resist any actual
reduction in the money rates of pay.

Form I is a crude mechanism which might, however, put
some brake on excessive rises in wage costs and thus effect some
mitigation of the problem of stagflation. It has the advantage
that the job of the Pay Commission would be confined to judging how much a given claim would in fact raise the cost of a
unit of labour. Forms II and III provide more sophisticated
mechanisms for adjustment of rates of pay in such a way as to
promote employment more directly; but in these cases the Pay
Commission would have the much more difficult and responsible duty of assessing future market conditions in the employment sector under review. Form III is more radical than Form
II. If it were acceptable, it would be the most effective in
replacing the wastes of the present anarchic system by impartial
wage awards. Whether or not it could be made acceptable
would turn above all on the confidence which the trade unions
placed in the constitution and understanding of any proposed
Pay Commission.

These forms are in any case presented in the most tentative
fashion. My present purpose is simply to suggest that, if we
really wished to do so, it should not be impossible for social
democrats to devise a decent and effective system for pay
determination.

VI The Problem of Sanctions

The three forms of institutional arrangements just described all
rely upon a distinction between the legal bargaining powers
which a party to a dispute would normally enjoy and those
which would be available if action were taken to resist an
arbitral award. The final and perhaps decisive question thus
remains to be considered. By how much and by what methods
would the parties' bargaining powers be affected? Or, in other
words, what penalties or sanctions would be imposed on any
party which opposed an award?

My answer to that question will be based on the assumption

that there is a widespread measure of support, including the support of the majority of workers and trade unionists, for the system which I have outlined. An arbitral system of the kind which I have outlined would in fact be greatly to the benefit of workers and trade unionists; but it could be operated only if that were understood and there were a consensus in its favour.

Assume then that the case for relying on impartial arbitral awards rather than on the present disruptive use of mono-polistic bargaining strength is generally accepted. This does not mean that one can totally ignore the problem of sanctions against those few who from time to time may be moved to oppose such awards. There is widespread agreement that rob-bery is wrong; that does not mean that there should be no penalties against robbers.

What then are the penalties which, given a favourable clim-ate of opinion, might be imposed? One must, I think, distinguish between penalties which would be suitable to curb the opposi-tion to an award on the part of the employer and those suitable in the case of opposition by employees.

In the case of employers, as has already been suggested, it would be possible simply to make it unlawful for the employer to employ anyone except on the terms of the award, which would be treated as if its terms were part of the individual con-tracts of employment of the workers. This is an extreme penalty since it means that the employer must accept the award or close down his business; and one could add for good measure that if he closed down his business his employees would be eligible for redundancy payments. The design of effective penalties for the recusant employer presents little difficulty.

The design of sanctions against recusant workers and trade unionists is a much more difficult matter. It is above all neces-sary to avoid penalties which rest in the end on the imprison-ment of strikers as criminals or as being in contempt of court. There are, however, a number of possibilities which do not involve any such consequences.

Any supplementary benefit paid to support the families of any workers on strike in opposition to an award could be treated as a loan to the worker concerned, to be repaid by deductions, like PAYE, from future earnings; any PAYE tax rebates due to anyone on strike against an award could be postponed until the strike was over; it could be ruled that anyone on strike against an award should be treated as having thereby terminated his contract of employment, with the result that he would sacrifice any accumulated rights to redundancy pay and could not in any case claim to be unfairly dismissed if he were not re-engaged when the strike was over; legal immunities against claims for damages in tort arising from actions taken in contemplation or furtherance of a trade dispute would be rescinded in the case of such action taken against an award, the payment of any such damages being made by deduction at source from future earnings; and similar immunities enjoyed by the trade unions themselves could be rescinded if the trade union itself supported such action against an award.

VII Conclusions

There are in fact many possible forms of penalty; but I do not want to close on this sour note of a catalogue of possible sanctions. I emphasise once more that this chapter is not an exercise in trade union bashing. My argument is that everyone, including trade unionists, stands to gain by an arbitration system under which the task of the union leader would remain, as it is now, to negotiate wages and conditions with the employers but, in the last resort, to put a case to an impartial body rather than to organise an exercise in costly industrial warfare. Such a system would work only if it were generally accepted as being a Better Way; sanctions would be an issue only in the exceptional and *ex hypothesi* generally unpopular case of refusal to accept an impartial award.

And this system would indeed constitute a Better Way for all concerned. The children of workers and trade unionists receive no education when the schools are closed; workers and trade unionists are deprived of medical treatment when the hospitals are closed; workers and trade unionists are unemployed and shiver when fuel supplies are cut off; workers and trade unionists are unemployed when the Chancellor adopts restrictive financial policies in order to curb the inflationary effects of excessive wage claims; the generality of workers and trade unionists suffer a decline in their real standards of living as a result of the inflation of the money cost of living when specially privileged groups manage to get one jump ahead in the rat race and to raise their own wage rates and the costs of their own products more rapidly than the average. I commend my system of ultimate appeal to an independent Pay Commission as a Better Way and Fairer Way for trade unionists to exercise their great influence in society, above all in the interests of their own members.

7

Socialism and Incomes Policy

by William McCarthy

The thesis I want to argue is that there is a necessary link between incomes policy and socialism – although the nature of
the relationship is not what it is usually said to be. By incomes
policy I mean attempts to gain support for guidelines and
criteria which influence the pace and distribution of increases .
in personal income.

Normally a connection is admitted between incomes policy
and socialism on one of two grounds. First, it is argued, usually
by those on the Right of the Labour party, that incomes policy
is required to deal with the inegalitarian consequences of so-
called 'free collective bargaining'. In effect it is seen as a way
of redistributing income towards the lower paid; a device for
mitigating the worst effects of 'capitalist trade unionism'.

Alternatively, it is maintained, usually by left wingers, that
incomes policy will only be required when we arrive at the
socialist state. Once Labour has control of the means of production, and has expropriated the expropriators, it will need
to decide the relative size of investment and consumption. A
further decision will then be needed on allocation and distribution. In the case of consumption, this will require policies on the
distribution of income. Under socialism these things will be
resolved by rational discussion – there will be no room for free
collective bargaining and not much for trade unions to do.
Meanwhile, attempts to influence the pace and distribution of

pay can be safely denounced as revisionist reformism since militant wage bargaining helps to advance the ultimate collapse of capitalism. These two approaches may respectively be termed amateur egalitarianism and half-baked democratic centralism. Neither has anything to do with the real case for incomes policy. Both mistake the nature of its relationship to the principles and practice of democratic socialism in Britain today.

This derives from the fact that, for the foreseeable future, Labour governments will have to operate within the confines set by a small, stagnant and uncompetitive economy, against the background of a world wide economic depression and the long run decline of capitalist institutions – especially in the West.

This means that if socialism is to have any future and rele-vance in Britain it must help a future Labour government to do two things: improve the overall performance of the economy and decide the best use to be made of scarce resources. I remain a socialist because I believe that the traditional socialist prin-ciples of public intervention and control, plus the basic socialist belief in equality and social justice, remain of crucial relevance to both these tasks. But before this can be seen to be so, socialists must face the full implications of the age of continued scarcity. This is where incomes policy comes in.

In the past, part of the difficulty has been that traditional socialist theorists, so effectively summarised in *The Future of Socialism*, all assumed this problem away. In their various ways our founding fathers, from Marx to Morris, believed that the continued existence of scarcity was a device used by capitalism to perpetuate itself. This was because they were convinced that what Marx termed the 'methods of capitalist production' (or what would now be termed its technological potential) had made surplus a practical possibility. All that was required, in Marx's language, was to break the 'fetters' represented by the 'capitalist system of property relations'. Once this was accom-plished, 'production for use not profit' would satisfy all society's material needs. As Clause IV suggests: 'upon the basis of the common ownership of the means of production, distribution and exchange'.

And before anybody says that only Marxists believed this, let me say that similarly naïve assumptions can be found in the works of Blatchford, Shaw or the Webbs. Indeed, even Keynes encouraged the notion of potential surplus in the General Theory, when he looked forward to the 'euthanasia of the rentier'. Keynes thought this would come about fairly quickly, once a plentiful supply of capital had reduced interest rates to zero. In more recent times very similar views were expressed by Anthony Crosland as late as 1956. For at the end of *The Future of Socialism* he wrote as follows:

> With personal consumption rising by 2–4% a year and likely to double in 20 years, it will really not much matter a decade from now whether we plan to produce rather more of this and less of that, or exactly what prices are charged for this commodity or that. The level of material welfare will soon be such that marginal changes in the allocation of resources will make little difference to anyone's contentment. If they wish, let the violent economic planners battle the matter out. The rest of us will grow progressively more indifferent.[1]

What distinguished Tony from other socialists was that as the 1960s advanced he rapidly abandoned the assumption of potential surplus. He came to see that even with high and sustained levels of economic growth the demands of investment, private consumption and welfare would continue to advance the date when it could be said that abundance had arrived. And as sustained growth became increasingly difficult to achieve, he became more and more interested in how the principles of socialist intervention could be used to improve the overall performance of the economy in conditions of continued scarcity.

At the same time, he also came to realise that the equally important principles of equality and social justice were required to provide us with the basic guide lines for welfare policy. Thus, by the time of *Socialism Now* in 1974, he was stressing the need to limit and define what a new Labour government could expect to achieve in the welfare field: 'we must ruthlessly select priorities. We must prepare in advance a limited programme of radical measures which does not promise more than we can actually perform'.[2]

There followed a short list of priority areas, which bears re-reading today. Unfortunately, there was no similarly thorough treatment of the role of incomes policy in helping to make available resources needed to carry out Crosland's programme. Tony never wavered in his belief that incomes policy was an important element in the armoury of any future Labour government but, in my experience, he tended to see it as an unfortunate and even temporary expedient. 'Would that it were not so,' he says in a later essay in *Socialism Now*.

I do not think we can make this assumption any longer. I would like to argue that a continuous and enthusiastic commitment to incomes policy should now be accepted as the distinguishing characteristic of the serious socialist.

In some ways, the higher lunacies of Thatcherite monetarism should make it easy for this to be appreciated throughout the Labour movement. For it must surely become increasingly evident that without some agreement on the guidelines and criteria which are to influence and regulate the pace of income advances, we shall always be in danger of being pitchforked into alternative ways of controlling the claims that will be made on scarce resources. And the only alternatives that are available violate socialist principles of equity and social justice, since in the end they depend on higher and higher levels of unemployment and the deliberate fostering of inequality. It is also clear that the present government believes that these measures will have to be supplemented by a sustained attack on the legal basis of trade unionism. They hope that, taken together, all these measures will drive down the level of wages to the point where demands of organised workers are found to be compatible with the needs of international competitiveness and profits.

But we are not concerned here with the fallacies in this argument. The point is that if socialists reject such policies they must put something more acceptable in their place. For socialists, no less than conservatives, must find some way of restricting the claims which wages and salaries make on the national income. Since experience shows that, given the British economy's capacity to deliver, unfettered collective bargaining lays claim to the lion's share of the GNP, leaving other essential socialist priorities far behind.

Unfortunately, one of the central weaknesses of left wing advocates of the so-called 'alternative economic policy' is that they are so reluctant to admit this. Thus they are refreshingly radical and unorthodox in their critique of the last Labour government's policies for improving the performance of the economy, but pathetically weak in what they say about making the best use of scarce resources. Indeed, their position often seems to be that a future Labour government could escape the need to make hard choices of any kind if only it was prepared to impose a sufficiently all embracing battery of import controls.

In fact, of course, the degree of reflation they favour would mean an unrestricted consumption boom and a rapidly escalating price level, unless it was accompanied by an effective policy for restraining incomes. There would be very little left over for expanding the social wage, before competitiveness declined still further and the boom came to an end.

Yet acceptance of incomes policy, as an essential element in any socialist programme, does more than help us avoid past illusions. More important still, it directs our attention at some of the necessary characteristics which will be needed to make future incomes policy work more effectively than has been the case in the past, even under Labour governments. Indeed I want to argue that it enables us to draw no fewer than six important conclusions about the scope, content and limitations of future policy. The rest of this chapter is concerned to state them in a somewhat summary way.

First, it is clear that there is a sense in which we have to think in terms of a permanent incomes restraint. This does not mean that we can never allow another 'free for all'. From time to time there may be no way of preventing this – say, if incomes policy guidelines fail to gain any significant degree of support from trade union members. It means that, as and when this happens, it will be recognised as a defeat for both the government and socialism. There will be no pretence that it hasn't happened (as in the spring of 1975). Nobody will say that all we have to do is to stand firm behind our discredited guidelines (as in the autumn of 1979). It will be realised that a new policy is required, and required quickly.

Second, if a continuing influence is what is required, there will be a great reluctance to sacrifice the long term for the short. This means that incomes policy objectives will be modest and realistic, aimed at building up long term support. Once again, this does not mean that the aims of particular policy periods will always be recognised as modest and realistic by all trade unions and employers. It does mean that the government will seek to avoid using dramatic squeezes and restraints – especially when it would be so much more sensible to operate on the exchange rate, or by means of import controls. This is partly because experience shows that tough periods of incomes policy almost always generate what might be termed a return to the 'Dunkirk Spirit'. This means they are justified by reference to wartime analogies about 'backs to the wall', or 'finest hours'. Before you know where you are, the troops are expecting an early victory, or at least a respite from the battle. Thus the expectation of relaxation, and even an early return to some form of 'free for all', is very soon upon us.

One of the major mistakes made by the last two Labour governments was that they allowed such beliefs to gain currency – indeed high ranking members of the 1964–70 government actually encouraged them, because they thought they might help to win the 1970 election. Even during the unprecedented accord of the middle period of the last Social Contract (1975–77), there was a persistent attempt to pretend that both the government and the TUC were engaged on a once for all exercise to 'get the economy right'. This was partly because the 1976–77 norm of 5 per cent could not have been sold on any other basis. But this brings me to my third lesson, which relates to the factors which have to be taken into account in arriving at guidelines and criteria.

Here, I am afraid, one must make somewhat summary use of that fascinating but elusive concept, the 'going rate'. By the going rate I mean the rate of pay increase which intelligent men on both sides 'think they can get away with'. In most years this can be culled from a process of prolonged and exhausting pub crawling during the September meeting of the Trades Union Congress. It can then be further refined by visits to annual meetings of the CBI, the IPM and a carefully constructed network of personal contacts.

Ceteris paribus, it is unrealistic to seek to use incomes policy to reduce the general level of settlements more than 25 per cent below the going rate. This may be possible for a year or two – with sufficient dousings of the 'Dunkirk Spirit' – but it is not worth it in the end. If it is said that this is not much to claim for incomes policy, and if this is all it can do, is it worth it? The answer is yes! The most immediate benefit derived from a successful incomes policy is the prevention of the escalation of the going rate. This is what usually happens in periods of relatively free collective bargaining – although it would require a much longer chapter to spell out why this is so.[3] What incomes policy promises is the prospect of containing and modifying the incipient pay explosion that lies at the heart of our present system of pay bargaining, without the need to ruin the economy in the process.

Given the need to be modest and realistic about overall targets, the fine print of incomes policy can be allowed to vary to meet the circumstances of each round. The main need is always to deal with outstanding problems affecting pay structures and systems, as they have developed in the previous round. Once again it is necessary to know a great deal about the concerns and needs of employers and unions in this respect, and another chapter would be required to spell out the pros and cons of alternative policies.[4]

But this brings me to my fourth lesson: the need to provide some scope for outstanding exceptions and special cases. In the past, incomes policies have usually come to grief for one or two reasons: over ambition and inadequate provision for exceptions and special cases. The difficulty is that where policy targets are over ambitious – as they were throughout the 1964–70 period – the only way the policy can be saved from its evident impracticality is by allowing more and more exceptions and special cases. The danger then is that everybody expects to obtain a settlement above the level of the general increase. When this happens we may say that a policy is suffering from the 'colander syndrome'. It has more exceptions than a colander has holes, and is just about as likely to hold water. This is what happened during the latter stages of the 1964–70 incomes policy, resulting in a proliferation of phoney productivity deals.

Fortunately, as was demonstrated during the greater part of the 1974–79 period, the colander syndrome can be avoided if the general settlement level is modest and realistic. The danger then is that insufficient allowance will be made for the occasional genuine exception, or outstanding special case. This is usually because, in reaction against the colander syndrome, policy makers have fallen for some extreme version of what is usually termed the 'domino theory'. This is what happened under the Tories from 1970 to 1974. At times the Callaghan government came close to making the same mistake.

In essence those in the thrall of the domino theory believe that if they allow any exceptions on any grounds their policy will collapse. The above the norm exception will immediately establish a new going rate, which will destroy all hope of achieving the much publicised overall target. Once again, experience indicates that this need not happen, if what is permitted is seen to be broadly in accordance with the policy criteria. In any case the truth is that it is essential to try to navigate the narrow channel that lies between the colander and the domino. One must try to provide for an element of flexibility and the odd 'special case'. I believe the record shows that this is difficult but not impossible.

I also remain unconvinced that it is possible to develop and operate a permanent incomes policy without allowing for some variation in the level of settlements. It is not reasonable to expect employers to observe a policy indefinitely if it does not allow them any scope to deal with severe labour shortages or to improve performance. There must also be some way for groups to justify a lasting change in their relative position. Both the major miners' strikes of the early 1970s had this essential and reasonable objective at their centre. It was the fault of the incomes policy at the time that it failed to provide for a peaceful solution in either case.

The trick is to combine carefully defined exceptions criteria with a realistic general settlement level and adequate institutions; and to specify the upper limit allowed under each one of the criteria in a given year. I appreciate that sceptics will reply that this kind of policy has never been tried; I can only say that on the record of the past I think we shall come to it in the end.

But this brings me to my penultimate lesson. It is surely time to recognise that all low pay targets are time bombs ticking away at the heart of permanent incomes policy. They inevitably squeeze differentials in a way that leads inexorably to a subsequent pay explosion. Thus the low pay priorities of the Heath period led to the 1974 revolt of the miners – because they eroded the value of their Wilberforce Award. The supplementary settlements which produced the pay explosion at the end of the first period of Social Contract were all justified by reference to the flat rate threshold payments of the previous year. The £30 low pay entitlement, in the winter of 1975, contributed to the escalation of the following spring. The £6 limit, and the cut off at £8,500 a year in the same policy period, all helped to ensure the rejection of the 5 per cent target in the last year of the Callaghan government.

In other words, since 1973, low pay targets have undermined five periods of incomes policy and it is time that they were put to rest. Of course, as was stated at the start of this chapter, there is a school of thought in the Labour party that has always confused incomes policy with income re-distribution; but I would claim to have demonstrated that socialists do not have to rest their case for it on such a doubtful assumption. In any case it should be realised that low pay targets are an extremely inefficient way of dealing with the problem of low pay – let alone the wider problem of family poverty. A much more effective means is available in negative income tax, and this is not self-defeating. As has been said, the job of incomes policy is to influence and modify the overall level at which personal incomes expand. It cannot perform this task if it is also expected to act as an instrument of amateur egalitarianism.

So I come to my sixth and final lesson, which is in some ways the most obvious. It cannot be said too strongly that the best guarantee of success in incomes policy is that the great majority of trade union leaders are prepared to co-operate in making it work – largely because they know that most of their members regard it to be fair and necessary in the circumstances. Fortunately, the policies of the present government are likely to assist in the re-development of such a response, but in the long run support will depend on the extent to which general agreement can be reached between a future Labour government and the TUC on other aspects of economic and industrial policy.

This will not just be a matter of returning to less deflationary economic objectives, or agreeing to extend government intervention in industry. The unions will almost certainly insist on price controls and import controls, along with restrictions on the ability of the self-employed to escape the restrictions of conventional incomes policy. They will also demand the repeal of Conservative trade union legislation, and the restoration of traditional trade union immunities in the context of a trade dispute.

Not all members of the Parliamentary Labour Party will be

equally enthusiastic about what will be involved if there is to be agreement on another Social Contract, and there can be no denying that in some ways what will be needed will be more palatable to the Left than the Right of the party. To my mind, this only serves to reinforce my central theme.

8

Labour and the Unions

by Giles Radice MP

I

I greatly admired Tony Crosland as a leading Labour politician. Though I never had the opportunity of seeing him at work in a government department, I was deeply impressed by his performance in the House of Commons. He was one of the few MPs who were as authoritative in opposition as in government. Always supremely well briefed, he nearly always dominated debate, not so much by the passion of his rhetoric but by the force of his argument. His death in office was one of the biggest losses sustained by the last Labour government.

But, though he was always kind to younger MPs, Crosland's main influence on me was not primarily as a politician but as a political thinker. *The Future of Socialism*, which I first read when I was an undergraduate, was one of the formative books of my political life. I was overwhelmed by its originality, the broad scope of its compass and by its style and verve. When *The Conservative Enemy* was published in the early 1960s, I was already looking for a 'hopeless' constituency on which to cut my teeth. Though I had already read many of the essays in the work, I can still remember devouring it without stopping throughout one night and saying to myself when I had finished, 'Yes, this is my kind of Labour party.' Thereafter, whenever I got the opportunity to hear Tony speak or to read one of his articles, it was always top priority. I was one of many for whom Tony Crosland was a kind of political prophet.

II

Crosland did not write much about the trade unions. Whereas the Webbs (perhaps with the assistance of 'total abstinence and a good filing system') published two major works on the subject, Crosland's most considered statement is contained in his brilliant but brief essay 'Industrial Democracy and Workers' Control'.[1] This comparative neglect was partly because of his background; Crosland came to the Labour movement through Oxford and the war, not through the trade unions. It was partly because his expertise lay in other fields – economics, politics and sociology – and he never liked to write about matters which he had not studied deeply. It was also chance; Crosland was never asked to be secretary of an inquiry into the trade unions, as he was of the Co-operative Independent Commission, and he was never Secretary of State for Employment or Industry (though he would have excelled in both positions).

It was not that he did not consider the trade unions or their members important. On the contrary, Crosland had a respect, almost a reverence, for his working class constituents and their needs. He deplored the folly of the McGovern débâcle in the 1972 Presidential election. He criticised Labour's 1970 election campaign because it did not highlight issues of 'popular concern' (comprehensive education, working class housing, social welfare) and he praised the Scandinavian socialist parties because they combined so successfully the espousal of these social issues with liberal progressive causes. For Crosland, the unions were an essential part of this world of which he was so proud to be a spokesman. Crosland was a member of the GMWU and was a close friend of Derek Gladwin, Southern Regional Secretary of the union and a former constituent. He was a strong supporter of trade unionism and saw the connection between the Labour party and the unions, not only as a symbolic link, but also as a means of creating the basis for social democracy.

Crosland was well aware of the post war growth in trade union power. In *The Future of Socialism*, he argued that full employment had given unions a new bargaining strength at all levels and that this 'revolutionary change in the balance of power' was one of the decisive factors in the transfer of economic power away from the business class.[2] In *The Conservative Enemy* he wrote that 'The Trade Unions, skilfully exploiting the existence of a seller's market for labour, have established a remarkable degree of control over those management decisions which directly affect the day-to-day life of the worker'.[3] In *Socialism Now*, one of his counter-arguments to the neo-Marxist thesis of a transfer of power to a small oligarchy of private manufacturing firms was that the power of the unions had increased. 'They wholly defeated the Labour government, and effectively frustrated the Tory government, in major confrontations over industrial relations legislation; while the miners and others, in an open battle over wages in 1972, forced Mr Heath into a humiliating reversal of his chosen economic policies.'[4] He concluded: 'Some of the commanding heights of the economy are now to be found in union headquarters in Euston Road', though he noted that 'the dominant heights are for the present in the capitals of Saudi Arabia and Kuwait'.

Crosland was not afraid of this trade union power but he wanted to see it used in a constructive way. In *The Future of Socialism* he was critical of the limited nature of union objectives: 'generally the Unions have contracted out of responsibilities other than the traditional one for wages and conditions; or, rather, they have not widened their interests and influence to a degree in any way commensurate with the increase in their economic power.'[5] He advocated three major areas for advance – a more equal distribution of non-pecuniary privileges and a lesser social gap between staff and labour, effective consultation at the point of production and an extension of what he called 'high level industrial democracy' over national industrial decision making. Such an expansion of their role would mean internal change – in both the number of the officials and the employment of research staff.

For most of his political life he was against workers' participation in management. He was strongly influenced by the case put forward in Hugh Clegg's book *Industrial Democracy and Nationalisation* that union power rested upon remaining independent of and outside management.[6] He accepted Clegg's thesis that, while management plays the role of government, trade unions have to act as the opposition so that they can protect the rights of employees and enforce popular control over management decisions. The Crosland–Clegg line did not rule out a considerable development of union influence – indeed, they argued that it was by extending trade union control as an external, independent force that industrial democracy could most effectively be increased.

However, in *Socialism Now*, Crosland modified his position. He noted that there had been a dramatic upsurge of interest in industrial democracy which he ascribed to aspirations running ahead of power. He argued that the most important priority was to strengthen bargaining at shop floor level 'which is where it matters most'. He also supported the idea of higher level 'predictive' bargaining over company decisions. But, whereas the earlier Crosland had been against worker representatives on the board, the Crosland of the 1970s gave it his reluctant consent. He was influenced by the change in TUC attitudes and by what was happening on the continent (I suspect that David Lipsey also had a hand in his conversion).

But, though his views may have shifted slightly, he continued to raise objections to the idea. He asked how deadlocks were to be resolved where there was parity representation and how unions were to preserve their credibility with members when they were forced to associate themselves with unpopular management decisions. He also warned advocates not to expect too much: 'The worker-directors may become as remote from their rank-and-file as some local councillors or members of regional hospital boards are now. They may find themselves becoming dangerously compromised and equivocal in their loyalties.' He concluded that 'one must see participation in management as one element, and not the most important, in a total programme for industrial democracy and greater equality of working conditions'.[7]

With respect to the relationship between the Labour party and the unions, Crosland made a number of penetrating comments. In a 1973 article in the *Observer*, he wrote that 'Labour's special link is, and must be, with the organised working class and its solid base in the trade union movement. Both party and unions represent the same aspirations of their members and their families; and the area of common interest and mutual need is, and always will be, enormous.' But he went on to stress, 'that does not mean a *complete* identity of interest. Labour is not a sectional or one-class party, nor did most of the pioneers see it as such ... the Labour party should not automatically agree with everything that union leaders say, still less be dictated to by them. For all our special links with the unions, we are a national party, responsible to the people as a whole'.[8]

If Crosland was pro-union (he was against the controversial proposals for a 'conciliation pause' of *In Place of Strife*), that did not mean that unions should be above criticism, or that Labour politicians should always support their demands, or that Labour politicians should not, in their turn, make demands of the trade unions.

After the 1959 election defeat, Crosland advised the trade unions to look to their image for their own sake as well as the party: 'this image is suffering mainly because the Movement gives no firm lead on the issues which are currently troubling the public.'[9] A clear national view was required on such issues as the ETU, unofficial strikes, demarcation disputes and the rights of the individual member; and unions needed to spend money on public relations and to broaden their approach by organising white collar workers. In 1973 Crosland reminded the trade union leaders that public spending had to be paid for and that anti-inflation policy was inadequate without an incomes policy. He was insistent that 'it is the purest wishful thinking to suppose that in an increasingly planned economy (especially when a growing part of the population is employed in the public sector) governments can adopt a *dirigiste* attitude to the control of prices but a *laissez-faire* attitude to the determination of incomes'.[10]

III

To judge by opinion polls (though not by their growing membership), trade unions are now very unpopular. One of the main themes of the Conservative election campaign in 1979 was hostility to the trade unions; there is little doubt that the events of the winter of 1978–79 and the ensuing reaction against trade unionism played a part in Labour's election defeat. Given this background, it is hardly surprising that a number of those who call themselves social democrats (including Roy Jenkins and Peter Jenkins of the *Guardian*) have questioned the Labour party's close ties with the unions.

Their argument is roughly as follows: the trade unions are a powerful but highly conservative force. Restrictive practices hold back industrial innovation and lead to over-manning, while excessive wage agreements are at least partially responsible for our high rate of inflation. Labour's need 'to do a deal' with the unions over incomes policy results not only in excessive public spending commitments and over-generous labour legislation, but also in a Labour government turning a blind eye to union shortcomings, particularly their treatment of individuals. The critics also stress that the Social Contract relationship which developed between the 1974–79 Labour governments and the TUC is bad for Parliament and democracy because it gives excessive power and influence to an organisation which is not elected by the people. For all these reasons, Labour – and particularly Labour's revisionists – should loosen their links with the unions.

It is worth considering these criticisms in more detail. As Crosland noted, trade unions have become far more powerful since the war. The increase in power has, however, very often gone not to the national trade union organisation but to the shop floor. In many industries, shop stewards negotiate not only wages and working conditions but also employment and disciplinary issues. We should also note that, as a result of technological change, small groups of workers now have the ability to bring whole industries to a halt.

Yet trade union power is limited. Though shop stewards negotiate on a wide range of topics, the scope of their influence remains restricted to shop floor issues. Over most areas of industrial decision making there is no joint regulation at all. And collective bargaining at shop floor and at other levels is usually an attempt by trade unions to redress past grievances and complaints rather than to decide the future.[11] So unions are still mainly reactive bodies which can stop things happening but are seldom in a position to initiate.

It is certainly true that trade unionists have sometimes resisted changes essential for the health of the enterprise. Such industrial conservatism is highly regrettable and, in the longer run, self-defeating. The sooner trade unions give priority to raising productivity, the better it will be not only for the living standards but also for the job prospects of their members. But to blame trade unionists exclusively or even mainly overlooks the basic point that, within the existing organisation of industry, managers, not trade unionists, hold the reins of command. The managers make the investment decisions, choose the technology and oversee the design, making and marketing of the product. Significantly, NEDO reports have shown that the relative failure in the *design* and *selling* of British manufacturing products is the crucial factor in our economic decline. This failure has led to the closure of plants and unemployment, which has, in its turn, created a defensive employee attitude to subsequent attempts to increase productivity. The result is a vicious and intractable downward spiral of low labour productivity, low profitability and investment and shrinking market shares – a disastrous phenomenon for which trade unions bear only a part (and then only a small part) of the blame.

The charge that unions cause inflation is more plausible. Wage increases are undoubtedly an important, and on occasion (as in 1974–75) the predominant, factor in the generation of inflation. But union negotiators are more often than not reacting to other inflationary pressures, including rises in fuel and food and raw material prices, the impact of government policies on taxation, the money supply and the exchange rate, as well as the capital requirements of large corporations.

Did the Labour government's attempt to secure an incomes policy through the Social Contract lead to the politicians giving too much away to the trade union leaders in exchange? Taken overall, Labour's 'inducements' can hardly be said to be excessive. The Employment Protection Act of 1975 was a long overdue piece of industrial relations reform which extended employee rights in a number of crucial areas, including maternity, redundancies and unfair dismissals, though it was less successful over union recognition. The substantial increases in old age pensions and the introduction of child benefits represented a welcome though hardly extravagant advance, while the employment creation schemes did not compensate for the increase in unemployment after 1975.

The legitimate criticism of the Labour government was not that overall they gave away too much but that they failed to realise that they were dealing with bargainers. In 1974, Labour repealed the Tories' Industrial Relations and Housing Finance Acts and immediately increased pensions; the TUC merely agreed in a very loose way to restrict settlements in line with the cost of living. It was only when, in 1975, inflation rose to 30 per cent and there was a run on the pound that the TUC agreed to accept a tighter policy – and then only for a limited period. By 1978, after three years of an incomes policy which had inevitably created anomalies and distortions, the Labour government asked for an unrealistic 5 per cent policy – and had nothing to give in return. In any future relationship, gains and concessions have to be carefully balanced from the beginning.

Was the Labour government's relationship with the trade unions bad for democracy? The short answer must be no. Democratic governments have to rule with the consent of the governed. In a modern society, this means that they have to pay particular attention to the powerful industrial interest groups, especially the employers and unions. The new factor is that, for the first time in peacetime, the trade unions have been fully accepted into the charmed circle of the powerful. Where the Labour government can be criticised is for nor ensuring that there was an effective forum for *public* scrutiny of government's relationships with the industrial interests. Hopefully, the new parliamentary select committees (sadly not set up under a Labour government) will perform this function. But to argue for greater public accountability is very different from saying that there should be no relationship at all.

With respect to trade union treatment of individuals, the issue of the closed shop raised in the most acute form the clash between trade union and individual rights. Through the Labour government's repeal Acts of 1974 and 1976, it became legal again for an employer who was party to a closed shop agreement to refuse to employ and to dismiss employees who refused to join a trade union, except on grounds of religious conviction. In one sense, the libertarian argument is only partly relevant to industry; for without collective organisation the individual employee would be powerless. The closed shop helps unions build up effective countervailing power to management, thus giving protection to individual members. It also accords with the belief of most trade unionists that those who benefit from union action ought at least to join the union and give support when required. Finally, it removes a source of industrial conflict.

However, whatever the advantages of the closed shop, the Labour movement can not afford to ignore the question of individual rights. The Labour government recognised this when in 1974 it persuaded the TUC to set up an independent review body to consider allegations of arbitrary union behaviour and, in 1979, to give advice to its members on the application of the closed shop. The Department of Employment Closed Shop Survey, which revealed that the vast majority of recent agreements specified exemptions, provides evidence that the voluntary approach to the question was already beginning to work at the time when the Conservative government introduced legislation over the closed shop.[12]

I have tried to show that the conventional criticisms of unions are either exaggerated or wrongly conceived. But even if they were correct they would not add up to a convincing argument against Labour's ties with the trade unions. Any Labour government, indeed any modern government, has to have some form of dialogue with the unions. An existing link makes that dialogue more likely to succeed; if you are going to do business with someone, it is almost always a decided advantage if you have formed a relationship beforehand.

Viewed in perspective, Labour's link with the unions remains amongst the party's greatest assets. Although there will be times – as in May 1979 – when union unpopularity rubs off on Labour (and *vice versa*), it gives the party an organic connection with an immensely powerful (and growing) body of opinion – the millions of trade unionists whose views the Labour party ignores at its peril. The relationship with the unions also makes Labour a more credible governing party in modern Britain than the Conservatives. In this context, it is significant that the most successful social democratic socialist governments are those which, like the Austrians, the Swedes and the Germans, have close links with the unions.

This is not to say that the exact shape of existing constitutional arrangements within the Labour party should be preserved for all time. I well remember Tony Crosland making the point to a Young Fabian meeting in the early 1960s that the overwhelming preponderance of trade union votes at conference was a historical anachronism; certainly this is an area which the Labour party must consider. Neither should a link rule out a constructive relationship with other bodies, including not only one issue pressure groups (like the Child Poverty Action Group or Shelter) but also the employers as well. Indeed, in a recent

Fabian pamphlet, I argued that, before legislating on planning agreements, the next Labour government should try to make a deal with the CBI, by which in return for a government commitment to as stable an economic environment as possible (consistent tax policies, a reasonable return on investment, a realistic exchange rate and possibly import controls), major companies should let the Department of Industry see their corporate plans.[13]

Tony Crosland wrote, 'We must remember that the unions and the Party have their own distinct fields of responsibility, and their own distinct duties and obligations to their members and electors; neither is, nor should be, the creature of the other.'[14] The relationship between party and unions is based on common need and mutual interest, but it is also in part a bargaining process between two bodies with different roles. That means that Labour politicians, as leaders of a broad based, national party concerned with national solutions for national problems, have to have a carefully considered view of what they want from the unions and not merely react to what trade unions want. It is to this aspect of the relationship I now turn.

IV

The context in which the next election will be fought will almost certainly be one of grave economic crisis. It is true that by 1982 the oil revenues should be making a major contribution to the national budget. But even so it is improbable that the dispersal of these revenues in the shape of tax cuts will do much to halt or disguise Britain's industrial decline. Unemployment is likely to be at least two million, while inflation will certainly be no lower than in May 1979. All this will be against a background of world economic uncertainty, probably growing shortages of oil supply and possibly also international tension.

The Labour party will, therefore, be entitled to make the kind of demands of trade unions that are normally only justified in wartime. Firstly, unions will have to commit themselves to a long term incomes policy. Certainly we need to consider what went wrong last time. A Labour government must not again ask for a too restrictive phase in the fourth year of the policy. It must also keep in closer contact with the unions. But, for their part, trade union leaders must recognise that, by paying lip service to a 'return to free collective bargaining', they themselves helped undermine the incomes policy. Administering an incomes policy may be difficult but it is just not possible to run a modern economy effectively without one.

Secondly, as in wartime, there must be a wholehearted trade union commitment to increased productivity, to flexibility of labour and to the expansion of training. It is true that the Manpower Services Commission, set up by a Conservative government and expanded by the Labour government, was the brainchild of the TUC. But at shop floor level acceptance of new attitudes has been less than total. As a result, the productivity, flexibility and skills of our industrial labour forces are not as good as those of many of our rivals.

Thirdly, unions must improve their own government, structure, organisation and services. In a democracy, these internal matters are the responsibility of trade unions. But Labour politicians are entitled to remind the trade union movement that the TUC is still too weak for the good of the movement, that there is still too much competitive 'multi-unionism', that work groups are still not fully integrated into union structures and that union services are still woefully inadequate. These deficiencies are not only against the interests of trade union members; they also do damage to industry and, therefore, to the community as a whole. If the unions can initiate a Labour movement inquiry in the Labour party, why not a similar one into the trade unions?

In return, the unions are entitled to ask for government intervention in industry. Government intervention has not always been very successful in the past but, as with incomes policy, it is impossible to run a modern economy without it. Action will be required to save firms and industries which are vital to the economy, while public investment will also be needed to help set up firms in the new, advance technology sectors. Provided trade unions are prepared to adopt a positive approach to productivity, labour flexibility and training, they should be able to expect greatly increased government and industry support for industrial training and technical education. Employment creation schemes, which have already proved themselves cost effective, should also be expanded. In addition, work sharing in the form of a reduction in the number of hours worked, the lowering of the retirement age for men, less overtime and more educational and training sabbaticals will have to be considered – though always with an eye to what our competitors are doing.

If our industrial performance continues to deteriorate, the case for import controls (for which many trade unions argue) may become irresistible. The disadvantages are obvious: the danger of retaliation, the difficulties of ensuring an improved industrial performance, the inflationary pressures. The advantages are more problematic: in many cases it will do little more than provide a breathing space. But, by the mid-1980s, our industrial decline may have gone so far that there will be no alternative. The task will be to introduce controls in a way which maximises their advantages and minimises their disadvantages.

Here, the Labour movement faces a dilemma. On the one hand, the selective import controls which the TUC supports are likely to protect only those firms and industries which are already uncompetitive and may be extremely difficult to 'turn round'. On the other hand, though general import controls may be less 'feather bedding', they will have to be accompanied by both a tight incomes policy and restrictions in public spending – as the Cambridge School admits. In addition, our industrial competitors are likely to find general import controls even less acceptable than selective controls. These are problems which will have to be argued out *before* Labour comes to power.

With regard to social justice, there are unlikely to be extra resources to spend on more generous social programmes or reduced taxation. But trade unions, committed to a long term incomes policy, can reasonably ask for a concerted attack on the concentrations of inherited fortunes which so distort the distribution of wealth. This is partly a question of ensuring the Capital Transfer Tax introduced by the last Labour government becomes effective. There is also a strong argument for a wealth tax, though this needs to be co-ordinated with the existing Capital Gains Tax and the Investment Income Surcharge. The TUC have also called for a smaller difference between top and bottom incomes because of its divisive nature. As part of an overall approach on wealth and incomes, it may become possible to establish what the Royal Commission on the

Distribution of Incomes and Wealth called 'a broad consensus over pay relationships'. Only in this context will it become possible to devise an effective strategy to help the low paid – though experience over the last fifteen years has shown how difficult it is to change established differentials through an incomes policy.

Another crucial issue is likely to be industrial democracy. I have written elsewhere that 'more industrial democracy ... should help to reduce that feeling of alienation so characteristic of British industry and increase the sense of commitment to the enterprise so necessary to economic recovery. It should also provide a framework within which it should be possible to minimise the area of conflict and maximise the areas of co-operation. It should become easier to remedy some of the main faults of British industry – a resistance to change and an ineffective use of investment, including manpower.'[15] So the gains for the community are likely to be enormous. From the point of view of the employees, more industrial democracy, by giving workers and their representatives a real say in the running of industry, would represent a major step to an improved working life.

The problem is, as Crosland pointed out, to devise a system which preserves union independence while genuinely increasing employee influence over industrial decision making.

So far the trade union movement, unlike some of its continental counterparts, has been unable to make up its mind on the issue. All unions agree that the only basis on which industrial democracy can be built is a well organised shop floor. Some, however, believe that an extension of collective bargaining alone is enough to bring trade unionists into the heart of industrial decision making, while others argue that an additional dimension – employee representation at boardroom level – is also required. It was this division which was the main reason why the last Labour government failed to make any real progress on this front.

However, the Labour government's White Paper provides a useful starting point for discussion between the party and the unions. Its main recommendations (the establishment of the right to discuss strategic issues in companies employing more than 500 people, followed later by the introduction of an additional right to employee representation on supervisory boards of companies employing more than 2,000 workers) provide an imaginative synthesis of the two differing viewpoints. In addition, its emphasis on a flexible and phased introduction of industrial democracy, with most arrangements being worked out by those involved and with statutory rights only being invoked as a last resort, is very much in line with the voluntaristic traditions of British trade unions.

The White Paper also came up with ingenious answers to two tricky problems. With respect to the single channel of representation issue, it proposed that in both forms of industrial democracy (extension of collective bargaining and employee representation at boardroom level) a joint representation committee of trade unions (an idea first proposed by the Bullock Committee) should represent the employees. However, the White Paper suggested that any homogeneous group of a hundred or more employees should have a right to appeal to the Advisory, Conciliation and Arbitration Service. Whether the appeal device will get round the non-union problem remains to be seen.

On the issue of 'parity' between employee and shareholders representatives, the White Paper came down in favour of the employee representatives having a third of the seats as a 'reasonable first step'. If legislation had been introduced in the 1970s, a third might have been enough. But in the crisis conditions of the 1980s, it is doubtful whether the arguments against 'parity' can be fully sustained.

There remains the problem of multi-nationals. It is only fair that those who work for foreign controlled enterprises should have the same rights as those who work for domestic firms. However, that right does not necessarily give employee representatives the ability to influence decisions made at head offices outside this country. And what happens if the foreign management says 'If you introduce industrial democracy in our firm we will have to go elsewhere'? These difficulties can only be dealt with in a regional (perhaps European) or international (say, UN) context.

There is one further topic which must be high on the Labour party–trade union agenda – and that is staff status. The differences between blue and white collar workers (differences sometimes sustained by their unions) in increments to income, in length of holidays, in sick pay and in other mostly trivial though equally divisive areas (such as separate dining rooms, toilets, car park and 'clocking-on' arrangements) cannot be justified.[16] The time has come for the Labour party and the TUC to draw up a programme containing both legislative and collective bargaining elements which will eliminate these unfair distinctions.

There are overwhelming arguments for the link between the Labour party and the unions. But both sides must recognise their different roles — and both sides must accept that the gravity of the crisis facing the country means that the agenda for discussion cannot be artificially limited. Only if the relationship is completely honest and candid will the Labour party–trade union link be able to fulfil its potential in the 1980s.

Part 4

9

Democratic Socialism and Equality

by Professor Raymond Plant

No political demand can ultimately succeed — unless it is imposed by brute force — without being rooted in some powerful ethical system ... An effort in politics has to be confirmed in philosophy. Daniel Bell

Theories of socialism without critical moral philosophy are as undesirable as they are impossible. Bernard Crick

There are many aspects of Anthony Crosland's work which are of interest to the political theorist: his views about the transformed nature of capitalism, his account of the managerial revolution, his critique of the current vogue for participatory democracy, but most of all his account of equality, the ideal which, with Hugh Gaitskell, he regarded as the central socialist value. In this chapter I shall be concerned to investigate and assess his own distinctive view of equality and its relationship to socialist thought. But of course, with Anthony Crosland, not just socialist thought, but action as well — the translation of seemingly abstract ideals into politically defensible policies. I remember discussing equality with him over a bacon sandwich in the lumpers' canteen on Grimsby docks during the 1966 election campaign and, while he was adept at analysis and argument, he rightly reminded me that an ideal of equality had to be capable of being made relevant to improving the condition of people such as those in Hope Street in his cherished Grimsby constituency.

I

Unlike many of their political opponents, democratic non-Marxist socialists have to be very sensitive to the moral values on which their political attitudes and policy prescriptions rest. The traditional Conservative may, following the advice of Michael Oakeshott,[1] eschew the pursuit of rationalism in politics – the self-conscious pursuit of ideas such as equality and social justice – and prefer instead to pursue the 'intimations' present in the existing tradition of political activity. He may claim to follow what he tendentiously regards as common sense and practical experience and not be unduly bothered by the security of the moral basis of his position. However, this cannot be a position which can appeal to the radical. To the radical socialist, 'common sense', 'experience' and 'tradition' are likely to be seen as persuasive honorific titles given to privileged special pleading. Modern Conservatives, more influenced by Hayek than by Oakeshott, may equally abandon the search for just principles to govern the distribution of benefits and burdens in society. Taking the view that any attempt to constrain the market in the interests of 'the mirage of social justice' is likely to be totalitarian, they manage, as Hirsch argues, to take the issue off the political agenda:

> One broad solution which is propounded by the economic libertarian school of Hayek and Friedman is to deal with the distributional issue by taking it off the agenda ... The economic outcome is legitimised, not as just but as unjustifiable. Those who have drawn trumps in the existing allocation of economic endowments are merely fortunate, those who have drawn blanks unfortunate; all will be damaged by attempts to get a legitimated distribution by deliberate adjustment.[2]

Again here there is no need to worry about the moral basis of the distribution of benefits and burdens following on market transactions. In arguments with the traditional or the radical Right, a clear view about the nature of the egalitarianism to be defended by democratic socialists and its moral basis would seem to be at a premium.

Equally, the democratic socialist, unlike the Marxist, has to give a central place to his values in his political life. Marx was very clear that his critique of capitalism did not depend on moral assumptions but on historical and economic analysis and in this he was followed by Kautsky and Lenin. In Marx's mind, at least from the time of writing *On the Jewish Question*, moral values and corresponding social and political attitudes are rooted in material economic interests with the corollary that there can be no political appeal which can act as a counter-vailing power to those interests, challenge them and transcend them. Indeed in his *Critique of the Gotha Programme* Marx criticised democratic socialists precisely on the grounds that they did not see issues of social justice and equality as being fully determined by the existing productive relations and the class interests based upon them. For the Marxist, the pattern of ownership of the means of production determines the character of the distribution of goods and services in society and there is no role at all for an independent appeal to values such as justice and equality to criticise the pattern of distribution. In this sense, there is a certain amount of common ground between Marxists and the radical Right.[3] It is no accident therefore that the founder of revisionist socialism, Edward Bernstein, made the *moral* demands of socialism central to his thought.[4] The importance placed upon moral values and political principles is an explicit affirmation of the role of democracy in democratic socialism: people have to be persuaded and convinced, argu-ments put and visions of society defended if the democratic process is to work and the Marxian tie between values and material interests is to be broken. In our own day and in our own country it was Anthony Crosland who placed the *ideals* of democratic socialism at the centre of the political agenda.

II

We have to have either more equality or less, or the present amount: and politicians, in deciding which of these is the correct objective cannot but make some supposition about the welfare of the community. They have no excuse merely because these can be shown to be of an ethical nature for avoiding this responsibility.[5]

An egalitarian principle of distributive justice was central to Crosland's socialist vision. He saw the principle as constituting the main dividing line between socialists and non-socialists,[6] and as a principle which is likely to remain at the very centre of the political arena because problems of distribution will cease only with the abolition of scarcity. It is arguable that scarcity is a fundamental feature of human social life given the positional character of many of the goods which human beings desire,[7] so that the possibility of human relationships assuming an altruistic co-operative form is not a serious political option. In a situation of scarcity, individuals are always going to be concerned with the pattern of distribution of goods which prevails and the nature of the justification of that pattern. To that extent, therefore, Crosland is right to see problems about equality and social justice as endemic to political and social life.

Equality is, of course, a highly complex and contested social ideal and discussion of it can soon become very elusive. For my purposes here I shall distinguish three types of equality: equality of opportunity, equality of result and democratic equality. In *Socialism Now*, Crosland points out that he and other revisionists 'adopted the "strong" definition of equality – what Rawls has subsequently called the "democratic" as opposed to the liberal conception of equality of opportunity'.[8] This is an important statement because Crosland has often been taken as endorsing without qualification equality of opportunity. For example, Norman Birnbaum in an early reaction to *The Future of Socialism* took this view in *Socialist Commentary* in September 1959 and this misconception was repeated recently by Stephen Lukes in his *Essays in Social and Political Theory*.[9] It is also important, as we shall see, because Crosland links his own views on equality with those developed by John Rawls in his *A Theory of Justice* and in the course of this chapter we shall have cause to look more closely into this relationship.

The 'liberal' conception of equality as both Crosland and Rawls call it is fairly clear: it is straightforward equality of opportunity. Such a conception of equality would allow for fair competition for scarce social resources, income, status, power and so forth; certainly Crosland sees such a view as having an important place in his vision of a social democratic society on the grounds that it would make for a mobile dynamic society and this would have a disturbing effect on the class structure.

Equality of opportunity represents the meritocratic policy of widening the social basis of recruitment to positions of privilege in society. The aim is to provide equality of competition even if this leads to inequality of outcome. In *The Future of Socialism* Crosland gives a good description of the positive aspects of equality of opportunity:

> The essential thing is that every citizen should have an equal chance – that is his democratic right, but provided that the start is fair let there be maximum scope for individual self-advancement. There would be nothing improper in either a high continuous status ladder ... or even in a distinct class stratification ... since opportunity for attaining the highest status or topmost stratum would be genuinely equal.[10]

Such a view certainly appears radical. It rejects the idea of recruiting to scarce social positions from an hereditary class, it is efficient as a way of matching skills to jobs and would lead to a continuous cross-over in class membership. Some have taken the view that such a society would be marked by extreme insecurity and ought to be rejected on the basis of the psychological damage it would be likely to do. Crosland rejects this picture painted by some sociologists and psychologists as unduly pessimistic.

However, there are some difficulties with the notion of equality of opportunity taken on its own which make it in his own words 'not enough' for socialists. The major difficulties lie in attempting to equalise starting points, so that the competition for privileged positions is in fact fair, and in justifying those privileged positions in a manner consistent with socialist principles. On the latter point it is argued by some critics that the idea of privilege is inconsistent with the equality of respect which is owed to each individual in virtue of his common humanity and that equal respect points towards greater equality in the conditions of life, that is wealth, income, status and power. On this view the socialist should be concerned not with opening up recruitment to privileged positions to wider sections of the population but rather with narrowing as much as possible the differences in the conditions of life between individuals. Instead of a hierarchical society based upon recruitment by merit, those who believe in equality of outcome wish to argue

in favour of a progessive narrowing of hierarchy. The justification of equality of outcome can emerge from the discussion of
equality of opportunity in another way. The whole basis of
equality of opportunity depends upon the start of the competitive race being fair, but there are very clear limits within which
this is possible. First of all, granted that the family is the basic
social institution in our society, the influence of any action
taken in the field of health, education and welfare is going to
be mediated through the family with all the differentiating
effects this will have upon the start of particular children in life.
Moreover, studies of educational inequality and attempts by
governments to correct these through programmes of positive
discrimination have suggested that such programmes are less
successful than had been hoped. Reflections such as this have
led one major researcher in this field to argue that, 'instead of
trying to reduce people's capacity to gain a competitive advantage over one another, we will have to change the rules of the
game so as to reduce the rewards of competitive success and the
cost of failure'.[11] There are therefore these twin supports for a
conception of equality in terms of greater and greater equalities
in outcomes: inequalities, even when fairly competed for, are
inconsistent with socialism and in any case the competition can
never be made fair.

There are, however, difficulties with placing equality of outcome at the centre of a socialist framework of values. It may
well be inconsistent with political and civil liberties and it
embodies very weak demands in terms of efficiency. The first
of these points has been well put by a proponent of such a view
of equality. As Frank Parkin says, in *Class, Inequality and Political
Order*,

> ... socialist egalitarianism is not readily compatible
> with a pluralist political order of the classic western
> type. Egalitarianism seems to require a political system
> in which the state is able to continually hold in check
> those social and occupational groups which, by virtue
> of their skills or education, might otherwise attempt to
> stake claims to a disproportionate share of society's
> rewards. The most effective way of holding such groups
> in check is by denying them the right to organise politi-
> cally or in other ways to undermine social equality.[12]

For social democrats, such a conclusion renders the conception of equality which requires such drastic curtailments of political liberty suspect. The other aspect of equality of outcome is one on which Crosland has much more to say and which leads on to the third conception of equality, what he and Rawls call the 'democratic conception' of equality. Equality of outcome fails to recognise that certain inequalities may have essential economic functions. It is concerned to ensure a single status society on the basis of equality of respect but neglects the fact that without differential rewards certain jobs, the performance of which is to the benefit of everyone, may not get done. Democratic equality attempts to do justice to some of the arguments directed against mere equality of opportunity while at the same time being sensitive to the fact that there may be the need to pay differential rewards.

Crosland goes some way with those who wish to argue that equality of opportunity is suspect as a socialist ideal. He takes the view, which Rawls was later to develop, that not only does equality of opportunity lead to the development of a hierarchy of merit but the qualities which such a hierarchy may reward are arbitrary from the point of view of the moral demands of distributive justice. High rewards are given on the basis of merit to talents and abilities which are to a very large extent morally arbitrary in the sense that the individual is not fully responsible for them and they are in large part the result of genetic endowment and fortunate family background. In *The Future of Socialism* he puts the argument without equivocation: 'No one deserves either so generous a reward or so severe a penalty for a quality implanted from the outside and for which he can claim only a limited responsibility.'[13] The point is repeated in *Socialism Now*: 'By equality, we meant more than a meritocratic society of equal opportunities in which the greatest rewards would go to those with the most fortunate genetic endowment and family background.'[14]

So equality of opportunity is not a sufficiently rich conception on its own for a socialist view of equality; but equally he rejects equality of outcome because of its indifference to the fact that greater economic rewards for some may have a vital economic function. On the face of it, his position appears paradoxical. He rejects pure equality of opportunity and its resultant meritocracy and yet is in favour of differential rewards rather than equality of result. However, the resolution of the paradox is to be found in the justification he gives for differential rewards. Departures from equality are to be justified not by appeals to merit or desert but rather on the basis of a rent of ability – the amount of money (or for that matter non-material incentives) which would be necessary for individuals to perform tasks without which the whole community would suffer. There is a trade off to be found between equality and incentive but it must be a real trade off based upon a rent of ability and not on the basis of merit. Such differential inequalities need not lead to hierarchies such as were found to be characteristic of meritocracies because what the tasks are which will require incentives will depend upon circumstances and will vary. A good example of this would be the increased value to the community of coal miners in the light of actions by OPEC and the uncertainties about the nuclear industry. Because of this, it is impossible to say in advance what inequalities will be functional in an economy and at what level they will have to be set:

> How large this should be is of course impossible to lay down in general terms. If we believe in equality we can only say that we shall balance the possible loss to equality against the possible gain from exploiting the ability. The balance of loss and gain will depend upon the supply price of different grades of ability.[15]

On the basis of considerations of this sort we could say as an approximation that Crosland had a belief in equality, with inequalities being justified if, and only if, differential rewards work to the benefit of the community as a whole and we can assume that access to jobs which command differential rewards would be on the basis of genuine equality of opportunity. Of course, not all incentives or differential rewards are properly to be regarded as increasing inequality. Some socially important tasks may well involve considerable welfare costs for those who perform them. They may for example be dangerous or done permanently at night and extra payments for the performance of such tasks might be better seen not as *increments* of income but more as *compensation* for the 'dis-welfare' suffered in doing the job. The extra payments bring the worker up to the level of welfare experienced by others and as such the differential payment is a way of securing equality of welfare rather than being a departure from it. However, it is of course true, and Crosland takes the point, that most differential payments do involve a trade off between equality and economic efficiency and as such he has to make assumptions about the necessity for incentives, that there is a need for a rent of ability which will create in-equalities – otherwise socially important tasks will remain undone. At this point, egalitarians of result have criticised those who have made a case for differential and inequality producing payments. It is quite central to the case of those who believe in complete equality of result that incentives are ultimately un-necessary and the need for them is merely the effect on human motivation of the competitive ethos of capitalist society. Lukes, in defending egalitarianism of result makes this point:

> A further weakness of the theory [of democratic equality] is its assumption that unequal rewards are the only pos-sible means of mobilising qualified individuals into adequately performing important jobs. It leaves out of account the intrinsic benefits of different positions in relation to the expectations, aptitudes and aspirations of different individuals ... and it fails to consider func-tional alternatives to a system of unequal rewards such as intrinsic job satisfaction, the desire for knowledge, skills and authority, of public service etc.[16]

Certainly any egalitarian who cares about the possible range of inequalities which the rent of ability criterion would set up has to be interested in the possibilities which Lukes suggests. At the same time, though, the fact that these are not material incentives does not mean that they do not embody inequalities of life con-ditions and are morally speaking in much the same position as material incentives. It must also be said that the evidence cited by Sen in *On Economic Inequality* about the success of the applica-tion of non-material incentives in China during 'the Great Leap Forward' is not encouraging.

Presumptive equality with inequalities justified in terms of a rent of ability is a distinctive view of equality which falls be-tween equality of opportunity and equality of result. It is a view of equality which enables Crosland to answer a persistent question put by Conservative critics of the egalitarian ideal: how much equality ultimately? In his recent book, *Inside Right*, Ian Gilmour puts the question thus:

In constantly demanding more equality, while refusing
to specify how much, the revisionists are like a general
continually ordering his troops to move east irrespective
of whether the terrain is flat or mountainous, fertile or
barren, well drained or swamp, and ignoring the casual-
ties they suffer or inflict and the amount of equipment
they may lose. But then ideologists do not make good
generals.[17]

This is really a rather unsubtle criticism. The question should
not be 'how much equality?' but 'how much inequality?'
Democratic equality (presumptive equality combined with a
theory about justified inequalities) cannot specify in advance
and for all time the range and nature of the inequalities which
will be made legitimate by the rent of ability criterion. Differential rewards are to be paid after empirical investigation of the
economic function of a particular task and the supply price of
the skills to fulfil it. This will clearly vary from time to time and
place to place, depending upon the kinds of natural advantages
and disadvantages which a society may incorporate and the
stage of its economic development. The idea that this could be
specified in other than piecemeal and empirical terms and subject to constant scrutiny and revision is ludicrous. It would
make as much sense to ask a market oriented Conservative how
much competition precisely he is willing to allow in the market.
Usually he will answer that occasionally the national interest or
whatever will require intervention in the market but, of course,
he could never say in advance and in detail what this would
amount to. Similarly, the democratic egalitarian cannot say in
advance and for all times what divergences from equality are
to be justified in his terms.

III

So far I have contrasted three conceptions of equality and have
argued that Crosland comes closest to asserting a principle of
presumptive equality coupled with a view about the range of
justifiable inequalities which are required as a rent of ability if
important economic functions are to be performed.

I now want to turn to the moral justification of such a

principle. In *The Future of Socialism* Crosland does not spend very much time on this issue and I will argue that what he has to say is inadequate, but the issue is not of marginal importance. What matters in society is not the sheer fact of inequality but how these inequalities are perceived, in particular whether they are perceived as fair or unfair, just or unjust. If a particular set of unequal rewards can be defended on the basis of their fairness or justice, then the resentment which is directed towards them by those who do not share them is illegitimate. On the other hand, if this cannot be shown, then the resentment is justified. We need an argument based upon some kind of theory of justice to distinguish between legitimate and illegitimate resentment and to answer the Tory jibe that the pursuit of equality in order to lessen social resentment is the politics of envy. Among social theorists Runciman has asked this question most pertinently:

> Is it legitimate to speak of people's perceptions of in-
> equality as 'distorted' or to describe a disproportionate
> awareness of inequality as 'envy'? Or is there no criterion
> which could be brought to bear by which the use of any
> such term could be better justified than any other?[18]

This is not merely an academic, philosophical issue because it is at least arguable that issues of this sort play a major role in industrial and social discontents which are important in restricting economic growth and not only this, it is of central importance to the coherence of Crosland's own intellectual position. Colin Welch, in a vehement attack, has pointed out the issue which Crosland has to face here:

> To achieve any sort of durable financial success in such
> a world were it possible, is to expose oneself not only to
> Mr Crosland's icy disapproval but, more important, to
> the envy and resentment of the masses – ugly and uncon-
> structive sentiments which, so far from rebuking, he fully
> endorses, tries even to share, and proposes to assuage by
> levelling down the objects of envy. Did it not cross his
> mind that the greater the relative equality prevailing, the
> more all surviving inequalities (and he permits some)
> will be resented?[19]

This kind of assault can only be countered by an argument

which shows that the inequalities are unjust and the resentment legitimate.

However, the difficulty goes deeper than this. Crosland held the view that social resentment was a disruptive force in industrial relations and that the elimination of the objects of resentment would itself help Britain's economic performance. Such a view seems to underlie his endorsement of something like an early version of the Social Contract in a speech in Copenhagen in 1971 in which he developed the view that an incomes policy would only work in a society in which greater social equality is being pursued.[20] An incomes policy introduced against a background of *unjustified* inequalities is not going to command the assent of workers. The same point has been made powerfully by John Goldthorpe in a number of studies in which he suggests that:

> ... the existence of inequality, of an extreme, unyielding and largely unlegitimated kind, does militate seriously against any stable normative regulation in the economic sphere because it militates against the possibility of effective value consensus on the distribution of economic and other resources and rewards.[21]

Unless the structure of inequalities does have some accepted moral basis, workers are unlikely to moderate wage claims. The so called 'wages jungle' is one part of a wider system of inequality which lacks justification. Inequality may be a brute fact: what matters is our perception of its legitimacy and justice and this is why, as Crick points out in the epigraph to this chapter, socialist theories must rest upon some kind of moral philosophy, in this case a theory of justice.

It is perhaps worth noting in passing that present Tory policy is going to have to face up to this issue at some point. Under the influence of Hayek, and more remotely Hume, the tendency has become to try to argue that since there is no basis for agreement over the distribution of economic rewards, we should depoliticise the distributional issue, abandon the search for justice in the pattern of reward and leave it to the market place. However, this is probably unrealistic and is inconsistent with Toryism's traditional outlook, as has been well explored by Irving Kristol in his essay 'When Virtue Loses All Her Loveliness'.[22] To legitimise the market outcomes is to neglect notions such as merit and desert (Hayek and Hume are clear about this) but it is precisely notions such as these which are dear to many conservatives. Those who doubt this should read Welch's *Encounter* essay discussed above.

We need some kind of moral consensus to legitimise steps towards equality and moves away from it. Without this consensus we shall face a legitimation crisis and governments will find it difficult to act, particularly in the economic sphere. As Goldthorpe says: 'those who are prepared to accept social inequality more or less as it presently exists must also be prepared to accept disorderly industrial relations', with all the consequences which these have in terms of economic growth and development.

The difficulty with Crosland's position on this basic moral point is that he takes the view that his conception of equality is in some sense arbitrary and that it is far from being a consensus value. He argues that conceptions of equality lack objective validity, are not amenable to proof or disproof and must be accepted or rejected according to 'the moral predilections of the reader'.[23] In an article in *Encounter*, Vaizey points out that Crosland's egalitarianism was arbitrarily determined, without pointing out the problems to which this gives rise. A moral appeal which relies on the moral predilections of the reader is all very well, but it will hardly suit the radical because the predilections of the majority may well be in another direction. Indeed Crosland goes out of his way to emphasise this. The point is made repeatedly when he claims in many of his writings that the position of the worst off can only be significantly improved in a situation of economic growth because only then will those better placed be able to maintain their standard of living in absolute terms while allowing for relative improvements in the position of the worst off. This implies that egalitarianism is not a central consensus value otherwise this would not be necessary.[24] In addition, he draws an explicit distinction in *Socialism Now* between consensus values and egalitarian ones.[25] So a sheer appeal to the moral predilections of his readers is on his own account not likely to take us all the way. On the one hand, we have the need to see the distribution of benefits and burdens as legitimate and just in order to minimise social resentment; on the other, we have no clear moral basis to underpin the conceptions of justice and equality invoked.

Earlier I mentioned the fact that Crosland linked his view of equality, 'democratic equality', with the work of John Rawls whose *A Theory of Justice* has had such a profound effect in Britain and the United States. In *A Theory of Justice* Rawls attempts to construct an argument which will provide an objective basis for democratic equality but which seeks to relate to and in a sense theorise our ordinary reflective moral consciousness. In this sense it claims not to stand apart from everyday moral reflection but to stand in reflective equilibrium to it. Obviously a project of this sort must have a fascination for a social democrat and some commentators have noticed the need for precisely this kind of work. Stuart Hampshire, for example, in his review of Rawls's work in *The New York Review of Books*, argues as follows: 'In England, books about the Labour party's aims, for example those by Douglas Jay and Anthony Crosland since the war, needed just such a theory as this stated in its full philosophical generality.'[26] The need for such a project to round out Crosland's own intellectual position I hope already to have shown and others have noticed the importance of a Rawlsian perspective to his work.[27] Despite limitations of space and the problems with the theory, I hope to say something about the salience of this relationship.

In *A Theory of Justice* Rawls points out the extent to which our everyday views about the justice of a particular distribution of benefits and burdens will be influenced by our interests, the particular stake which we will have in a particular pattern of distribution. An argument which merely appeals to the unreflective predilections of the public is likely just to reflect these interests. In order to break out of this subjectivism, which is not likely to support radical proposals, we must stand back from our interests. The most appropriate way in which this can be done would be in terms of a hypothetical social contract in which we try to envisage what individuals in a state of hypothetical equality and in ignorance of their own talents and abilities would choose as principles to govern social life. To make a claim about justice, as opposed to a subjective claim about where one's own interests lie, means on this model that it would have to embody a principle to which the person making the claim would have to have subscribed without knowing in advance whether he would be a beneficiary or a loser under the operation of the principle. In this model Rawls's individuals are compelled to choose principles of distributive justice in total uncertainty of how the principles will apply to them. The model tries to translate into cash terms what we mean by fairness when we use the term in adjudicating various claims. In Rawls's view, the contractual model is the best device for elucidating fair and impartial judgment. Granted the model, Rawls argues that his hypothetical individuals would adopt a 'maximin' strategy, choosing from among all the principles the best of the worst possible outcomes they could experience under the operation of various possible principles. Utilising this stategy, Rawls argues that the 'contracting parties' would choose principles of justice to which he gives the name 'democratic equality', the view with which Crosland allies himself in *Socialism Now*. Rawls's two principles of justice are:

1 Each person to have the most extensive system of equal basic liberties compatible with similar liberties for all
2 Social and economic inequalities to be arranged so that they are (a) to the greatest advantage to the least advantaged consistent with a just savings principle, and (b) attached to offices and positions open to all under conditions of fair equality of opportunity

The first principle secures co-extensive principles of liberty, so central to democratic socialist thought; the second is a principle of presumptive equality with inequalities being justified if, and only if, they are to the benefit of the least advantaged members of society. Again we see the point which Crosland made much of, namely that differential rewards may be necessary and where they are necessary they are to be paid not on the basis of personal merit or desert but rather on the grounds that they are functionally necessary to the economy and to the benefit of the least advantaged members of society. Of course, it is impossible to do justice to the immense subtlety and complexity of Rawls's theory here, but what he is claiming is that it is possible to develop a model of rational decision making which will correspond to our reflective notions of fairness and impartiality and that this model is rich enough to yield substantive principles of distributive justice of a democratic egalitarian sort which will provide a bench mark for assessing the justice or otherwise of a particular set of rewards. Only a procedure of this sort will enable us to break out of a purely subjective approach to problems of distribution which means that it is impossible to escape from the charge of pursuing the politics of envy without merely resorting to a relabelling of one's own attitudes. Only some kind of theory of justice which develops our intuitive, but not worked out notion of fairness or impartiality will enable socialists to demonstrate in principle what kinds of grievances are to be regarded as legitimate and what pattern of inequalities are to be regarded as just. This is central to the intellectual coherence of democratic socialism and practically important in handling the problem of resentment against inequalities which as we have seen may be crucially important in incomes policy.

The trouble is, of course, that all of this does look far too academic. Samuel Brittan has pointed to the intractable nature of the problem faced here. He admits that some kind of justification has to be given to the structure of distribution and that it is important to develop a moral consensus over this, but equally the kinds of moral arguments deployed seem very remote from the general moral consciousness of individuals:

> ... if the rational arguments for accepting a system that does not aim at complete distributive justice are too abstract or sophisticated to command assent; and if there is an emotional void that cannot be met merely by rising incomes and humanitarian redistribution unrelated to 'merit', then the outlook for liberal democracy is a poor one.[28]

The Rawlsian answer is that the contractual model does develop ordinary reflective notions of fairness, but this can be doubted as can the logic of the arguments in favour of the two principles at least as developed by Rawls. This is by no means a closed question but Brittan's point still remains true; such arguments and devices *appear* too abstract. Are we then left with an appeal to the moral predilections of the electorate, which, as Crosland clearly realised, are quite frequently not of an egalitarian sort? It is just not possible to string together a set of consensus attitudes towards legitimate inequalities because the basis of the legitimation is just not there. Indeed, if we follow Goldthorpe, the development of consensus about a legitimate pattern of distribution *depends* upon moral values and does not itself exist apart from them:

Such consensus in turn cannot be achieved without the distribution of economic resources and rewards, and indeed the entire structure of power and advantage becoming in some way principled – becoming that is, more capable of being given consistent rational and moral justification ... In other words, the advancement of social justice has to be seen not as some lofty and impracticable ideal ... but rather as an important *precondition* of mitigating current economic difficulties.[29]

Crosland was surely right, therefore, to place equality on the agenda of socialism and to insist that it and increasing growth and welfare are inextricably linked. What democratic socialists still require are the intellectual resources to provide the rational and moral justification for the reward structure they favour, resources which can be translated into a political language which is accessible to all and not the rarified language of political philosophers. This is why it is perhaps important to look at some middle range justifications which could be given to democratic equality rather than to the vast overarching theory developed by Rawls.

In the first place there are good grounds for rejecting the Hayekian view that social justice is a mirage and its pursuit should be taken off the agenda of politics. His view that goods and services, benefits and burdens are not *distributed* by some identifiable human agency but rather by the impersonal forces of the market may be true but is irrelevant. Hayek wishes to draw the conclusion that because there is no distributor or agency, there can be no injustice, and the outcomes of exchanges have to be accepted for better or worse as *unjustifiable*. However, what is just and unjust is the way in which society reacts to the distribution. The misfortune of having a physical handicap is not an injustice, but justice comes into the picture in the way in which others react to those who have suffered such misfortune. In the same way as we seek to mitigate the effects on individuals of misfortunes in this sense, so we can seek to redress the misfortunes which are socially distributed and nurtured. The pursuit of social justice and the attempt to constrain the market in its interest is not a mirage and in a world of scarce resources, both physical and social, it is unlikely that the question of who is to get what and on what principle will ever become irrelevant to the political agenda.

Democratic equality also seems to be well defended against attacks on the Left from those who believe more strictly in equality of result. Equality of result is often justified, as we have seen, in terms of notions of common humanity and the respect owed to an individual. However, it is arguable that it is irrational, if one takes respecting individuals seriously, to prefer strict equality of result to democratic equality with its commitment to the idea of inequalities being justified if they help the whole community, including the worst off. Granted that differential rewards are being paid on the basis of rent of ability rather than desert, there is no disrespect towards those who do not achieve such differential rewards and in addition they can see that the rewards embody a principle which it is in their own interest to accept. The only ground on which it might seem rational to prefer equality of result would be some overriding commitment to community and social solidarity: that the gains in levels of welfare which might accrue from paying differentials would not offset the decline in social solidarity which the distancing effect of the differential payments would have. However, the advocate of democratic equality can counter this argument because one of the advantages of the theory is that it does attempt to give some content to the rather vague notion of community. Rawls has developed this point quite cogently:

> The difference principle [the second of the two principles of justice] ... does seem to correspond to a natural meaning of fraternity. Namely the idea of not wanting to have greater advantages unless this is to the benefit of others who are less well off. The family in its ideal conception and often in practice is the one place where the principle of maximising the sum of advantages is rejected. Members of a family commonly do not wish to gain unless they can do so in ways that can further the interests of the rest. Now wanting to act on the difference principle has precisely this consequence. Those better circumstanced are willing to have their greater advantages only under a scheme in which this works out for the benefit of the least fortunate.[30]

Differential rewards need not create social distance and destroy the sense of community in a society if they are paid on the basis set out in the difference principle and in terms of a rent of ability, and if those who are paid the differential rewards do not turn themselves into a self-perpetuating élite. However, changing social circumstances are always likely to *change* the groups of individuals to whom such rewards are paid.

Democratic equality seems well defended against the libertarian Right and the communitarian Left and it is equally clear why such a conception of equality should appeal to the worst off members of society and why a society organised on the basis of such a principle should command their allegiance. Democratic equality is clearly in their interests and will secure their welfare. The real difficulty, however, as Crosland's remarks about the difficulties of redistribution in periods of low growth make clear, is to provide reasons why the better endowed should feel loyalty to and vote in favour of a society organised on democratic egalitarian lines. This is clearly the basic moral problem here: how to justify egalitarian distributive principles to persons each of whom has a fundamental interest in receiving the greatest possible share of distributed goods. If there is no resolution to this problem any system of democratic egalitarianism is going to be relatively unstable because only the worst off members of society are going to have an incentive to support such a system and they are not going to be numerically significant enough (particularly if one adopts a relative view of poverty) to ensure the stability of a system of egalitarian distribution of the sort envisaged. However, there are two arguments here which are rather similar and could give reasons of self-interest to the better off to support a system of democratic egalitarianism.

It could be argued in the first place that the well being of the better endowed as well as that of the worst off members of society rests upon mutual co-operation. In order for the better endowed to be able to exercise their talents, capacities and powers and to derive satisfaction from doing so, there has to be a scheme of social co-operation. The surgeon can only operate if certain more menial tasks are performed; the philosopher can only think if he has a university and libraries, which again depend upon the services of a great many other people. Such co-operation can only exist between parties who recognise their mutual dependence only if they see the terms of their co-operation as fair. If this is not so there will be resentment and lack of co-operation. A fair agreement may not be optimal for any individual, but it is a necessary contract to ensure the smoothness of the relationship. The critic will of course argue that while this may be true, the concessions made by the better off under conditions of democratic equality seem to be much greater and indeed the system seems to be geared to optimising the position of the less well off. The answer to this surely is to take up Crosland's point about merits and deserts. If, as he argues, we bear only very limited responsibility for our assets (these being the result of genetic endowment and fortunate family background), then it is reasonable to ask those with these assets to better themselves only under a system in which so doing will help those who are less well off and whose less fortunate position is by parity of reasoning not fully their responsibility. Granted the point that society is a co-operative venture, if fate has stepped in and penalised some participants who use the assets they have got, then it may seem only fair that the advantages of the fortunate should be used in ways which help them and the less well off.

The other argument would be a more direct appeal to self-interest. It is the view that individuals will see the advantage of the pooling of natural talents in a scheme of mutual benefit, for the better off as well as for the worst off. Individuals will be aware that the community will support them in time of need whether in health, education or welfare, in exchange for an agreement between individuals to share their talents in a way which benefits others as well as themselves. Although this may seem to evade the problem posed earlier about the significance of the numbers of those who are poor and disadvantaged, the fact is that with the contingencies of life being what they are no individual could ever be sure that he would not have to draw upon this kind of help and therefore the better off would have an incentive to support it. There is a good deal of evidence that this is in fact the way people do feel about welfare institutions, particularly the NHS, and Titmuss in his *Gift Relationship* discusses this attitude in some detail.

IV

Anthony Crosland was quite right to see the issue of distribution as central to socialism and to see a form of egalitarianism as the form of distributive justice which sets off the socialist position from all others. I have tried to pin down precisely what his commitment in *Socialism Now* to a form of democratic egalitarianism means and to look at its justification. It has been a central conviction in this chapter that the search for greater equality and for normative arguments which could sustain it is not mere 'theology' but the central task of democratic socialism.

10

The Place of Public Expenditure in Socialist Thought

by Colin Crouch

The demand that public spending should be kept high and frequently increased – one of Anthony Crosland's central commitments – has long been one of the hallmarks of political movements of the Left in virtually all industrial societies. It provides one of the very few points of consensus linking parties as far apart as the French Communists and the West German Social Democrats, and extends to the progressive wing of the United States Democratic Party. Furthermore, it is a demand which has survived the radical changes in social circumstances from nineteenth-century poverty, through two world wars, the inter-war depression, post-war affluence and on to the recent return of global recession. Indeed, the commitment of the Left to public expenditure is so much a part of our accustomed political life that we take it entirely for granted.

However, during the past few years, policies of high public spending have come under new and heavy attack – intellectually from a newly confident school of Conservative economists and social commentators, and in practice through the policies of international economic agencies. In Britain – not a country with a particularly high level of public spending – the attack has been given added point by the violent ideological hostility to all public spending apart from the police and the armed forces expressed by the current Conservative government.

It is therefore an appropriate time to reconsider the taken-for-granted commitment and to examine some of its paradoxes. This chapter does this, first by a brief historical review of how public spending came to occupy its prominent place in British socialist thought, and second by an examination of some of the inadequacies which have been revealed in the Labour movement's approach to the question.

There are clearly several areas of public spending – including one of the biggest single items, defence – which are in no way distinctively socialist. Public expenditure becomes a particular concern of socialists if it falls into any one or more of three categories. First and most straightforward, state spending may be used to offset the inequalities which exist in the operation of the market by enabling citizens to enjoy certain goods and services as of right (or for token payment) and irrespective of their ability to buy them at their market price.

Second, and closely related to this, there are several goods which citizens quite rationally seek but which cannot be provided by the market, or can only be provided at a cost so high that they would be available to very few people. A wide variety of goods comes into this category, ranging from clean rivers to the police force to grand opera. Defined this broadly, there is no *a priori* reason why socialists should have any global commitment to this category. There are, however, three reasons why they tend to embrace a wide range of causes within it. Firstly, given their dissociation from the interests of capital and their long standing belief in intervening in market processes in the interests of equality, socialists are more likely than the supporters of bourgeois parties to be sympathetic to appeals that there should not be complete reliance on market mechanisms for the provision of people's needs. Secondly, in many, if not most, instances even the clearest cases of public goods can actually be provided through market mechanisms for a small minority; if there are very few unpolluted rivers it will be the rich who will monopolise access to those that remain; several exclusive American housing estates employ private police forces. In general one can argue that where provision by public expenditure will potentially put within reach of everyone a good which would otherwise be accessible only to a wealthy minority, socialists will be prominent among advocates of that provision.[1] Thus, there is no particular reason why socialists should be particularly committed to the annual subsidy to the Covent Garden Opera, because even as subsidised it remains accessible only to very few. They should be, and are, heavily committed to the tradition of public service broadcasting exemplified by the BBC, because that makes available to a mass audience a richer variety of cultural experience than would result from radio and television services governed by commercial criteria alone. The dividing line is difficult to specify clearly, and there will be interesting and continuing debates over where it falls, but the rule of thumb given here will serve for present purposes.

Thirdly, socialists are interested in the use of public expenditure as a means of maintaining demand in the economy in order to secure full employment – in short, in Keynesian economic policy. Closely related is spending on job creation through special schemes, subsidies and investment incentives. This is because the strength of the Labour movement and the welfare of those it represents depend on full employment. This category differs from the previous two in that it may involve indiscriminate support for *any* public expenditure which increases demand,[2] something which the definitions of the two previous categories have deliberately tried to avoid. If one's aim is simply to boost demand, then it does not matter very much whether the expenditure goes on the salaries of top level bureaucrats, the production of kidney machines or the manufacture of hydrogen bombs.[3] Indeed, before 1945 it was often argued that the only way in which a capitalist economy would be able to sustain full employment would be through maintenance of a permanent war economy – a reasonable argument at a time when the only available examples of full employment had been Fascist Italy, Nazi Germany and the combatant countries of the Second World War.[4] Most socialists would reject the idea of indiscriminate support for public spending on the grounds that there are sufficient unmet needs under the first two categories, and that it is inconsistent with socialism's stress on the conscious choice of priorities to show unconcern about the objects of state expenditure. This is a sound and reasonable argument, though it is remarkable how often the Labour movement has, especially recently, allowed itself to be manoeuvred into a position where it is willing to support any spending provided it emanates from the state. Let us assume that the basic distinctive commitment of socialists is to those elements of public spending covered by categories one and two, together with items of demand stimulation and job creation which accord with some plan of economic and social development.

A Historical Perspective

Early working class movements were confronted by a world in which the two principal sources of power and the allocation of resources – the market and the state – operated in ways largely hostile to their interests. Labour's place in the market was weak and by definition subordinate, while workers were excluded from political citizenship. The aspiration of the early socialists was therefore to transcend both these by some system of social regulation based on co-operation and community. For all his refinements of and improvements on early socialist theory, Karl Marx did not really differ from this ultimate ideal, nor did he improve on the hopeless vagueness of its formulation. Instead, the idea of a marketless, stateless society barely shifted from its place as an unworldly utopia as Labour movements developed in strength and made their practical targets the amendment of the terms of operation of state and market. This was no less true of revolutionary than of reformist movements. No one needs reminding that the Bolshevik revolution failed entirely in its avowed intent of smashing and subsequently transcending the powerful, autocratic Russian state; instead it consolidated its position by using the resources of that state and by developing them even further – a process which continues today. Elsewhere the socialist and communist objective of challenging the state in order to transcend it has become in effect a policy of trying to adapt it and make use of it.

There are several reasons for this crucial change: the failure to develop, intellectually or practically, alternatives; the need, in desperate situations, to use whatever resources are at hand to gain some results; the naïvety of the Marxist concept of political power, which sees it as something generated solely by the class nature of society and not as an inherent process of social organisation. For our purposes, the most important point is that the consistent pressure of the working class Left in politics – the movement most alienated from the authorities of the state, the culmination and symbol of the existing social order – has been for that state to loom larger and larger within social life, rather than, as originally envisaged, to 'wither away'. In the countries of Western Europe, the reason for this has not been the success of revolutionary captures of the state but the advance of universal suffrage: the state was becoming responsive to a wider electorate than before, and this might be expected to force changes in the interests served by that state.

The existing bourgeois state, responding to an enfranchised and increasingly organised working class, could be pushed into making reforms that changed the unequal distribution of resources, through regulations, public ownership and public spending. This new sense of the opportunities presented by a changing capitalism was grasped by the revisionist wing of the socialist movement in Germany – a movement with objectives far more radical than present day social democracy, but which saw scope for achieving them through the transformation rather than the destruction of existing institutions. In Britain, it was the Webbs and their associates, working from rather different sources, who represented the most fully worked out philosophy of reformist socialism. They built on the existing tradition of British domestic and imperial government: a strong sense of the 'public interest' and of public service, an efficient tax collecting system, an increasingly professional bureaucracy, even some development of public enterprise, particularly in the imperial civil service in India. The Webbs believed that the state could be developed further to counter some of the gross irrationalities produced by the theoretically entirely rational system of the free market economy. Needs which the market system neglected, such as those of working class health and security, could be met through public spending, financed by redistributive taxation; through the state a form of collectivism could limit the disorder and avarice of individualism.

This was how the Webbs' policies joined with the aspirations of the Labour movement, with emphases that remain at the core of Labour politics. But it is also necessary to consider other elements in the Webbian programme. Along with others at that time, the early Fabians were concerned about popular health and welfare for reasons other than the interests of the people concerned; they were committed to a search for national efficiency.[5] The competitiveness of the economy, the need to maintain the Empire and to be prepared for war, were becoming important pre-occupations of a Britain which could no longer take world domination for granted. It was necessary to ensure that all the nation's resources, including the physical welfare of its people, were deployed as efficiently as possible. The role of the Boer War and the First World War in encouraging concern for the physical conditions of the working class is well known, and the Webbs shared fully in that aspect of welfare policy – motives similar to those which had led the highly conservative government of Bismarck to equip Germany with the world's first, if rudimentary, welfare state. In other respects, the extensions of public services advocated by the early Fabians, several Liberals and 'social Toryism' were aimed at providing capitalist industry with infrastructural facilities which could not be produced by the normal market process but which industry itself needed: good roads, a work force with basic education skills, publicly owned utilities.

This last point does not, as some Marxists would have it, automatically discredit this brand of socialism.[6] There is an alternative view of the matter. Capitalism is an inherently divisive and competitive system, incapable of providing some of its own needs. However much it might be in the overall interests of capital for certain unprofitable public services to be developed, the task of provision would have to be carried out by the state, with finance raised from taxation; and individual capitalists would be likely to oppose both the taxation and the extension of state activity involved. The main power house for change therefore had to come from outside capital's own political organisations. This was provided by the Labour movement, which wanted an extension of state spending primarily for purposes of its own.[7] From this a compromise has emerged. In many ways public spending was developed on capitalism's terms, but not entirely so. For example, one may take the argument that industry needs a workforce with certain levels and types of educational skills – from ordinary workers it needs basic literacy and numeracy, from others specialised technical skills, from others again more advanced scientific and intellectual abilities. One may therefore regard those aspects of educational spending which provide for these skills as being at least in part explained by industry's needs. But this leaves much educational activity unexplained. Once a service has been established, a range of other aspirations which do not necessarily have anything to do with industry's needs make themselves felt in policy making. Included among them have been essentially socialist pressures for educational opportunities to be opened to all and not just to those who could afford to pay for them; though probably more important have been pressures from within the educational profession itself.

Thus a socialist concern for public spending has been able to entrench itself in the politics of the society because it coincided with certain interests of capitalism which the latter found great difficulty in realising by itself. At the same time, bourgeois parties adjusting themselves to universal suffrage had to accept social spending themselves. But the ambiguities of this compromise left their mark on the development of public spending policies. The early welfare state plans assumed that there were no difficulties in implementing measures through the existing apparatus of the bourgeois state and its civil service. The measures were essentially *de haut en bas*, the people being the passive and sometimes obligatory recipients of what was considered good for them. This is seen most clearly in those aspects of public spending that simply redistribute resources among the working and lower middle classes, requiring them to consume services which they might not choose in the market.

This kind of paternalism is often attributed to the policy makers' belief that they know better than the people themselves what is good for them. But it is not just that; it is also a question of doing to people what is good for the system as a whole (empire, nation, capitalism, whatever) rather than for the people themselves. A significant legacy of this approach to public spending was the absence of any theory of widespread participation in the control of the new public services, apart from Parliament and various systems of token representation. An aspect of this, emerging clearly in the thinking of the Webbs and becoming firmly entrenched in Labour policy, was the strategy of concentrating the administration of welfare activity in the hands of employees of the state and local authorities, rejecting the system of voluntary action which had been growing up since the later nineteenth century, and which increasingly found its political supporters on the Right. This is a theme to which we shall return.

The basic cast of socialist thinking on public spending had been set by the early decades of this century, but the two major developments which firmly established a high level of public spending on social services as part of our national life took place during the Second World War: the adoption of an ambitious and systematic set of social policies (on health, education and social insurance) and the acceptance by the government of Keynesian economic policies, which provided a means for the financing of public spending and a clear philosophy for the use of public expenditure to maintain full employment. The basic concerns of those policies were those which had been brought to political life by the socialist movement: security for working people and entitlement to certain services as of right, irrespective of capacity to pay in the market. However, the policies also took their place in the overall national consensus, becoming, in T. H. Marshall's important phrase, 'aspects of citizenship'.[8] It is significant that a war time coalition government introduced the policies, and that the two men most closely associated with them, Lord Beveridge and Lord Keynes, were Liberals.[9]

The welfare state and the use of public spending to provide a wide range of non-marketable services probably remain the most important practical contributions made by democratic socialism. Socialist economic policies have had nothing like the same success in becoming indelibly implanted in the practice of government. While subsequent Labour governments have been responsible for an extraordinary number of institutional innovations, there has been nothing to compare with the contribution to social philosophy and practical politics of the actions of the 1945 government in implementing the policies which had emerged from the war period. This remains the high water mark of the impact of socialist thought on public spending and related questions.

But the ambiguities of the earlier period were carried forward in the post-war policies. As well as being designed to provide certain services, public spending was part of overall demand management; and the needs of macro-economic policy rather than the emergent needs of the services or political decisions about their desirability would determine whether spending would rise or fall – though in practice it has never been as simple as that. Also, while constituting a challenge to the earlier form of capitalist economy, Keynesianism in other ways furthered the aims of capitalism. By solving the problems of under-consumption and unemployment, it actually increased the scope of the market economy, bringing idle resources into use and giving to capitalism a stability which it had never known before. It is this ambiguity which helps explain the contradictory attitudes towards full employment and Keynesianism among business interests. They like the stability and expanding markets which it provides but resent both the freedom afforded to their workers by full employment and the constraint imposed on themselves by a large public sector and high levels of taxation.[10] Such ambivalence is part and parcel of the compromise embodied in public spending policies as they have developed.

The Keynesian and Beveridge revolutions did little to alter the basic mould in which British socialism's approach to public spending had been set: services provided for the people by the state and its bureaucracies, and with a continuing remoteness from the people themselves. Indeed, the more remote the services and the less interest which people took in them, the more readily could their development be subsumed under policies of demand management.

By the mid-1950s, the new stability imparted to western capitalism by these measures and by the post-war economic recovery led the reformist wing of the Labour party to align itself more closely to the compromise as such, rather than to remain, as did the party's left wing, unreconciled to an economy which was still primarily capitalist.[11] Anthony Crosland and others in the Gaitskellite movement considered that the capitalist economy no longer needed structural transformation, but that existing weapons of economic regulation could, through taxation and public spending, be devoted more consistently to the over-riding priority of social equality.[12] A further important contribution to this line of thought came from the USA in the form of J. K. Galbraith's book *The Affluent Society*.[13] In his analysis of the contrast between the private affluence and public squalor which developed in a rich society that neglected to provide for those services which the market itself did not generate, Galbraith provided a clear perspective for those who, while accepting the main contours of existing economic and social arrangements, remained sharply critical of several aspects of them from the standpoint of the Webbian tradition, showing concern for the neglect of collective needs in an individualistic society.

Whatever its deficiencies, this was a powerful and coherent philosophy, well tailored to the needs of that particular stage of capitalist development; perhaps too well tailored, in that the end of the age of easy economic growth has robbed it of so many of its initial assumptions. It is difficult to find anything on the party's Left from that time to compare with it. Buried in foreign and defence policy and in sorting out its relations with communism, the Labour Left had virtually nothing to offer on these questions during the 1950s and early 1960s beyond demands for indiscriminate nationalisation.

In so far as the Crosland–Gaitskell faction dominated the party (and essentially it did, whatever the vagaries of particular conference votes), the policy of public spending through the agencies of the existing state now reached its apogee as the distinguishing mark of reformist socialism, because it no longer shared place with the earlier demands for the structural transformation of society. The strategy was clearly distinguished in principle from that of the Conservatives, who did not share the goal of equality, and many of whom continued to believe that it was a major task of politics to reduce public expenditure. But it is easy to see how the policy attracted the taunt of being indistinguishable from Conservatism – the notion of Butskellism. Policy disagreements with Tory governments, if not their idealogues, became matters of more or less social spending, with the debate much dependent on technical judgments of feasibility.

In fact, Tory neglect of the social services – private affluence and public squalor – was a major theme in the 1964 general election. According to the major study of electoral behaviour in Britain, it was the clearest policy divide between the parties, and one on which Labour had a distinct advantage in public opinion.[14] Further, the Labour government elected at that time expanded public sector spending, primarily in the social services and in support for industry; a policy continued by its immediate Conservative and further Labour successors. In the past decade or so, several areas of glaring under-provision have been rectified; new areas of policy have been opened up; and public service staffs have become an important lobby for the further expansion of their numbers and salaries. At the same time, and in the context of international economic crisis, the basic consensus over public spending and Keynesian economic policy has burst asunder. Full employment has gone; so has the constantly expanding economy which Crosland had in 1956 felt able to take for granted as the background to politics, and the association between uncontrolled public spending and inflation has been used by international finance and the Conservatives to launch a wholesale roll-back of public expenditure. To tackle these problems and their relation to developments in socialist thinking, it is necessary to move from this historical overview and consider the range of problems now confronting the public spending commitment.

Contemporary Challenges

First, there is the battery of charges from the Right, asserting the essential profligacy of high levels of public spending. Second is the need for socialists to be prepared to criticise aspects of the commitment to public spending. And finally there is the problem of remoteness and public alienation from public services. The problems are all linked, and can all be interpreted against the pattern of historical development discussed above.

The challenge from the Right
First, the central arguments from the Right. In debates on public spending socialists are used to defending principle against expediency. To take an example familiar from the debates of the early 1960s, the free market produces plenty of fruit machines but leaves schools poorly equipped. By increasing public spending, governments are able to ensure that widely recognised social needs are met, perhaps at the expense of the more effete frills of the private market system. But recently the Right has developed some moral arguments of its own, regarding a high level of public spending as evidence of moral decadence on two grounds: that governments do not subject themselves to the discipline of spending within their means, and that public spending is a form of electoral bribery.[15]

Some years ago the American political scientist Anthony

Downs tried to demonstrate why it was that public services would always be either under-provided or under-financed.[16] While individuals make a distinct contribution to financing public services through taxation, their return in the form of enjoyment of services is indistinct and uncertain. Therefore, while electors may be willing to vote for public services, they will be unwilling to give adequate financial support to them and will prefer to keep more of their money for private consumption, over which they have individual control. The new Right has accentuated part of this argument to claim that public services will always be *over*-provided and under-financed. They claim that politicians will initiate spending projects to 'buy' votes, while governments, unlike private persons, do not have to ensure that their spending is balanced by income. If there is public resistance to higher taxes, then governments can go on spending by the simple expedient of printing more money. This introduces the whole monetarist argument about the causes of inflation.[17] There is of course some truth in this, and it is only the most obtuse among socialists who argue that in no circumstances should public expenditure be contained in relation to national income – though it is relevant to notice that the major historical case cited of a government being unwilling or unable to raise taxation to meet its expenditure is the Johnson administration's deficit financing of the Vietnam War, hardly an instance of socialist public spending!

But the Rightist argument here is not quite as strong as it seems. First, it is assumed that governments can go on indefinitely with deficit spending, even if this is associated with increasing inflation. This is simply not true. A high level of inflation is itself a source of pressure on governments to act, through public concern at rising prices, the threat to investment levels, balance of payments crises and difficulties in raising credit. Why should it be assumed that governments are vulnerable to popular pressures for public spending and low taxes but not to these other pressures – some of them also being democratic forces?

There is a further argument. It will probably be universally conceded that high levels of inflation are undesirable, but it is by no means clear that the evils consequent on a low or moderate level of inflation – setting aside certain unresolved technical debates on how long inflation can be contained at moderate levels – are greater than those of trying to eliminate it from the system altogether.[18] Thus, if Downs was right in his argument about popular unwillingness to support an adequate level of public spending, it may well be that it is only through a certain amount of inflation that public spending can be kept high enough to fulfil important social purposes.[19] Once the issue has been posed this way, it ceases to be an economic one and becomes one of basic values, and the Right is forced back into its ultimate, long standing position of claiming that all private spending is inherently superior to public spending. Against this, socialists argue that many basic services are not marketable and they emphasise the arbitrariness introduced by the ultimately indefensible inequalities of income and wealth distribution which determine our ability to secure goods and services in the market.

As for efficiency, the Right's view that the internal rationality of the market is superior to that of the political process has far more to commend it than socialists are usually prepared to acknowledge.[20] However, there are two points to be set against it. Firstly, the substantive outcome of the free market may well be inefficient if (i) it makes inadequate provision for infrastructural goods and services which are not fully marketable but on which economic activity depends, for example, if it fails to provide an educated work force; or (ii) it leads to arbitrary concentrations of wealth, the owners of which are so rich that they have no incentive to act efficiently. To try to refute such arguments by claiming that the market is the sole guide to efficiency is to reify an indicator and to make an argument true by definition. Secondly, even if the distortions of under-provision and gross inequality which the market produces are efficient, it remains in the last analysis a question of value over which reasonable men can disagree whether one prefers the narrow efficiency of the market or is willing to compromise some of this in order to secure some goals which the market will not achieve at all.

At this point, the Right uses its second 'moral' argument against public spending. Whereas I have here assumed that public spending is directed at certain widely recognised needs, the new Right sees it as a set of bribes: governments spend money in order to win electoral support from specific sections of the population. Closely related to, if more sophisticated than this argument, is the recently popular thesis of the political trade cycle.[21] Politicians, it is argued, increase public spending before an election and reduce it (or raise taxes) afterwards, thereby distorting the rhythm of the true economic trade cycle in an inflationary way. This is not an argument which one can dismiss out of hand. There are plenty of examples of carefully targeted expenditure in the recent political histories of, for example, the USA, France and Italy; it is not too far fetched to regard the EEC Common Agricultural Policy as being, in part, a mechanism whereby the whole of western Europe subsidises the Gaullist party's hold on the loyalty of French farmers – though this has little to do with any electoral trade cycle. What also are we to say of the Conservative party's stance in the October 1974 election when, in the context of a general call for reductions in public spending, the housing spokeswoman, Margaret Thatcher, promised an open ended subsidy to maintain the mortgage interest rate at $9\frac{1}{4}$ per cent? Or the way in which the current Conservative government and local councils are trying to win the votes of council tenants by offering them the right to buy their houses at unrealistically low prices?

I would here venture an argument which might seem to be merely partisan pleading but which I believe can be substantiated: electoral bribery will be more an element in public spending the less comprehensive the general welfare system of the country (or party's policy) and the less it is oriented to the goal of reducing inequality. Conversely, the more socialist and far reaching the system, the less will it be vulnerable to corruption. It is when spending is carried out in an *ad hoc* way, with few guiding principles, as a small item within a system primarily governed by market processes, that politicians have the kind of discretion available deliberately to target their spending on electorally sensitive groups. And 'bribery' will be most manifest when the spending policy departs from egalitarianism and is directed at groups already privileged in market relations – Mrs Thatcher's promised mortgage subsidy being a good example.

A further and distinct aspect of the new attack on public spending concerns its alleged negative consequences for the level of investment. The issues here are primarily economic, and beyond the scope of this paper. The attack, made most prominently by Bacon and Eltis, has been effectively refuted on empirical and other grounds by Moore and Rhodes, and by Bosanquet.[22] However, it still raises important questions about the nature of British Labour's general stance on public spending.

Nearly all Western societies have effected some kind of compromise between the capitalist economy and the thrust of socialism, and part of the compromise consists in the uneven penetration by social reforms of different areas of the society. Important though the process is, it has not yet been subjected to any detailed study, and in our characterisations of the political balance of any particular society we usually make some overall assessment, ignoring differences between sectors. In the United Kingdom the main achievements of socialist reform have been in the scope of the welfare state and (until recently) in the general consensus of full employment. Left virtually untouched by socialism has been the question of investment and indeed, apart from fitful short lived experiments, the whole area of economic planning. Important here has been the dominant role of the City of London, which, being primarily an international institution, has been almost immune from domestic political pressure.[23] One consequence of this lack of integration is that investment has been the casualty of the system, being sacrificed to both public spending needs and to the defence of the currency.

In stopping short at this point, government economic policy has not changed to the extent perceived necessary by Keynes himself as a consequence of the adoption of his demand management techniques. In an admittedly brief and ambiguous passage at the end of the *General Theory*, Keynes spoke of the probable need for a 'comprehensive socialisation of investment' if full employment demand management policies were to be sustained.[24] In the absence of this, British governments have had to manage the economy through the infamous process of 'stop-go', hindering both investment and public spending. Alternatively, there has been 'over-full' employment and an inflationary level of public spending. The Labour movement's power has been concentrated at the point of making effective demands for spending, with little leverage at the level of investment and production decisions.

What Labour governments have in effect done has been to assume that the private sector could operate adequately, generating growth, despite the changed context of a capitalist economy which has to bear the 'burden' of public expenditure. I say 'in effect' because, at the theoretical level, the party's thinkers have always advocated planning to tackle these and other problems. But, central though planning has been to the party, it is remarkable how poorly developed the policy has always been.[25] On the Left, it has been subsumed under a general advocacy of nationalisation, with very little detailed attention being given to how it would operate.[26] The social democrats, given their general belief since the 1950s in the malleability of capitalism for their own ends, have always underestimated the problems of finding adequate and powerful instruments, especially failing to come to terms with the role of the City. For example, in 1964 Labour recognised that the Treasury's policy pre-occupations inhibited planning, but this was seen as a problem of departmental mechanics and was tackled by the establishment of a separate ministry, the Department of Economic Affairs (DEA). But the Treasury was only reflecting the priority of exchange rate stability dictated politically by the crucial position of the financial sector within the economy. The consequence in the postponement of devaluation, the wrecking of planning targets and the dismemberment of the DEA constituted one of the great wasted opportunities of recent economic history.

A Labour movement with power in the area of public spending and a capital with power over investment lead, in times of prosperity, to a reasonably happy compromise, but in times of difficulty to a stalemate of which inflation is the main consequence. As the economic situation has worsened, its unsatisfactory consequences have become more marked.

An indication of how the compromise can turn out differently, and in some ways more constructively, emerges from comparisons of British and Swedish experience. In Sweden, too, investment has been left to private capital, largely beyond the reach of Labour's powerful political forces, and in the past few years this has become an issue of controversy linked with problems of inflation control as in Britain. But in other aspects of economic policy, Swedish Labour has in the past been able to achieve things not possible in Britain.

In 1948 the Swedish unions propounded what has become known as the 'active manpower policy', and by the late 1950s important elements of the programme were adopted by the

Social Democratic government.[27] The policy rested on the identification of different degrees of profitability in different sectors of the economy. The aim was to encourage workers to move from the less productive to the more productive sectors. Fiscal policy would be *more* restrictive than in the initial stages of Swedish Keynesianism, keeping demand high enough to ensure full employment in most of the economy, but not in the least productive sectors. There would, for example, be increased indirect taxation through a sales tax, diminishing the extent to which firms could pass on increased wage costs in price rises. Meanwhile, the unions would pursue a 'solidaristic wage policy', insisting through centralised bargaining on equal increases for equal work regardless of an employer's ability to pay. Through this pincer movement, firms would be forced to become more efficient or to close down. The unions were prepared to propose such a policy which obviously threatened higher unemployment because they were confident that a Social Democratic government would maintain a policy of overall expansion for the economy, constantly creating new job opportunities, while also vastly expanding selective manpower policy, including information, retraining and financial support during the process of transition from old to new jobs. As Marting comments:

> In this way, a process of structural change in industry would be encouraged, increasing the proportion of efficient, low cost activities capable of paying standard rates without putting increased pressure on prices. At the same time, manpower policy would assure that the costs of structural change would be shifted from the workers involved to the society as a whole.[28]

And all within a fiscal policy becoming more restrictive and less inflationary because of the degree and type of government intervention involved and because of the integration between union and government policy that could be expected.

Some of the reasons why Sweden found such policies attractive have to do with the position of the country. In the 1950s it was, unlike Britain, still in the process of industrialisation, a small economy heavily dependent on the price competitiveness of its exports; and with a union movement which did not have its strength rooted in craft identity in declining industries. But there were also political factors. The Swedish government was able to pursue the policy of constant expansion necessary if labour was to have confidence in the active manpower policy, without constant interruptions to secure the value of the currency. This increased direct control over economic variables enabled the Swedish government for a considerable period to pursue full employment with relatively low inflation. Indeed, the Social Democrats believed in running the economy without constant budget deficits, and in some respects they shared the monetarists' view of the need to avoid inflationary money growth. They accepted the need for a policy of overall restraint rather than an easy-money policy, under which the efforts to prevent inflation and inflationary distortions of the market by incomes policy and various controls were likely eventually to fail. They also noted that the stable-money policy would be followed by a certain amount of unemployment if nothing were done about it. They did not use the monetarist expression 'the natural rate of unemployment' to describe this, and preferred fiscal to monetary instruments of regulation, but basically the content of the analysis was the same. However, unlike the monetarists, the Swedish economists, under the leadership of Gösta Rehn, recommended measures to reduce the actual as well as the 'natural' rate of unemployment, to be achieved by means leading as far as possible to allocative results similar to those which would be produced by the market, but better in terms of the level of unemployment consistent with a constant rate of inflation, preferably close to zero. They argued that without an efficient administrative and legal apparatus for that purpose, governments would be tempted or driven by political pressures to apply distortionary measures of an awkward kind.

To draw attention to Swedish experience is not to argue that Britain should or could simply have adopted the same policies; certain specific structural characteristics of Swedish political economy were important to its acceptance. But it illustrates the advantages of having public spending incorporated into a policy of overall economic regulation.

A further question which tended to be ignored by socialists in those years of capitalism's acceptable face in the 1950s was the possibility of companies avoiding those countries which imposed either heavy taxes to finance public spending, or restrictions on industrial activity in pursuit of social goals. For example, France and Japan have both acquired considerable advantages in cost efficiency by irreparably scarring the physical environments of their countries.[29] And as internal protest in those countries grows and the appalling consequences of the destruction become manifest, there can be escape to third world countries less liable to object. Thus many Japanese firms have removed to South Korea. The scope for companies doing this is not infinite; the very public spending which leads to high taxes often provides industry with the infrastructure which it needs, while there may be advantages of natural resources or the location of work force skills which lead a company to remain in a particular country whatever its policies; but the danger is real enough.

The internationalisation of the world economy is among the most significant political facts of our time, and it is experienced doubly by Britain. As the result of loss of Empire and economic decline, Britain is more vulnerable than it once was to international forces, at a time when those forces are becoming generally more powerful. This happens in two ways: through the growth of the multinational corporations, and the rising importance of international monetary organisations. The ability to operate internationally is almost entirely a monopoly of the interests of capital; capital is highly mobile and there is no democratic international polity. The international organisation of various essentially left wing lobbies and pressures is therefore becoming crucial to the interests of socialists within individual nation states. Movements of this kind have begun: there are occasional instances of transnational trade unionism. But the task remains extraordinarily difficult; for some time to come the general internationalisation of economic affairs will work against using public spending as an instrument of socialist policy.

This conclusion is bitterly ironic. As recently as the early decades of the twentieth century, capital was organised on a vehemently nationalistic and imperialist base, and during the First World War it was a wider commitment to an idealistic internationalism which weakened and divided the socialist movements of individual countries. Now the positions are reversed. It is capital which is supranational and labour which is trapped within national boundaries, but again it is labour which is on the weak end of the conflict. Since the nation state is the central instrument for the implementation of socialist public spending policies, socialists are, whatever they might believe, strongly and hopelessly wedded to the cause of the autonomous nation state.

British socialists need to seek international agreements and joint action on policies which involve public spending, to ensure that at least a range of similar competitor economies are subject to a similar scale of public spending demands, for example, by seeking social policy advances at the level of the European Economic Community. An element of caution is necessary: work through remote, bureaucratic international bodies cannot be pursued as an alternative but only as a supplement to attempts at building a genuine international base for the Labour movement and other pressure groups of the Left. The future of socialist public spending in Britain depends on such developments.

It must be stressed that these measures are *not* needed because Britain has an unusually large amount of public spending; in comparison with most competitor nations, this country ranks as little better than mediocre, whether one takes as one's index total public spending, spending on social services, or the share of government revenue in the gross domestic product. An additional question which now demands analysis is why the level of public spending in Britain so often seems to lead to crises of confidence in sterling, when the Scandinavian countries, the Netherlands, Germany, Austria and, to a certain extent, even France are able to maintain larger state revenues and bigger volumes of public spending without the crises which attend Britain at somewhat lower levels. Is it a question of the particular composition of our public spending? Or, perhaps more likely, is it merely because of the unusual role of sterling as a recipient of 'hot' money, which is likely to be moved out of the economy suddenly in response to facts about an economy which international currency advisers dislike? Or is it that the general weakness of the British economy makes it exceptionally vulnerable to anxieties on such an issue, which matter far less in an economy that is strong? It is important that we learn the answers to these questions, since vulnerability to irrational fears about the level of public spending has been an important source of instability in the currency, leading to further economic weakness, and, as a reaction, to public spending cuts.

Defects in the system

Another way of beating off the challenge from the Right is to ensure that the pattern of public services we have deserves wholehearted support. Only too often this is not the case, but socialists often seem unwilling to accept any re-examination of the system we have inherited, being committed to defending any item of public spending apart from armaments, almost regardless of whether in its existing form it continues to serve much useful purpose. In the late 1940s an unusually favourable political conjuncture enabled a whole range of ambitious social services and spending items to be introduced; any surrender now of an item in that programme seems a concession to the enemy, even if the overall system has become ridden with imperfections and vulnerable to attack.

Take the present state of council housing. Envisaged at a time when virtually the only other choice for the great majority of people was to be the tenant of a private landlord, it now has to be evaluated in a society where the majority of families own their own homes. Council housing is not administered primarily in the interests of the people who inhabit it, but on behalf of an entirely depersonalised 'public'; the inhabitants are not that public, but merely tenants. Thus millions of people are unable to paint their front door or call the plumber to repair a cracked lavatory basin because their houses have to be looked after by the authority which is responsible to the metaphysical 'public' for their care. Further, they have to pay a rent which, at the end of the day, leaves them with nothing, while the owner occupier eventually has ownership of his house; and for mortgages undertaken before the 1970s, the level of monthly repayments may well be lower than the monthly rent on a similar council house. Tackling the problem of how to do things otherwise is admittedly not easy; but much of the Labour party acts as though there were no problem at all.

Another question concerns the use of hidden, unquantified and sometimes unacknowledged subsidies which arise through various services being allowed to run at a deficit. If pressure is to be applied to a nationalised industry to keep open an uneconomic plant in the interests of reducing unemployment, then some attempt should be made to assess the cost of that decision, the industry receiving specific grants in compensation. This is preferable to the industry making do as best it can and reporting at the end of the year a variously attributable overall deficit which has to be met by an unexpected subsidy. Some progress has been made on this kind of problem in recent years. For example, while at the Department of the Environment, Anthony Crosland instituted a review of transport subsidies which made it possible to work out precisely who benefited from various deficit operations – in the main rather wealthy long distance commuters.

Politicians often find it convenient for responsibility for a given item of expenditure to be shuffled around and diffused, in the hope that, at the end of the day, it might be lost altogether, Although Conservatives favour explicitness of subsidy in principle, they have done little to honour it in practice – for example, the Heath government used crude blanket price restraint in the nationalised industries, with dire consequences for their investment programmes. It may be argued that by covert subsidies a minister can 'do good by stealth', funding good causes for which he could not get direct support. The attraction of this reasoning is deceptive; the more that a system becomes permeated by actions of this kind, the more of an inchoate jumble public spending becomes; *and* the more remote from the public.

It has always been socialism's claim that it improves on, not that it fudges and botches, the efficiency of the market. This is best achieved by planned, calculable interventions in a market process which is otherwise left to do its work. Economic pricing, whether directly or through analogues, remains an invaluable means of weighing the relative costs of alternative courses of action.

Many of our problems here are the result of the inevitable co-existence of public spending with private markets. Unless we are prepared to seek the abolition of virtually all markets – which would be impracticable as well as undesirable – we need to pay special attention to what happens at the interface between public and private, those aspects of public spending which cover items of expenditure very similar to those which people normally buy in the market. An example of what I mean is the subsidy on school meals. Large numbers of materially comfortable people are able to devote relatively little of their family resources to feeding their own children because they assume that their children's 'main meal' is being provided at highly subsidised prices by the local education authority. Because rises in the price of school meals to parents are political decisions which have a widely publicised effect on the retail price index, there is considerable ministerial reluctance to make them; it is far easier to make cuts in school building programmes, in-service training for teachers or the extension of nursery education, because these attract little public opprobrium, even though their long term effects on the quality of the public education service are far greater.

There remains a good case for education authorities *providing* meals, but why should the price to parents be held so relatively low? Of course, one result of higher and more frequently fluctuating school meal charges would be that more children would be eligible for free, or reduced price, meals because of the low pay of their parents. But the larger the number of people qualifying for a selective subsidy, the less the degree of any stigma attached to it.

The exact size of any saving from a change of this kind needs to be established; it may be that it would not be great enough to make the change worthwhile. I quote it just as an example of a general question: to what extent does the pattern of public expenditure and subsidies which we have inherited resemble the pattern which we should develop if starting afresh to create a welfare state responsive to the main needs of the 1980s? It really is essential that the Labour movement begin an exercise of this kind – *not* with the aim of reducing overall expenditure or of cutting taxes – but in order to ensure that we are using public spending in the most effective ways possible. Otherwise the suspicion that some of the time we are defending the indefensible will weaken us against the Conservative enemy of the public services.

Remoteness and bureaucratisation

Our willingness to re-examine the existing network of subsidies and services may be partly both consequence and cause of a final problem: the continuing and possibly growing remoteness of public services, including even the social services, from ordinary people. This aspect of the way in which public expenditure is organised and dispensed is becoming increasingly important as large numbers of people experience the welfare state as a tax 'burden', and as the bureaucracy needed to administer services becomes more impenetrable. Working people have more control over the money they spend in the private market than over the public spending compulsorily levied on them through taxation and dispensed by bureaucrats and politicians. This is something to which social democratic parties have failed to respond, to the advantage of their opponents. It is only by a verbal conceit that the 'public' arena can be regarded as a genuine communal property in any sense of the term. It was all very well for the early socialist visionaries to regard the democratic welfare state, or an individual local authority, in these terms, but it will not do for our generation. We know too much about the obstacles to mass participation in formal politics, about the techniques whereby politicians and bureaucrats deflect and fob off attempts at finding out what they are up to, about the sheer difficulties experienced even by men of probity and good will in rendering any large scale organisation transparent and open to influence. The response of many local councillors when told that they ought to open up channels for community paticipation is to say, with righteous indignation, that they are themselves the embodiment of that. They have constitutional law on their side, but not social reality.

One can regard the issue as being between bureaucracy and community; but another formulation, which takes the debate back to an earlier period, is that between statutory and voluntary action. Thus, A. H. Halsey, pondering these same problems in his 1977 Reith Lectures,[30] quoted what he called 'a lament' by R. H. S. Crossman, writing in 1973, 'for the eclipse of voluntarism by bureaucratic organisation':

> From the 1920s on, the normal left wing attitude has been opposed to middle class philanthropy, charity and everything else connected with do-gooding. Those of us who became socialists grew up with the conviction that we must in this point ally ourselves with the professionals and the trade unions and discourage voluntary effort particularly since it was bound to reduce the number of jobs available to those in need.

> I am now convinced that the Labour party's opposition to philanthropy and altruism and its determined belief in economic self-interest as the driving dynamic of society has done it grievous harm. For, ironically enough, the party, trade unions and the co-operative

were all a hundred years ago inspired by a profound and passionate altruism – a belief in a new Jerusalem – linked with an urgent sense of duty – a conviction that it was an essential part of socialism to practise what one preached by volunteering to help comrades in distress.[31]

Crossman was of course giving only half the story; the social services dispensed by Victorian charity were at least equally remote from the recipient community as the institutions of the welfare state – distributed at the whim of upper class patrons with a keen desire for receiving gratitude and deference from the recipients, and with a constant tendency to apply their own smug criteria of desert to the supplicants.

Further, complaints that the welfare state removes responsibility from people for their own lives is often a concealed Conservative demand that the less able and less wealthy be left to drift by themselves so that the rich and cunning can monopolise the services of education, health and security which can be extracted from society.

Seen as the choice of a universal, systematic welfare service available to all as a right of citizenship, the ultimate victory of the approach of the Webbs over that of the Charity Organisation Society was almost entirely gain and was a worthy victory for socialism over liberalism and conservatism. However, in the above quotation, Crossman reminds us of earlier Labour movement traditions that were also expunged. Having quoted that passage, Halsey continues:

So the movement which had invented the social forms of modern participatory democracy and practised them in union branch and co-op meeting, thereby laying a Tocquevillian foundation for democracy, was ironically fated to develop through its political party the threat of a bureaucratic state. So much is this so now that when Norman Dennis protests against these emerging tyrannies with the authentic voice of a deeply rooted English socialism, he is heard with approval by Keith Joseph, and dismissed as a nuisance by the Labour establishment. Mr Dennis has written, for example, a completely convincing demolition of British planning practices, from the standpoint of democratic socialism in the English tradition which I have described.[32]

Dennis (a former Labour councillor in Sunderland), in dealing with urban planning in the north east of England, was confronting a political process that we now know from the revelations of the Poulson case to have been riddled with corruption, by no means unrelated to problems of large scale public expenditure by remote and unscrutinised authorities.[33]

In criticisng public bureaucracy and extolling voluntary action, Halsey is not in fact evoking Victorian charity but active participation by the community itself in the running of its services, making democracy more real than is possible through existing statutory authorities, and tapping the well-springs of commitment to community responsibility which exist in British society. Something very similar to this was the vision of the welfare state promulgated by its greatest exponent: Richard Titmuss. For Titmuss, the welfare state did not mean a system of impersonal expenditures by public bureaucracies and employed professionals, but the conscious, altruistic dedication of the members of a society to ensuring that all its citizens enjoyed the basic means to health and happiness. In his last work, *The Gift Relationship*, he contrasted such a vision with the practice of a capitalist market oriented society by contrasting American commercial blood banks with the British voluntary blood transfusion service.[34] But how characteristic of the welfare state is the blood transfusion service? Titmuss did show convincingly how the capitalist element in US medical practice has helped to drive out voluntary effort. This serves as a useful antidote to the more frequently voiced claim that it is the welfare state which has eroded a voluntary commitment that would exist in a society without government social policy. His hope was that institutions like the voluntary blood transfusion service would reinforce the ties of community loyalty that in turn produce further examples of altruism. In this his argument is similar to the more rigorous formulations of Fred Hirsch: a market society depends for social stability on certain bases of trust and on the willingness of people not to pursue their own interests to the extent that the free market model implies.[35] But the tendency of a society organised on increasingly capitalist lines is to drive out such restrained or other-regarding behaviour; it certainly cannot create it. Thus Hirsch described capitalism as living on a 'depleting moral legacy' of codes of restraint and deference inherited from pre-capitalist institutions.

At this point one wants to be able to claim that socialism can create a new, egalitarian base for altruistic, community-regarding behaviour. But to the extent that socialism has meant the establishment of centralised professional administrations, so much of the evidence points the opposite way. Centralised bureaucracy depends on but drives out a depleting moral base just as does capitalism, forcing voluntary participation to the margin and treating it with arrogance and contempt. This is often as true of its approach to elected representatives as it is to voluntary helpers. As a result, community effort declines further and even more tasks have to be undertaken by the public authority. If we want socialism to reproduce the moral base of community life, we have to look beyond the existing mould of social policy administration.

Of course, there is no way in which we can avoid the need for a large state bureaucracy and fiscal machinery for the efficient operation of social services. Neither should we assume that professional employees are incapable of providing a genuine dedication to the purposes of the services which they administer. But all that granted, I am still driven to the conclusion that the welfare state now needs a major shift towards community level bases controlled by volunteers assisted by small teams of locally based professionals wherever this is practicable. Trends in this direction have already started. There is now some kind of public participation, albeit of a grudging kind, in local authority planning processes; adult education services in many areas are being administered by community based voluntary committees; if the Taylor Report had been implemented by the last Labour government, there would have been a major increase in the role of parents in the governance of schools; community health councils are struggling to scrutinise the activities of NHS bureaucracies; there are interesting experiments in tenant management of council estates.[36] And ideas have started to shift within the Labour movement; a former Labour minister, Evan Luard, and a Labour MP, Giles Radice, have made useful contributions to a debate that was in danger of being monopolised by Liberals and non-party activists.[37]

Moves of this kind constitute the best available means for making the notion of a 'public' service something more substantial than a verbal ploy; for realising Titmuss's vision of a welfare society rather than an administrator's welfare state;

and, not least, for finding for public spending the constituency of support which it will desperately need in the current climate of monetarist economic policy, international recession and threatened 'tax revolts'.

The policy has its dangers and problems. First, participatory exercises can be introduced by authorities as meaningless tokens, within which a few self-appointed local worthies serve simply to give increased legitimacy to the bureaucracy. Reformers may be able to ensure basic minimum standards in the structure of the institutions which become established, but for the most part the effectiveness of participation will depend on the energy and vigilance of those concerned, and on the opportunities and constraints presented by the social and economic structure of society at any particular time.[38] As Crosland pointed out, the dangers of new channels of participation being meaningless are reduced if they exist at the genuinely local level, where people have a direct identity with institutions.[39]

A further problem concerns the inequalities which develop if matters are left to voluntary initiative. People from the educated, wealthy, professional and managerial classes have more time, more resources and the appropriate skills to devote to voluntary action in the interests of their communities. They will therefore lobby and work hard to ensure that funds come their way; they will, for example, ensure that their children's schools attract the best teachers and have the best facilities. Against this, control vested tightly in the hands of bureaucracy will ensure an even handed distribution based on formal criteria of need. As Crosland put it: 'There are times when only the despised local councillors and bureaucrats stand guard on behalf of the majority.'[40]

Much, but not all, of this argument has to be conceded. The assertion that existing bureaucratic procedures are egalitarian can be contested. There is now a good deal of evidence to suggest that several public services already embody built in advantages for the better off. For example, much town planning legislation operates to protect the environmental amenity of wealthier areas far more than it does that of the poor. Class differentials in political effectiveness existed long before increasing public participation came on the scene.

Beyond that, the undoubted superior capacity of the better off to take advantage of participatory opportunities has to be counted as a cost of the reforms, to be set against their many merits. And as Richard Titmuss used to remark in a slightly different context, one argument for universal public services is that if the middle classes have to make use of them rather than escape from them into the private sector, they will deploy their energies and resources to improve them, and from that everyone will gain. Also, initiatives developed in enterprising communities may spread to become general practice.

A different problem concerns the relationship between voluntary participation and the professions whose skill is necessary in several services: medical practitioners, social workers, school teachers, planners, housing managers, municipal engineers and so on. Most of the practitioners of these occupations work according to an ethic of devotion to the task in hand, to the achievement of substantive results within their service. They do not present the same problems as the blind forces of the market or the obtuseness of formal bureaucracy. And they do have forms of knowledge which limit the challenge that the layman can make to their authority and their decisions. However, they do tend to wield that knowledge as a mystique to shield them from criticism. Asserted but unargued 'medical' or 'educational' reasons may be an excuse to enable the professional to do what suits him. Penetrating this cover, and doing so in a way which achieves a proper balance between the rights of lay participation and the proper knowledge of the professional, is not easy. This problem is not limited to the area of public spending; it is inherent in any relationship between professional and client. But it is exacerbated by the nature of a public service.

In a private sector relationship the client pays the professional a fee, and if he is dissatisfied with the service given he goes elsewhere. Within the public service it is far more difficult because a government or local authority department is paying the fee or salary, and a transfer will need to be negotiated through its administration. People can sometimes change schools, less easily their general practitioner, never their housing manager.

Conservatives have recently suggested a method of easing the problem of transfer, at least within the school system, with the idea of educational vouchers which parents may use to 'buy' education at a school of their choice. Is this an alternative to participation? Vouchers have certain distinct advantages. Parents are required simply to make a decision about their own child; they make that decision themselves and can act on it immediately; the effect on a poor school of a sudden removal of children can be salutary, and fear of this occurring could be a pressure on teachers to keep up their standards. Against the directness of this form of 'voting with one's feet', participation can be a difficult process, requiring organisation, constant commitment to working for other people's as well as one's own children; and an attempt at improving an existing institution rather than moving from it to a known success.[41]

However, participation, if it can work, is likely to lead to more balanced improvements. The viability of a system for increasing choice depends very much on the choice which a given geographical area can provide; the number of secondary schools within reasonable distance of a great many children's homes is no more than one. Further, participation can do something to remedy the problem of inadequate knowledge already referred to; teachers and parents can work together to discuss educational problems. In contrast, a system of vouchers is likely to lead to panic removals from schools in response to rumours and misunderstandings. (The attempt by the Conservative junior Education Minister, Rhodes Boyson, when an opposition spokesman, to publish crude 'league tables' of schools' examination results suggests that there is no shortage of people willing to foment rumour and misunderstanding in this area.)

A final gain from increased participation in the government of welfare state institutions is the creation of a powerful lobby for the continuous improvement and strengthening of the social services and the maintenance of a high level of public spending. This will be vital in the years ahead. While defects remain in our existing pattern of public services, there can be no doubt that the essence of the socialist commitment to social expenditure, so central to Anthony Crosland's thought, remains valid. It is impossible to envisage an egalitarian politics, concerned with man's collective and unmarketable needs, which will not need to divert resources from the unequal, individualised market process so that they can be put to communal use by popularly responsive public agencies. It is largely in the adequacy of our existing institutions to match up to the challenge of responsiveness that improvement is so badly needed.

I I

Liberty and the Left

by Professor Maurice Peston

One of the more curious characteristics of recent political debate is the claim by the Right that they are the defenders of liberty which is subject to attack from the Left. While they admit that equality is not high on their list of priorities, if it appears there at all, they say that this is offset by the value that they place on freedom of the individual. Indeed, they go so far as to argue that pressure for greater equality, no matter how well motivated, is itself an attack on freedom.

I call this a curiosity because it has not been a uniform characteristic of those on the Right that they immerse themselves in the struggle for freedom. And even those who have written a great deal on the subject have not always seen their responsibility as going farther than that, namely to do something about it. At the same time, the leading figures on the Left have found it possible to fight both for liberty and equality. Far from the two being incompatible, they have seen them as complementary to each other. Anthony Crosland was one such figure and I start with two quotations from *The Future of Socialism*.

> I have listed only the social and economic aspirations. But of course underlying them, and taken for granted, was a passionate belief in liberty and democracy. It would never have occurred to most early socialists that socialism had any meaning except within a political framework of freedom for the individual. But since this political assumption is shared by British Conservatives as well as socialists, no further reference is made to it.[1]

It might ... still be argued ... that inequality represents a negative protection of freedom against certain imminent dangers ... [that] might stem from the inevitable growth of a state bureaucracy impinging heavily on the lives of individual citizens ... This is a serious point, though with only a limited application to the case presented in this book. It is scarcely relevant at all to most of the inequalities which have been discussed ... But it is an argument against carrying equality of wealth to a bitter extreme in which no one can be even temporarily self-sufficient, or have access to private resources on which to maintain himself while declining to conform.[2]

Another remarkable statement on the subject comes from Clement Attlee. He wrote in 1937, in *The Labour Party in Perspective*, as follows:

The aim of socialism is to give greater freedom to the individual. British socialists have never made an idol of the state, demanding the individual should be sacrificed to it ... State action is advocated by socialists not for its own sake, but because it is necessary to prevent the oppression of an individual by others, and to secure that the liberty of the one does not restrict that of others, or conflict with the common good of society. Those who attack socialism on the ground that it would mean the enslavement of the individual belong invariably to the class of people whose possession of property has given them liberty at the expense of the enslavement of others. The possession of property in the capitalist society has given liberty to a fortunate minority who hardly realise how much its absence means enslavement. The majority of the people of this country are under orders of discipline for the whole of their working day. Freedom is left behind when they 'clock in' and only resumed when they go out. Such liberty as they have got as workers has been the fruit of long and bitter struggles by the trade unions. But a far greater restriction on liberty than this is imposed on the vast majority of the people of this country by poverty. There is the narrowing of choice in everything. The poor man cannot choose his domicile. He must be prepared at the shortest notice to abandon all his social activities, to leave the niche which he has made for himself in the structure of society, and to remove himself elsewhere, if economic circumstances demand it. ... The liberty which it is feared socialism may restrict is the liberty of the few ... My conclusion is that men and women will be more free, not less free, under socialism. Freedom will be more widely disseminated. There will be no attempt made to impose rigid uniformity. There will be no forcible suppression of adverse opinion. The real change will be that a man will become a citizen, with the rights of a free man during his hours of labour just as his leisure time. This does not mean that he will have the right to do just as he will. He will have freedom within the necessary restraints which life in a complex society imposes.[3]

There are several comments to be made immediately. Firstly, Tony Crosland is doing more than justice to Conservatives in saying that they shared the assumptions of political democracy. While many Conservatives were in the forefront of the struggle for parliamentary democracy, many more were not. Moreover, subversion of political democracy whether it be revolt in Northern Ireland or the use of the power of an unelected House of Lords was Conservative practice not Labour. Secondly, Tony Crosland used the expression 'taken for granted'. I am bound to say that that was not only characteristic of most of the founding figures of socialism in this country, but is even more a characteristic of the leaders of the Labour party today. The Labour movement's history is so much a criticism and a reaction to the *status quo*, it has depended to such an extent on the exercise of freedom and the fight to establish freedom within the capitalist system, that we have simply taken it for granted that freedom is central to our work. The result is that our opponents have been able to capture the motto of liberty for their banner and have tried to depict Labour as the party of restraint. They have placed us on the defensive when, as I shall show, their own position is an extremely weak one.

Thirdly, there is Clem Attlee's emphasis on the connection between freedom, in the sense of what a person is able to do, and his economic position. Attlee saw this in terms of the way the poor man is restrained and in the way the rich man is at liberty to do what he likes, the two being obviously connected. One man's economic freedom is another man's economic slavery.

Fourthly, attention must be paid to Tony Crosland's 'while declining to conform'. There is no need to doubt the importance of economic freedom; a starving man's chief expression is likely to be 'feed me'. But beyond the bare economic minimum it is surely true that the right and ability to criticise and not conform is more fundamental than any other.

When we are discussing liberty, we mean two sorts of things. On the one hand, we refer to what you can do in the sense of what you can buy, where you can work, where you can live and things of that kind. But we are also talking about something in a different, but frequently related domain, namely what you can say, what you can write and, in the extreme case, what you can think. In addition, we can characterise freedom positively, as we have just done, namely what you can do or say etc. But it can also be characterised negatively in terms of protection against what can be done to you or even said to you. (I hasten to add that I am considering all of these things at the level of common sense, and I am not proposing to get into the philosophical deep water of freedom versus determinism.) In connection with all of these definitions of freedom, I would assert three propositions: (i) most people have more freedom today than at any time in Britain's history; (ii) in the twentieth century this freedom has stemmed more from the activities of the socialist movement in this country than from any other political movement; (iii) it is not the socialist movement in this or in any other advanced society which today threatens freedom. To quote an American philosopher, Sydney Hook:

> There is not a single democratic country where the public sector of the economy has grown substantially over the years, either through socialisation or through governmental controls and subsidies (whether it be England, Sweden, Norway, Holland or the United States) in which the dire predictions concerning the extinction or even the radical restrictions of democratic freedom have been realised.[4]

In all those countries, apart from America, socialist parties have had periods of power, have been defeated electorally, have accepted that defeat, have gone on to fight new elections and been re-elected etc. At no stage have the socialist parties threatened the system of parliamentary democracy, a statement which, as far as Britain is concerned, cannot be said of the Conservative party. One need merely refer to that party's attitude to Ireland throughout most of the last century and this.

I must at this point mention the distinction between socialism and communism. Without getting involved in the most tortuous doctrinal matters, socialism for me is represented by the policies of the Labour party or the Swedish Social Democrats or their equivalent in Norway and Holland. The problem for many of us debating in this field derives from the double confusion between communism and socialism, and worse than that, between Stalinism and communism. I quote two other recent writers on this subject. Professor Arrow (a recent winner of the Nobel Prize for Economics) has said, 'If the Soviet experience were in fact representative of socialism there could be no dispute that democracy is incompatible with socialism.'[5] Professor Glazer has added, 'No state governed by a communist party is democratic. Every state governed by social democratic parties is.'[6]

Thus, I hope it is clear that, in defending the socialist record on liberty, I am in no sense defending Soviet communism. I would be willing to argue somewhat about communism itself and freedom, because it is apparent that much of the lack of freedom in Russia derives from a much longer tradition than Stalin's, going back as it does to the early days of the Tsars. However, despite the oppression of the Tsarist regime, there was much more freedom of speech and writing in Tsarist days than there ever has been since Stalin's rise to power (simply compare Tolstoy's experience with Solzhenitsyn's). If we look more generally at Eastern Europe, the original tradition of liberty was stronger there than in Russia and, in my opinion, is still alive. The power of that freedom has been expressed in the attempts of the Hungarians, Czechs and Poles to devise a superior form of communist society. It is apparent that they were succeeding and, perhaps, that there would have been no insuperable problem for them in transferring their successes into something recognisably free and socialist if it had not been for Soviet military intervention. Surely the Dubček experience shows that there is hope for liberty under communism, but there is no hope for liberty under Stalinism. A prime objective of Stalinism is to supress socialists and socialism.

One last point on international comparisons concerns freedom in non-socialist, that is capitalist, countries. It has been argued that capitalism is the basis for freedom and leads inevitably to it. One can point immediately to two examples to contradict this. First of all, there is the experience of capitalism in South America, in which expression in all forms is rigidly controlled and in which, for the vast majority of people, there is no economic freedom either. The second example is, of course, the South African one, which emphasises freedom for a small minority and a modern form of serfdom for the majority.

More generally on the subject of capitalism, it is important not to confuse capitalism's historical role in promoting freedom with some necessary characteristics of it once it has been established. Marx himself was at pains to emphasise capitalism's function in generating freedom compared with medieval society. It is also true that capitalism went hand in hand with the Renaissance, and the Age of Enlightenment, although some of us would argue that it was the Renaissance which gave rise to the conditions for capitalism rather than the other way round. However, the important thing is that what happened historically is not something which is also logically necessary. This is most easily seen by noting the extent to which capitalism, having been based on freedom, and having one great philosopher of freedom in Adam Smith, went on to restrict freedoms of all kinds. May I also add on the history that, while freedom for a minority is an ancient ideal, freedom as applied to all is a much more modern conception.

Most of the argument of this chapter has been in the Labour tradition of considering actual experience with a view to throwing some light on the connection between the economy and society and freedom. Both the Marxists and the radical Right are correct in saying that we do have a tendency to empiricism and pragmatism and lack a general theory. Against them it may be said that it is better to argue, albeit in a slightly *ad hoc* way, about the real world than to get a great deal of intellectual pleasure from theories which in the end do not account for actual experience. None the less, there are a few remarks in general theoretical terms that need to be made. Their purpose is to show that the analytical difficulties of freedom apply to all socio-economic systems.

To start with, we must pay some attention to the so-called paradox of freedom. In any free system is one free to advocate, and even achieve, its overthrow? Is capitalism or socialism not free if one is prevented from changing it? If one is free to criticise, but not to act, is that freedom an illusion? Since all systems must be able to change and must be flexible, freedom for some people, if not for all, becomes a precondition for survival. However, the exercise of freedom can itself lead to the destruction of the system in its original form. I throw these out as questions but, at the level at which they are asked, we are all aware that they appear to be unanswerable. None the less, they are central to any consideration of social democracy in the future.

Since socialism and capitalism are different economic systems, it can hardly be expected that they will differ only in trivial ways or in ways that have no political significance. The distinguishing characteristics of a fully socialist economy (in the traditional sense) must be public ownership of capital and public enterprise. The system may be decentralised and market oriented; people may have some private possessions; but in the main they will not own productive capital or be free to open private businesses. Similarly, while a fully capitalist system cannot operate without a legal base, implying some kind of public sector, and its firms may be centralised and paternalistic in operation, capital itself must be almost entirely privately owned and privately disposed of. (Incidentally, it is for these reasons that those of us who are advocates of the mixed economy are attacked by both sides, each of which sees us as inevitably contradicting ourselves in the kind of economic system we favour.) At either of the extremes of full socialism or capitalism liberty will be a problem, but not in the same way.

We can immediately note two examples of a general kind. It is a matter of logical consistency that economic freedom to open a private business, accumulate capital, and bequeath it to one's successors, must be severely limited in a purely socialist system. It is also logical that political freedom to restrain private enterprise and the way capital is used must be severely limited in a capitalist system.

Each side then creates its own paradox. The socialist seeks equality partly because it enhances freedom, but he limits freedom in order to achieve equality. The capitalist seeks economic freedom, but this on the part of some may create such inequality as to reduce towards zero the freedom of others. That one may be a conscious process and the other the result of the working of a system is neither here nor there as far as the actual diminution of freedom is concerned.

Consider further the paradox of capitalism. If firms are free to combine and grow, they may so dominate markets as to prevent the entry of new, competing enterprises. If individuals are free to accumulate wealth and leave great inheritances to their offspring, each generation will start unequally, and the rich may increasingly reduce the freedom of action of the poor. In both these cases economic power may be turned into political power to maintain monopoly, and economic inequality. It is difficult to see why this would not lead to significant political restrictions, to counteract which the weak and the poor may also combine economically and politically. The advocates of *laissez faire* capitalism see this danger and propose to legislate against it. Their free system depends on the maintenance of the most stringent restraints on current economic and political behaviour. But how are they to legislate? Where do they get their power from? What group exists powerful enough to prevent competitive capitalism turning into monopoly capitalism and then to exercise its power in that way rather than to achieve monopoly gains for itself?

Consider next the paradox of full socialism. State enterprises do not run themselves. People must be given the power to run them. If they have that power, they will be able to employ it for other purposes. Again, it is not impossible they will use it to suppress criticism, to maintain themselves in position and to influence the appointment of their successors. Once more it may be predicted that economic power will be transformed into political power, and that the latter will be exercised in an illiberal direction. In addition, it cannot be taken for granted that an alternative source of power necessarily exists and will be exercised to preserve freedom. Freedom (and for that matter equality), therefore, is continually in danger in both pure systems, and neither guarantees its preservation. Since each of the pure systems has a tendency to develop towards a perversion of itself, it is possible to conclude that the mixed system, which is what both Clem Attlee and Tony Crosland were discussing, is the correct one. It does not provide the best of all worlds, but it actually succeeds in avoiding the worst. It offers what to some is an intellectually unsatisfactory combination, but this is because it is a system which provides a continuous balancing of economic and political power. The pursuit of equality and the preservation of liberty clash all the time, but neither can overwhelm the other within the mixed economy. The eternal vigilance quotation can be extended to cover both eternal vigilance for freedom and eternal vigilance for equality.

To continue in a rather philosophical vein, there is a necessary connection between freedom and order or restraint. May I quote Adam Ferguson, who wrote his *Principles of Moral and Political Science* in 1792. He said:

> Liberty or freedom is not, as the origin of the name may imply, an exemption from all restraint, but rather the most effectual application of every just restraint to all the members of a free state, whether they be magistrates or subjects. It is under just restraint that every person is safe, and cannot be invaded, either in the freedom of his person, his property, or innocent action ... The establishment of a just and effectual government is of all circumstances in civil society the most essential to freedom; that everyone is justly said to be free in proportion as the government under which he resides is sufficiently powerful to protect him, at the same time that it is sufficiently restrained and limited to prevent the abuse of this power.[7]

Ferguson begs a great many questions (and is not, of course, to be regarded as a philosopher of the Left), but he does draw our attention to the way that freedom is predicated on restraint, and that the restraint must in some sense be just. To take the most important freedom, once physical survival is guaranteed, freedom of speech is predicated on the existence of a language which itself functions according to rules. The corruption of language, something which we observe with horror in our society today, is itself an attack on freedom. A similar point may be made about logic in its general form or in its specific form of mathematics, the corruption of which is also part of the armament of those who fight against freedom.

Debate in any of its forms requires rules of order. It is two sided, as is rational discourse altogether. Expression needs a reader or listener, and symmetrically implies a willingness on the part of the speaker to listen or the writer to read. A desire to persuade or influence surely involves logically a recognition of the possibility of being persuaded or influenced. Threats, shouts, jeering and the like are incompatible with freedom of speech even though in our society people are free to behave in that way. Above all, freedom of speech means that all may speak, but not that all must speak simultaneously.

Freedom of action too presupposes a certain order allowing the same action in its turn to others. Freedom of movement implies a law which permits that movement, and *prevents others from interfering with it*. That approach to freedom which lays emphasis on access to material goods and services has behind it a concept of order which protects each person in his or her due access to these things. A free-for-all actually means only freedom for some. Recognition of the connection between freedom and restraint does not diminish the value of the former, and certainly does not lead to the conclusion that freedom is an illusion. My freedom to drive a motor car is not diminished by the rules of the road (especially the one that makes us all drive on the left). The rules enhance the freedom which is surely quite real. The question of what restraints are necessary for freedom is unavoidable as is whether some conditions for freedom along a given dimension are conditions against freedom along another. I have already referred to freedom of capital accumulation in capitalism and to power accumulation in socialism, both of which may reduce the freedom of most members of society.

Let us take the matter further, concentrating on freedom of thought and expression. Is freedom of that kind endangered by freedom to talk nonsense, to distort argument, to corrupt evidence? Should and can the permissible rules of discourse be narrowed to rule out such behaviour? The Voltairian cry ('I disagree with everything you say but I defend to the death your right to say it') makes sense when applied to rational discourse, but does it also make sense when applied to the irrational? I ask this question every day when I look at our newspapers, and in the case of one or two of them I am uncertain whether I would apply the Voltairian dictum. But in the end, I suppose, the answer here is crudely utilitarian, namely that an attempt to distinguish sense from nonsense and to restrict the latter might be desirable, but it would be impossible to know where to stop. Playing safe, and most wanting to protect true freedom, prevents the initiation of any restraint on expression. There is also a logical point not unrelated to a similar proposition in moral theory. It is that doing right is only admirable if it were possible to do wrong. Sense and nonsense must both be permitted if freedom of expression is to have any meaning at all.

None the less, although none of us would suppress a particular newspaper, much as we might detest it, it ought to be remembered that that great advocate of freedom, Winston Churchill, was quite capable of threatening the *Daily Mirror* and of banning the *Daily Worker*. The case made was that it was wartime and we could not afford to take risks; an excellent example of the paradox that a war for freedom had to be based on the very serious limitation of freedom. All that needs to be added is that, even in times of peace, advocating revolution, sedition or insulting the Royal Family are limited or even totally banned. And most people would accept a concept of national security as overriding an individual's freedom even though simultaneously it is supposed to give rise to conditions for that same freedom. It may also be noted, to add to the paradox, that newspapers themselves are quite capable not only of suppressing points of view they dislike but also of strongly playing down news supportive of such opinions. Their freedom to print everything is in practice a freedom to print only some things.

I must now consider what used to be called 'The Road to Serfdom', but may now be referred to as 'The Path to the Gulag Archipelago'. It is argued that, with certain obvious exceptions to do with the preservation of law and order and national security, government action necessarily limits the freedom of the individual and inevitably leads to further action of the same type. Ultimately the scope for the individual is reduced to zero. He must conform to the demands of the state or end up in a concentration camp. Put as bluntly as this, and especially when examined in terms of specific examples, the argument seems ludicrous. It has been applied to the founding of the National Health Service, to the progressive income tax and to the working of the Price Commission. The more extreme holders of this view actually believe that since (say) 1945 Britain has moved a long way in a totalitarian direction. Others who are aware that freedom of speech, as a right which exists and as a right which is exercised, has never been stronger in this country confine themselves to dire warnings of what may happen.

The easiest response lies in considering the position of the protagonists of this view themselves. Those of us who hold to the eternal vigilance position may be deafened and bored, but we cannot complain of the extent to which Professors Hayek and Friedman and their acolytes fill the newspapers and occupy time on television and radio. It is impossible to resist pointing out the contradiction of how our increasingly enslaved society gives them scope to express their opinions.

There is, however, a more serious proposition to be put forward, namely that, far from social democratic intervention and the mixed economy being the way to Gulag, they are the best, if not the only, means of avoiding that destination. The mixture despite its imperfections and seeming contradictions does preserve freedom by using state action to meet social demands, notably those for the avoidance of poverty and extreme inequality.

Consider a decentralised capitalist system which is also a parliamentary democracy. This system will be subject to both random shocks and systematic change. Theoretical analysis suggests that it will spend a great deal of time out of equilibrium. There will also be a tendency for the following to emerge: (1) inequality of income; (2) inequality of wealth; (3) monopoly supply of goods; and (4) non-optimal supply of goods for which there are significant externalities.

In order to function at all this system will have a government which provides law and order and national security which in turn means that it will have a taxation process and a bureaucracy. Law and order must be taken in a broad sense to include enforcement of contract, redress for fraud and control over the monetary system. Equally, assuming we wish to be realistic, national security will involve public sector operations and expenditure on a large scale.

In these circumstances, it will be predicted that monopoly and externality will be on the agenda for political debate. The former undermines the very logic of the decentralised system and the latter, being a form of market failure, will at least be an embarrassment. In addition, those who suffer adversely from change in the system will also be tempted to place additional political activity of a countervailing and self-protective nature on the agenda for public discussion and action.

For example, three sorts of people will press for policies to reduce unemployment or mitigate its effects. One group will be those who experience or regard themselves as in danger of experiencing unemployment. A second group will be people whose social consciences cause them to suffer from the existence of unemployment. A third group will be those who suffer directly from the unemployment because of such anti-social behaviour as increased crime. The three groups together may comprise a sufficiently large fraction of the electorate to outvote the groups who wish to do nothing. These groups will consist of (i) those who would lose from unemployment policy, (ii) those who are convinced that unemployment policy cannot work and may actually intensify the problem, and (iii) those who are worried about the constitutional implications of an extension of state activity. It cannot be predicted *a priori* which side of the argument will be in a majority, but there is no reason to believe that this will never be the interventionists.

Suppose, however, that the anti-interventionists retain a permanent majority, but that the problem itself persists. Can it be assumed that there will be no political consequences? Will it not be more likely that those who suffer will use extra-political means either to achieve their ends or to damage those whom they will come increasingly to regard as their enemies? Again this does not mean that the disaffected minority will win, but it may imply that the law and order powers and activities of the state will be extended. In addition, if there is an agnostic group in society who initially abstained from voting, they may come to vote for intervention *faute de mieux* to preserve the political system and avoid the worst consequences of civil disorder.

More generally, questions concerning the working of any economic system are unavoidable. If the society is a free one, debate on its current performance will take place. To argue that certain matters were settled long ago and may not be re-opened will seem biased against those who were born relatively handicapped, so to speak, but will also seem to be a contradiction of freedom. There is a world of difference between exercising caution because we cannot predict accurately the full effects of our actions, and doing nothing at all. In particular, why should those who lose relatively or absolutely from the existing economic and political arrangements be the altruists who refrain from the exercise of political power on their own behalf?

My conclusion is that the decentralised capitalism so beloved of the radical Right is unstable in conditions of parliamentary democracy (and may be incompatible with any political system) but that if we are sensible we can convert it into the mixed economy. Within that system there will be continuous debate about the dividing line between public and private sectors, public and private expenditure. In addition, the limits to freedom and to equality will be subject to unrestricted scrutiny, never being finally justified. It will be impossible to guarantee perfect freedom or total equality, but those are at best mirages which may be pursued but never reached. Indeed, each is a totalitarian aim, just as is perfect truth.

To conclude by being a little more political, it is not surprising that in our own country many of those (notably in the Tory party) who preach the rhetoric of freedom of expression are foremost in their desire to suppress certain types of expression. Their passion for freedom accompanies an equal passion for suppression of others. Simultaneously, others of us may be more relaxed in our pleas for freedom, but devote little time to suppressing freedom either. The extreme Right in British politics undoubtedly preach freedom of expression of their own views, but how often do they stand up for the rights of others? When, for example, have they ever criticised those newspapers which support them as a matter of policy, but do not publish anything, unless they cannot possibly help themselves, which represents an alternative view? After all, immediately the Tories became the government, having been elected in 1979 on a platform of freedom, they became obsessed with secrecy, manipulation of the news and exerting pressures to play down views different from their own. It is not at all obvious from their first year in office that they would defend to the death anybody's right to criticise their economic policies, for example. Instead, they are much concerned with 'the irresponsibility of some trades union officials', 'not rocking the boat', etc.

Thus, a question that cannot be avoided concerns the *bona fides* of those who today preach liberty from a Right wing standpoint. Are they genuine libertarians or are they simply concealing their desire for high incomes and high inheritance behind a plea for freedom? In answering this question do not fail to note, which has been central to my argument, that now that the system does not function solely in their direction these very same people denigrate parliamentary democracy. When democracy operated so that workers were free to starve, it was a political system the Conservatives boasted about. Today, when the Labour party wins elections and, to a moderate degree, restrains the behaviour of some firms and individuals, we are told that there is something wrong with our political system.

In this connection the extremism of the radical Right is not in doubt – given the choice between capitalism and parliamentary democracy they will choose the former. If asked what is the permissible range of free political choice, they will answer, only those actions that preserve free market capitalism. It is for this reason that I suggest that freedom for them is a secondary consideration, while for us it remains so dominant that we take it for granted.

12

Democratic Socialism and Education

by Tyrrell Burgess

The school system in Britain remains the most divisive, unjust, and wasteful of all the aspects of social inequality.[1]
Anthony Crosland

Education has always been the Labour party's big disappointment. No Labour government has ever created a major Education Act. The party's most distinctive policy, comprehensive secondary education, has been a commitment for more than twenty years: it has still not been achieved, though for more than half that time there have been Labour governments. Nor has education itself lived up to the hopes of early socialists, by ending class differences or even assisting social mobility. Even in advanced societies, like Britain, the resilient evils of ignorance, incompetence and dependence remain. Most people now spend at least eleven years in compulsory education yet they emerge limited, unskilful and gullible.

The disquiet is not confined to radicals. For most people education is a permanent disappointment. It offers the hope of improvement to both individuals and society. It is sought as a remedy for personal and social ills. Yet its performance always seems to fall short. Individuals and society are alike disillusioned. It comes to be regarded with a mixture of hope, affection and frustration. As a consequence, public respect for education is characterised by booms and slumps. In boom times education is seen as a foundation of social and economic life and of its development in order and prosperity. Central and local government are encouraged to increase educational spending. Electoral promises can be summed up in one word – more. Public inquiries on the salaries of teachers unanimously recommend large increases. Almost at once a reaction sets in and people begin to wonder whether we are not spending too much or whether we are getting value for money. People complain that education is making little direct contribution to the problems of, say, unemployment or urban crime. Individual students and pupils are heard to doubt whether the outcome of their education offers enough compensation for the boredom of the process.

At present education seems to be in a minor slump. It is under fire from all sides and is on the whole defending itself rather badly. The criticism comes from pupils, students and their parents, from teachers and employers, from friends and enemies of education alike. It is possible here to indicate only the range and nature of this criticism. Let us start with pupils at school. There have been a number of serious studies of what pupils think and want, from the Schools Council inquiry eleven years ago, to John Raven's massive research published in 1977.[2] These reveal that pupils have clear and coherent views about what school is for and that they find that the schools themselves have other objects. In particular, pupils wanted an education which enabled them to deal with their personal problems, to get and hold a job, to apply their knowledge and to be the confident masters rather than the slaves of circumstance. Generally speaking, parents agreed with their children in this. There have been similar surveys of the attitudes of students. They too demand 'relevance'. They complain that their courses tend towards the mere accumulation of knowledge, are overcrowded with detail and give little time to think. Many see their educational experience as 'tricks and dodges' and their courses as consisting of anything that could attract a twenty minute question in the final examination. They may find that having knowledge does not at all enable them to apply it: even when theory and practice are integrated students may not be able either to apply the theory or to describe and defend their practice. Many come to fear that their courses are directed to no vocational end, and even those on a supposedly vocational course may see its relevance as spurious because they seem to get no nearer to the practice of their specialism. Other students complain of narrowness and stultification. They complain that final examinations frequently demand little more than memory, or hanker for more command over their educational experience.

Many of these criticisms are echoed by teachers. Those in secondary schools, in particular, see themselves as victims of external circumstance. They complain of the tyranny of society which requires them to be not so much educators as selectors, serving the division of labour, and of an examination system which is the expression of this tyranny. As John Raven found, teachers are conscious that they do not concentrate on the objectives they consider to be most important, and he rightly says that the consequences of this are insidiously demoralising.[3]

It is often claimed that the perversion of education by selection is supported by employers, who express their demand in terms of certificates, diplomas and degrees. This is true but it conceals the criticism which employers have of the system which offers these certificates. What employers typically say is that they take the possession of a certificate or a degree as a very general indication of a level of capacity and application. They do not see it as indicating the acquisition of any information or skill that can be used productively. They all assert that it is they who have to educate and train the young person who comes to them, whether he has CSE or a degree. Many go further and claim that the more education a young person has received the less fitted he is for the problems that he has to face as an employee. On this view an employer takes a graduate rather than a non-graduate only because he imagines that the qualification is an indication of capacity: he sees it also as a warning that much will have to be done to eliminate the incompetence systematically induced by the process of graduation.

These criticisms, by pupils, students and their parents, by teachers and employers, are not new. They reflect a long-standing belief that there is a serious imbalance in British education and training. The idea of the 'educated man' is that of a scholarly, leisured individual who has not been educated to exercise useful skills. Those who study in secondary schools or higher education increasingly specialise; and normally in a way which means that they can then practise only the skills of scholarship, to research but not to act. Their knowledge of a particular area of study does not include ways of thinking and working which are apt outside the education system itself. This is damaging both for individuals and for society. Education concentrates on analysis, criticism and the acquisition of knowledge: it neglects the formulation and solution of problems; doing, making and organising; and constructive and creative activity in general. It thus inhibits the satisfaction derived from personal capability and denies to society the benefits of competence.

To these specific criticisms are added more general ones. There are those who regard education as having developed to the point of being an expensive luxury. There are others who seek a solution in accepting it as a selective process and wish to concentrate on making the selection more 'efficient'. There are many, on all sides, who are concerned about the quality of education and ways in which this can be measured. Many reformers are bewildered by the realisation that the expansion of education has not itself led to a more rational, egalitarian or viable society. At the extremes there are those who believe that education can be saved only by removing it altogether from its institutional framework: they would 'de-school' education and society.

For social democrats the failure of education is especially critical. It is no coincidence that the greatest political philosophers, from Plato onwards, have also been philosophers of education. They have all recognised the intimate connection between the organisation of a state and the development of its citizens. If social democrats get education wrong, they are unlikely to make a general success of social democracy. It is this which makes people in the Labour party so uneasy when they contemplate the party's record in education. They instinctively realise that failure here is symptomatic of a general weakness in theory and practice. In other words, the challenge for social democrats in education is to create a system which not only meets the criticisms detailed earlier but stands as an example for the management of a public service in a democratic society. Fortunately the basis for such a system exists in Britain, and its development can be rooted in the theories and practice of social democracy.

Let us remind ourselves, firstly, what those traditions are. First among them is respect for the individual. The revolt against capitalism grew in part from the conviction that it was inefficient and wasteful, in part from the Marxist belief that it represented an outmoded stage of social evolution, but in England at any rate it derived overwhelmingly from a conviction that capitalism crushed and corrupted individuals, limiting their potential and stunting their growth. A second tradition is that of co-operation, the desire for harmony and cordiality in the management of human affairs. The tradition recognises that co-operation must be willing: if it is coerced it becomes merely the tyranny of the collective. Belief in individuals co-operating to create a society in which they can all live and develop leads to a firm commitment to democracy – not just as a means of changing governments peacefully, or of holding them to account (important though this is), but as a style of life and of social behaviour which is admirable and educative in itself.

The commitment to democracy has a profound influence on attitudes to the state. The social democratic tradition has always regarded institutions as existing for men, not men for institutions. Thus, even where it has extended the activities of the state it has continued to see the state not as a master, but as what R. H. Tawney brilliantly called 'a serviceable drudge'.[4]

Let us now turn to what these traditions mean in the provision of a public service like education. Education is a personal service. It succeeds with individuals, not with systems. In creating the service, therefore, we must start with the individual child and his parents: if things are not right for him, they will not be right at all. This means emphasising the responsibility of individuals and enabling them to act on this responsibility. The next point of concern is that at which the individual meets the service that is offered. In education this is the relationship between the individual child and his teacher or teachers. It is this relationship that ensures that education takes place. Decisions about it should be taken on the spot, by people competent to take them. They cannot even in principle be taken by those who are remote from the individuals concerned and certainly not at some national level.

Of course decisions about an individual child have to be taken in the context of the need to take decisions about a lot of other individual children. Teachers in schools have therefore to organise things to accommodate incompatible and perhaps conflicting needs. There will be many constraints, over time and resources, which have to be taken into account. These decisions may be hard, but they cannot be short circuited by directives and guidelines from those who do not know the circumstances.

Teachers and children come together in schools, so the next question is how those schools are to be provided. What is needed here is a democratically elected providing authority, so that the schools in an area can broadly reflect what the people of the area, both parents and others, think desirable. The kinds of school available and the range of choice, in other words the *system* of education, is not something that can reasonably emerge from the behaviour of individual schools: it must be settled by a providing authority. Otherwise, people who have general objections to what is done cannot make their objections felt. It is preferable if the providing authority itself raises the money to pay for its provision. In that way the people of an area can decide what it is they are prepared to pay for. They can trade off higher taxes against a better service. A providing authority with its own electoral and financial legitimacy is a critical feature of democratic government.

Finally, a public service, like education, must in some sense be a national service. There must be a minister responsible to Parliament for the broad direction of the service, the overall level of resources going to it, and the assurance that standards of provision are broadly similar. There must be, in education, information nationally about the outcomes of the service and provision for the resolution of disputes within it.

It is important to note the consequences of a system of this kind. In the first place it makes possible the growth of dignity and responsibility in the individual. Pupils, parents and teachers can all be offered personal initiative. Secondly, decisions about the curriculum are removed from a central Department of State and placed where they properly and rationally belong. Thirdly, the provision of schools and other institutions and the creation of the system as a whole can clearly be seen as a *service* to pupils and their parents. Fourthly, the separation of provision and overall regulation ensures that the system can be locally responsive and avoids an undesirable concentration of power which would arise if the providing and regulating authorities were the same. Such a system would be an apt basis for education in a social democracy.

Astonishingly, it exists in England today. Under the Education Act of 1944 the duty to see that children are educated rests upon parents, and the providing authorities must have regard to the principle that education should be in accordance with parents' wishes. Schools are provided by democratically elected local education authorities. These authorities are responsible for the 'secular instruction' given in schools, but may and do delegate this responsibility to governing bodies of individual schools. Head teachers are responsible for the organisation, management and discipline of their schools, and there is a long-standing tradition of independent responsiblity for individual teachers. The Secretary of State for Education and Science regulates, inspects and arbitrates. The system exists, and has done for nearly forty years. Why, then, is education still a disappointment? The brief answer is that although the system has been in place, its potential has never been widely understood, it has in parts been neglected, and in parts systematically undermined.

Misunderstanding has in fact grown with the years. For nearly three decades after 1944, for example, it was accepted that the provision of schools was a matter for local education authorities, and questions about this in Parliament were so answered. In recent years Members of Parliament have grown dissatisfied with this, and parliamentary pressure on ministers to intervene has grown. At the same time, other Departments of State have taken to sneering at the Department of Education and Science for not being able to 'deliver'. Secretaries of State have been under this uncomprehending pressure from Cabinet colleagues, and officials have faced similar pressure in inter-departmental meetings. It has grown with the fashion for using public expenditure as a method of economic control. This has powerfully reinforced the centralising tendencies of the Department of the Environment, particularly through control of local government finance. Education, with its different traditions and organisation, remains an anomaly, and one which takes the bulk of local government spending. The defence of these traditions by ministers and civil servants has become more half hearted in recent years. This is a tragedy, because education is the most rationally organised of all the public services. Not only does it follow closely the principles enunciated earlier. Equally important, the distribution of powers and duties within it gives to the Secretary of State just those functions which he, assisted by a small Department, can reasonably perform. Because the job is manageable he can reasonably be held accountable for it to parliament. At present, the Education Secretary is the only major Departmental minister who can reasonably be held accountable at all. All the others have jobs that are so vast and are supported by such huge bureaucracies that they cannot reasonably be expected to be accountable for any of it. The habit of ministerial resignation when things go wrong has entirely died out because nobody believes that the minister is in any real sense responsible.

It is important for democratic socialists to realise this. When making proposals for education or any other service they should ask where responsibility is best placed and if possible avoid creating new powers and duties at the centre. One often hears Labour MPs and members of the National Executive Committee urging new powers for a future Labour Secretary of State – within minutes of complaining that when there is a Labour government ministers quickly get into the hands of officials and are sluggish at carrying out Labour policies. They do not seem to recognise that more powers for a Labour Secretary of State mean more powers for a Conservative Secretary of State and that more power for any Secretary of State gives more power to the central bureaucracy. Social democracy is not to be established by those means.

Paradoxically, and alongside these centralising tendencies, there is one rational function of the Secretary of State that has been neglected. This is the requirement that local authorities prepare plans for the development of both schools and further education in their areas and submit them to the Secretary of State. By a curious quirk, the power to require these plans, in the 1944 Act, was limited to a single occasion for schools but is a permanent power for further education. It is not too much to say that the patchy growth of further education and the continuing neglect of part time education for those who have left school derive less from the failure of successive ministers to activate the provision for 'county colleges' than from the neglect of the plain duty in law to require local authorities individually to plan for provision. Worse, so far as advanced further education is concerned, the provision has been perverted. Never, since 1944, have local authorities been required to take seriously their duty to provide, for their own areas, a varied and comprehensive service. Instead the provision of advanced further education has been a matter for central direction and control. The consequence is that provision for such education is extraordinarily patchy, with some cities having several institutions and large parts of the country having none. To reinforce this maldistribution, there has grown up a complex and elaborate system of funding which is universally agreed to be unsatisfactory. At present reform is imminent – not in the direction of proper local responsibility, but of even more central control. It is a familiar story: the central bureaucracy neglects its proper powers and duties, takes more powers and misuses them, uses its own incompetence to insist on more powers still.

The legislative quirk that required school plans to be produced only after 1944 has proved equally damaging. The experience with the early plans was not happy. No sooner had they been produced than the explosion of the birth rate and the growth of new house building (both of which, astonishingly, seem to have been unexpected) meant that the plans were quickly outdated. Unfortunately, instead of taking the opportunity to develop a dynamic system of planning, ministers and their officials threw up their hands in despair. Planning became synonymous with the annual approval of building programmes. This meant that authorities were not required, as a regular activity, to maintain a process of thinking or consulting about their provision. The disadvantage of this neglect became clear. When Labour introduced its plans for abolishing selection at eleven, in 1965, the then Secretary of State, Tony Crosland, acted wholly within the spirit of educational legislation. He sent out a circular asking local authorities to prepare proposals and submit them to him. Unfortunately the exercise was a novel one, and even in those authorities that wished to collaborate it took much longer than it would otherwise have done. Unsympathetic authorities were given happy opportunities for delay. Even so, the method proved fruitful. The schemes produced were rooted in local circumstances. A wide variety of systems was established, giving valuable experience of different forms of organisation which are proving invaluable today as local authorities face falling school populations. Local initiative created local support. Conservative authorities became committed to their schemes of reorganisation. It is a matter for the greatest regret that, as reorganisation went on, and with a substantial majority in parliament, Crosland's Labour successors did not secure two small legislative changes. The first was to introduce a permanent requirement that local authorities should from time to time submit their school plans to the Secretary of State. The second was to make it unlawful to introduce procedures for selection for different kinds of schools during the years of compulsory education.

This latter requirement is precisely the kind of general decision that it is reasonable for a Secretary of State to take nationally. Just as in 1944 it was decided nationally that education should be in three successive stages: primary, secondary and further; so it is also reasonable for as basic a decision as whether or not to have selection for different kinds of school to be taken nationally. What is not necessary is for there to be central decisions about the kinds of school which are created to accommodate all the children. Nor is it necessary to have arguments of a general theological kind about what 'really' constitutes a comprehensive school. It is enough to be rid of the evil of selection at eleven. It is only with experience that we shall know what if any unintended consequences of this reform turn out to require other action.

The end of selection at eleven holds important lessons too for the curriculum. While it lasted it was a powerful perversion of the principle that the curriculum is a matter for individual schools. While preparation for the 'eleven plus' was common, children and their teachers in primary schools were dominated by external requirements whose purposes were remote from their own. Tests of intelligence, devised to help in the diagnosis of individual children and their learning difficulties, were perverted into an administrative device for allocating groups of children to particular schools. The demands of the tests meant that the children were being used to solve the problems of administrators, and education was prevented from solving the problems of children. Behind all the arguments against selection at eleven, whether they were social, psychological, personal or political, lay the conviction that in a social democracy the curriculum is not something to be decided without reference to individual children.

Precisely the same argument applies to the examinations taken at the end of compulsory schooling at sixteen plus. Here the damage is far worse. Even at its most oppressive the old eleven plus influenced only a part of the curriculum of primary schools. The examinations at sixteen plus dominate both the curriculum and the organisation of secondary schools to the point where the responsibility of schools has become a myth. What is more, the dominance is not that of a local authority or even of a Secretary of State, either of which could in principle be held accountable to an electorate, but of examining boards who are effectively accountable to no one. There are many respects in which the examinations are objectionable. In the first place they do not accommodate all sixteen year olds. The evil consequences of this may have been disguised when the examinations were attempted only in selective schools to which perhaps a quarter of the children went and when most children left a year before the examinations took place. Today the promise in the 1944 Act of secondary education for all is redeemed firstly by compulsory schooling to sixteen, and secondly, by the abolition of selection at eleven for different kinds of school. These two developments have heightened the anomaly of a system of school leaving examinations which accommodates many fewer than all school leavers.

Unfortunately, the available statistics are presented in such a way as to make it hard to see what is actually happening. In the academic year 1975–76, 557,000 young people left school who were aged either fifteen or sixteen on 1 January 1976. These 'young leavers' represented some three quarters of the age group. Of these leavers 109,000, or nearly a fifth, left without attempting either CSE or GCE, and these figures exclude pupils in special schools. Those who took GCE or CSE and were ungraded bring the total leaving without qualification to 132,000, or nearly one quarter.

The statistics also show those who left without 'higher grades' in CSE (Certificate of Secondary Education) or GCE (General Certificate of Education). The higher grades at GCE 'O' level are A, B and C – which are the standard of the former 'O' level pass. (In the words of the explanatory notes to the statistics, 'Grade D indicates a lower level of attainment and grade E is the lowest level of attainment judged to be of sufficient standard to be recorded'.) The higher grade in CSE is grade 1, which is equivalent to a higher grade 'O' level. In 1975–76, 226,000 young leavers left with GCE or CSE grades other than higher grades: none of these can be held to have 'passed 'at GCE 'O' level.

It means that the present system denies the public recognition of a 'pass' or higher grade to a total of 358,000 or well over three fifths of all young leavers. A further 164,000 gained only four or fewer higher grades – showing that they had performed creditably (they had 'passed') in this limited range of the total curriculum. Only 46,000 received a certificate which implied substantial performance in half or more of the range of subjects taken during their compulsory schooling – one in twelve of all young leavers. Clearly the present elaborate and costly system of external examinations is not designed to inform young leavers, their parents, employers or other educational establishments about the competence of young leavers or even about the range of experience which they have had.

There are those who accept this state of affairs on the ground that it is important to maintain 'standards' and that this is done by the achievement of the minority. (It is a version of what R. H. Tawney called the tadpole philosophy: that is, the unhappy lot of tadpoles is held to be acceptable because some tadpoles do in the event become frogs.)

Unfortunately the statistics conceal the examination performance at sixteen plus of those who could have left but did in fact stay on. It is these 'older leavers' (perhaps a quarter of the age group) who are usually thought to be the main beneficiaries of the system. About half of them, or a little more, generally qualify themselves for entry to higher education. Existing examinations act as a selection device and do little positively for those who take them and 'pass'. They do not in themselves ensure high standards and they seriously underestimate the capacities even of those who are successful in them. They do this for two reasons. The first is that they test mostly the lowest category of performance, that of 'isolated recall' or plain memorising. They test less well the higher levels of performance like the understanding of concepts or principles, the ability to generalise or synthesise, or unfamiliar application. They do not test for example the kinds of qualities, skills and attributes listed in the recent Green Paper as the aims of education: inquiring minds, respect for people, world understanding, use of language, appreciation of economic controls, mathematical and other skills, and knowledge of cultural achievements. The examinations exclude most human aptitudes and abilities, particularly those which are of most importance in managing a successful life, like persistence, courage, generosity, co-operation, human understanding.

The second reason why existing examinations underestimate

the worthy is that they are tautologous. A syllabus is set and examined: success in the examination is held to indicate success in the syllabus. But there is nothing here to tell us what effect on the individual has been achieved by covering the syllabus and passing the examination. In short, what existing examinations say about intelligent and creative people is on the whole trivial and demeaning.

Nor are they much more use in helping employers to appoint young people to particular posts. Many employers assert that the courses have positively unfitted them. Educators may rightly retort that employers themselves are lax about stating clearly what qualities and competencies they in fact require – beyond an often limited statement of some technical skill – and that there is more to life than the jobs which many employers offer. But this does not absolve educators from their responsibility to find better ways than existing examinations of recording and measuring the outcome of education.

Existing examinations also have unintended consequences within the schools. Generally speaking, teachers in England and Wales claim to be in charge of what they do. There is a tradition of independence within the classroom. The authorities do not prescribe syllabuses (except for the agreed syllabuses of religious education). Still less is there any central government regulation of curricula, syllabuses or timetables. But the claims of academic freedom advanced by British teachers are held in some scorn by European educators, who are in no doubt that the British system of public examinations exercises the most powerful of external controls. It is true that schools may choose between different examining boards, so the schools at least have the freedom to choose which constraint to adopt. It is also true that one of the public examinations – the Certificate of Secondary Education (CSE) – is controlled by teachers. But representation on central or regional examining bodies does not mitigate the constraint on individual schools which the examinations of these bodies impose. The system of public examinations largely controls the curricula as well as the internal organisation, management and discipline of secondary schools. They influence in detail the deployment of staff and their organisation in subject departments. In addition they powerfully affect the understanding of pupils of the nature of education and their confidence in themselves and its outcome.

Examinations are also used for purposes for which they are not at all apt, in particular for judging the general performance of individual teachers or schools, or the educational system as a whole, over time. The annual statistics of the Department of Education and Science are constantly being mined for evidence in the debate about standards, often with a good deal of sophisticated statistical tomfoolery. But the figures of entries and passes can yield evidence only of entries and passes, not of quality or achievement either in individual pupils or in schools. What we need to know about education is the difference which a particular course or programme has made to those who have followed it. A 'good' school is one which does well by the particular children who enter it. A successful student is one who has gone far from the point at which he started. An 'O' level grade B can be obtained for quite different performances: by the facile layabout who swots it up the night before and by the earnest plodder who transcribes notes for two years. Attempts to make general judgments about performance on the basis of such crude statements as 'grade B' are quite simply nonsensical. The temptation to do so, however, is natural with a system of national public examinations.

It is also important to remember that examinations are not cheap. They consume expensive human and material resources which would be better employed in education itself. It is impossible to discover the true cost of public examinations because much of it is represented by the time taken by teachers and students in invigilating and taking the examinations themselves, together with the preparation and organisation that the examinations require. It is not too much to say, however, that the whole of the last term of compulsory schooling is lost to education in order that public examinations may be conducted. This is too large a proportion of an adolescent's life. The direct cost is also formidable. In 1977–78, the local education authorities paid £13.5 million in entrance fees for candidates in GCE 'O' level and CSE. In the recent financial stringency, local authorities have cut back on teaching staff, on the maintenance of buildings, on books and equipment – that is, on everything that might directly educate young people – while the cost of taking examinations mounts year by year (even if the rate of increase is below that of the retail price index).

Perhaps the most fundamental criticism of examinations is not so much that they are exclusive, trivial, uninformative, expensive and misused, but that they are anti-educational. They effectively preclude any sharing by the young people themselves in responsibility for their own education and for recording its outcome. Yet some such activity is essential if learning is to take place. The one thing which all the diverse and sometimes incompatible theories of learning have in common is an insistence that learning takes place through the activity of the learner. Our system of public examinations removes initiative and activity not only from the learner but also (except in CSE Mode III) from those who are most directly responsible for his learning, that is the teachers in his own school.

A suggestive experiment by Held and Heim vividly illustrates this.[5] Two litter-mate kittens spent several hours a day in a contraption which enabled one kitten fairly normal freedom to explore its environment actively. The other was suspended passively in a 'gondola' which was moved in all directions by the movements of the exploring kitten. The gondola kitten was thus subjected to the same visual experience as the activity kitten but initiated none of the activity. When not in the contraption both kittens were kept with their mother in darkness. Tested after some weeks, the active kitten showed that it had learned to use its visual experiences for getting about (for example, by choosing the safer of two drops from a shelf) while the gondola kitten had not. Television to some extent makes gondola kittens of us all. Public examinations make gondola kittens of adolescents. The time is ripe for their abolition.

This can only be done if we take seriously the general principle that pupils are to be educated in accordance with the wishes of their parents and enhance the responsibility of young people themselves for their own learning. We need to make it possible for each of them to have something to show for the years of compulsory schooling, something that will give parents, teachers and employers an indication of capacity, achievement and ambition.

This would mean a radical change in the schools, but one for which there is already considerable experience. Already there have been many successful experiments, both practical and academic, in reporting and recording the outcomes of education.[6] Some teachers (though too few yet) have used the opportunity of CSE Mode III to create courses which relate to their own pupils. What is needed now is an indication that initiatives by schools to build on this experience would be nationally welcome.

One example of what might be done is given in the book by Burgess and Adams (see reference 6). It rests on making a reality of the choices which pupils are at present asked to make at the end of the third year of secondary school. Instead of giving them the passive choice between predetermined sets of options, there could be a serious period in which young people were asked to plan their own programmes. This would involve taking stock of their present position and indicating what they wished to be able to do by the end of compulsory schooling, two years later. This would present them with a problem of how to get from where they were to where they wanted to be, and the solution to the problem would be the course of study they proposed to follow. The process of negotiating a programme of study in this way, in which pupils, parents and teachers can all be engaged, would itself be highly educative. It, or something like it, is essential if we are to make a reality of the aspiration to meet individual needs or parents' wishes.

There is no doubt that such a development is possible within the schools. Pupils, parents and teachers are alike capable of it. To make it possible, however, there has to be action by the public authorities, and action in the reverse direction from the present tendency to unify examination systems and centralise control of a 'core' curriculum. What is required of the Secretary of State, acting nationally, is to end a visible evil (in this case sixteen plus examinations), not to consult endlessly in order to impose an imagined good.

Fortunately, the means for doing this are also readily available, and there has been long experience of them in further and higher education. The history of this development is instructive. When new university colleges were founded at the beginning and middle of this century, they were not at first allowed to offer their own degrees but had instead to offer external degrees of the University of London. This device, which was ostensibly designed to maintain standards, was quickly seen to be stultifying. Every university college sought to escape the 'tutelage' of the University of London. Since all British universities have been autonomous, standards have been maintained by different methods, largely by the exchange of external examiners.

Experience in maintained colleges has been different. Ever since 1922 there have been various devices (like the National Certificate scheme and the Council for National Academic Awards, CNAA) through which individual colleges have created their own courses, based on the needs of particular groups of students or particular local industries. These courses have then been given national recognition by a process which has come to be known as 'validation'. Even today the degree courses which are offered in polytechnics and other colleges of further education are all created by the institutions themselves and then validated by the CNAA. Each college prepares a submission to the Council which it then defends before a visiting party. This process not only greatly improves the submissions that are made, but offers the students, staff and the community at large some assurance of the programmes' worth.

It is this principle that should be introduced into schools. The necessary radical changes required in the *content* of education cannot come through external direction, whether by core curricula or external examination. They can come only through local initiative nationally validated. Education in a social democracy demands that validation should replace examination.

Again fortunately, the beginnings of a validating structure already exist. Every school has a governing body, and every governing body has responsibility for the curriculum. This responsibility can best be exercised not, as the Taylor Committee suggested, by removing from the staff of schools the responsibility for setting the schools' objectives but by being the body which arranges the initial validation of programmes proposed by individual pupils and their teachers. What it would then be left for the Secretary of State to do is establish a way in which these local arrangements can be recognised as having a national validity.

Education has hitherto presented problems for politicians. They dimly recognise that it is the *content* of education that is important, rather than any system. They also dimly suspect that central attempts to determine this content, whatever the prior consultation and agreement, must end in triviality and vacuity. This does not mean that education is or can be outside politics, but it does suggest that progress will be made only by recognising where various kinds of decisions and actions are apt. It has been the purpose of this contribution to show how progress in education can be achieved in the kind of society desired by social democrats.

Notes

1 **In Memoriam: I** Dick Leonard
 1 C. A. R. Crosland, *The Future of Socialism*, Jonathan Cape, 1956, pp. 521–2.
 2 *Ibid*, p. 524.

3 **Crosland's Socialism** David Lipsey
 1 C. Welch, 'Crosland Reconsidered', *Encounter*, June 1979.
 2 See e.g. A. W. Benn, *Prospects*, AUEW (TASS), 1979.
 3 D. Marquand, 'Inquest on a Movement', *Encounter*, July 1979.
 4 C. A. R. Crosland, *The Future of Socialism*, Jonathan Cape, 1956.
 5 C. A. R. Crosland, *The Conservative Enemy*, Jonathan Cape, 1962.
 6 C. A. R. Crosland, *Socialism Now and other essays*, Jonathan Cape, 1974.
 7 *Socialism Now, op cit*, p. 15.
 8 *Ibid*, p. 43.
 9 *Ibid*, p. 18.
 10 *Ibid*, p. 18.
 11 C. A. R. Crosland, *Britain's Economic Problem*, Jonathan Cape, 1953.
 12 *The Conservative Enemy, op cit*, p. 12.
 13 *The Future of Socialism, op cit*, p. 414.
 14 *Ibid*, p. 285.
 15 Anthony Crosland, *Social Democracy in Europe*, Fabian Tract 438, Fabian Society, 1975.
 16 *The Future of Socialism, op cit*, p. 383.
 17 *Ibid*, p. 57.
 18 Reprinted in *Socialism Now, op cit*, pp. 78–9.

19 In *A Social Democratic Britain*, Fabian Society, 1971, and *Protecting the Environment*, 1972, both reprinted in *Socialism Now*, *op cit*.

20 *Socialism Now, op cit*, p. 18.

21 Philip M. Williams, *Hugh Gaitskell*, Jonathan Cape, 1979.

22 C. A. R. Crosland, *The British Economy in 1965*, Hugh Gaitskell Memorial Lecture, University of Nottingham, 1965.

23 See *Socialism Now, op cit*, p. 104.

24 R. W. Bacon and W. A. Eltis, *Britain's Economic Problem: Too Few Producers*, Macmillan, 1976.

25 See *Sunday Times*, 22 May 1977.

26 *Socialism Now, op cit*, p. 47.

27 C. A. R. Crosland, 'The battle for the public purse', *Guardian*, 26 March 1976.

28 *Guardian, ibid.*

29 E. Luard, *Socialism without the State*, Macmillan, 1979.

30 G. Radice, *Community Socialism*, Fabian Tract 464, Fabian Society, 1979.

31 D. Marquand, *op cit*.

32 *The Conservative Enemy, op cit*, p. 227.

33 *Socialism Now, op cit*, p. 89.

34 'Socialists in a Dangerous World', reprinted in *Socialism Now, op cit*, p. 69.

35 See *The Future of Socialism, op cit*, chapter 5.

36 *Socialism Now, op cit*, p. 46.

37 *The Future of Socialism, op cit*, p. 105.

38 *Socialism Now, op cit*, p. 23.

39 *The Future of Socialism, op cit*, p. 113.

40 *Socialism Now, op cit*, p. 15.

41 *Social Democracy in Europe, op cit*, pp. 2–3.

42 *The Conservative Enemy, op cit*, p. 57.

43 Reprinted in *Socialism Now, op cit*, p. 68.

44 *Ibid*, p. 53.

45 *The Future of Socialism, op cit*, p. 520.

46 *Socialism Now, op cit*, p. 89.

47 *The Conservative Enemy, op cit*, p. 122.

48 *Ibid*, p. 127.

49 *Ibid*, p. 134.

50 *The Future of Socialism, op cit*, p. 524.

4 Labour and the Voters Dick Leonard

1 C. A. R. Crosland, *The Conservative Enemy*, Jonathan Cape, 1962, p. 144. Reprinted from *Can Labour Win?*, Fabian Tract 324, Fabian Society, 1960.

2 David Butler and Michael Pinto-Duschinsky, *The British General Election of 1970*, Macmillan, 1971, p. 190.

3 Kristi Andersen, 'Generation, Partisan Shift and Realignment: A Glance Back at the New Deal', in N. H. Nie, S. Verba and J. R. Petrocik, *The Changing American Voter*, Harvard University Press, 1977, pp. 74-95. See, particularly, the chart on p. 83.

4 David Butler and Donald Stokes, *Political Change in Britain*, second edition, Macmillan, 1974.

5 *Ibid*, pp. 39-47.

6 See Ivor Crewe, Bo Särlvik and James Alt, 'Partisan Realignment in Britain 1964-74', *British Journal of Political Science*, volume 7, number 2, 1977, pp. 129-90. This article was summarised and additional data added in 'What future for Britain's two-party system?', *The Economist*, 11 March 1978.

7 See, for example, David Butler and Denis Kavanagh, *The British General Election of October 1974*, Macmillan, 1975, pp. 244-5.

8 Crewe, Särlvik and Alt, *op cit*, p. 152.

9 The figures have not yet been published, but I am grateful to Professor Crewe for letting me have this information in advance of the publication of the book which he and his colleagues are writing on the 1979 general election.

10 Anthony King, 'Labour voters give Tories the nod', *Observer*, 22 April 1979.

11 See, for example, the account of the genesis of the nationalisation proposals implemented by the 1945 government in Samuel H. Beer, *Modern British Politics*, Faber and Faber, 1965, pp. 153-87.

12 Daniel Patrick Moynihan has drawn a graphic contrast from the Far East which is not without relevance, though he undoubtedly ignores certain extraneous advantages which Singapore possesses. He writes in his book about the United Nations, *A Dangerous Place* (Secker and Warburg, 1979, pp. 21-2): 'At the outset of the Second World War there were three great cities on the Bay of Bengal more alike than great cities usually are. Each had been founded by the British East India Company, and each was very much part of an international, trading, English speaking world. A generation later the first, Calcutta, had become a necropolis, city of the dead and dying. Vast, putrefying, forsaken. The second, Rangoon, had ceased to be a city, and was rapidly reverting to the village it had once been ... The third city, Singapore, very possibly had the highest urban standard of living in the

world ... Something had made the difference. And what was it if not a rational liberalism in economic affairs?'

13 For example, a MORI poll, reported at some length in *The Economist*, 10 January 1976, pp. 13 *et seq.*

14 Butler and Stokes, *op cit*, p. 198.

15 Dingle Foot, 'Why I joined the party with the human touch', *The Times*, 28 September 1974.

16 *Gallup Political Index*, Report number 225, May 1979, pp. 8–9.

17 Hans L. Zetterberg, 'The Swedish Election 1976', mimeographed paper read to the Ninth World Congress of Sociology in Uppsala, 14–19 August 1978, p. 15.

18 Anthony Crosland, 'Labour and "Populism" ', reprinted in *Socialism Now and other essays, op cit*, p. 100.

5 Social Democracy and the International Economy
I. M. D. Little

1 But extensive public ownership of land was advocated. This, of course, is not incompatible with individuals also having extensive rights in that land. Ownership is not a simple concept. The rights of a long leaseholder may include sale and bequest, and can come quite close to 'ownership' especially where it becomes politically almost unthinkable not to renew the lease of a sitting tenant.

2 C. A. R. Crosland, *The Future of Socialism*, Jonathan Cape, 1956, p. 29.

3 I use the term 'organised employees' here to indicate (a) that I am referring to professional associations as well as trade unions, and (b) that employees may exert power other than through official union action. But employees cannot exert power without some concerted action, which implies some organisation. I shall also use the term 'organised labour' in the same sense. Doctors, solicitors, estate agents, airline pilots are 'labour' in this sense.

4 In 1975, OECD output was lower than in 1973; that of the non-oil developing countries was about $3\frac{1}{2}$ per cent higher. Since 1975, the OECD area has again been in trade deficit, while the total deficit of the developing world has been reduced.

5 South Korea is an extreme example. Despite her heavy dependence on imported oil and on exports to OECD countries, her growth did not fall below 8 per cent in the recession. As in Brazil, inflation was high and also accelerated. But inflation can be more easily tolerated by governments which are not democratic.

6 W. H. Corden, I. M. D. Little, M. F. G. Scott, *Import Controls versus Devaluation and Britain's Economic Prospects*, Trade Policy Research Centre, 1975.

7 For a discussion and references, see Robert Solomon, *The International Monetary System 1945–1976*, Harper and Row, 1977.

8 cf Ronald I. McKinnon, *Money and Capital in Economic Development*, The Brookings Institution, Washington DC, 1973, chapter 8.

9 *The Future of Socialism, op cit*, p. 448.

10 *Ibid*, pp. 450–1.

11 *Ibid*, p. 451.

12 *Socialism Now and other essays*, Jonathan Cape, 1974, pp. 56–7.

13 Anthony Crosland, *Social Democracy in Europe*, Fabian Tract 438, Fabian Society, 1975, p. 11. This pamphlet was based on a lecture given to a seminar of members of the Costa Rican government. In all the developing world, Costa Rica has perhaps the highest claim to being socially democratic. Sri Lanka is another, perhaps the only other, claimant.

14 In fact, in the Fabian Tract (note 13 above), Tony Crosland presented inflation as a threat only to growth. But this was underplaying the issue. It is surely also a threat to democracy.

15 See, for example, *Socialism Now, op cit*, p. 29, where he pointed out that the trade unions 'wholly defeated the Labour Government, and effectively frustrated the Tory Government, in major confrontations over industrial relations legislation'.

16 *The Future of Socialism, op cit*, p. 12.

17 There are now many studies showing that, when increased exports are taken into account, the net number of jobs lost through the entry of labour-intensive manufactures from developing countries is remarkably small. The effect on developing countries is more serious, because the relative labour intensity of, say, garments in relation to steel, is greater in the developing countries.

6 The Fixing of Money Rates of Pay Professor James Meade

1 See Tibor Scitovsky, 'Market Power and Inflation', *Economica*, August 1978.

2 Income from employment (employed plus self-employed) as a percentage of Gross Domestic Product less capital consumption, average 1975–77.

3 See OECD Report of Expert Group on *Wage and Labour Mobility*, 1965; and W. B. Reddaway, 'Wage Flexibility and

the Distribution of Labour', *Lloyds Bank Review*, October 1959.

4 C. A. Pissardies, 'The Role of Relative Wages and Excess Demand in the Sectorial Flow of Labour', *Review of Economic Studies*, October 1978.

5 I am greatly encouraged in this view by the fact that it was the view of those ancient protagonists of the trade union movement, Sidney and Beatrice Webb, who in 1902 after a general discussion of the functions of the trade unions continued with their analysis as follows: 'So far democracy may be expected to look on complacently at the fixing, by mutual agreement between the directors of industry and the manual workers, of special rates for wages for special classes. But this use of the method of collective bargaining for the advantage of particular sections – this "freedom of contract" between capitalists and wage earners – will become increasingly subject to the fundamental condition that the business of the community must not be interfered with. When in the course of bargaining there ensues a deadlock – when the workmen strike or the employers lock out – many other interests are affected than those of the parties concerned. We may accordingly expect that, whenever an industrial dispute reaches a certain magnitude, a democratic state will, in the interests of the community as a whole, not scruple to intervene and settle the points at issue by an authoritative fiat. The growing impatience with industrial dislocation will, in fact, where collective bargaining breaks down, lead to its supersession by some form of compulsory arbitration.'

7 Socialism and Incomes Policy William McCarthy

1 C. A. R. Crosland, *The Future of Socialism*, Jonathan Cape, 1956, p. 524.

2 C. A. R. Crosland, *Socialism Now and other essays*, Jonathan Cape, 1974, p. 58.

3 The main reason concerns the crucial role played by certain key wage bargains at various stages in the round; see W. McCarthy, *Wage Inflation and Wage Leadership*, EESRI, Dublin, 1975.

4 See W. McCarthy, 'The Politics of Incomes Policy' in D. Butler and A. H. Halsey (ed.), *Policy and Politics*, Macmillan, 1978.

8 Labour and the Unions Giles Radice MP

1 C. A. R. Crosland, 'Industrial Democracy and Workers'

Control', *The Conservative Enemy*, Jonathan Cape, 1962, pp. 217–27.

2 C. A. R. Crosland, *The Future of Socialism*, Jonathan Cape, 1956, p. 349.
3 *The Conservative Enemy*, op cit, p. 218.
4 C. A. R. Crosland, *Socialism Now and other essays*, Jonathan Cape, 1974, p. 29.
5 *The Future of Socialism*, op cit, p. 349.
6 Hugh Clegg, *Industrial Democracy and Nationalisation*, Blackwell, 1951.
7 *Socialism Now*, op cit, p. 52.
8 *Ibid*, pp. 104–5.
9 *The Conservative Enemy*, op cit, p. 157.
10 *Socialism Now*, op cit, pp. 56–7.
11 W. E. J. McCarthy and N. D. Ellis, *Management by Agreement*, Hutchinson, 1973, pp. 102–3.
12 *Employment Gazette*, HMSO, Dec. 1979 and Feb. 1980.
13 Giles Radice, *Community Socialism*, Fabian Tract 464, Fabian Society, 1979.
14 *Socialism Now*, op cit, p. 83.
15 Giles Radice, *The Industrial Democrats*, Allen and Unwin, 1978, p. 214.
16 See, for example, Robert Taylor, 'Inequality at Work' in Nick Bosanquet and Peter Townsend (ed.), *Labour and Equality: a Fabian Study of Labour in Power, 1974–79*, Heinemann, 1980.

9 Democratic Socialism and Equality Professor Raymond Plant

1 Michael Oakeshott, *Rationalism in Politics*, Methuen, 1962.
2 Fred Hirsch, *The Social Limits to Growth*, Routledge and Kegan Paul, 1977, p. 182.
3 Robert Nozick, *Anarchy, State and Utopia*, Blackwell, 1975.
4 Edward Bernstein, *Evolutionary Socialism*, Schocken Books, New York, 1961. Reference may also be made to R. Plant, 'Continental Social and Political Thought 1900–18' in C. B. Cox and A. E. Dyson (ed.), *The Twentieth Century Mind*, Oxford University Press, 1972.
5 C. A. R. Crosland, *The Future of Socialism*, revised edition, Jonathan Cape, 1964, p. 137.
6 C. A. R. Crosland, *Socialism Now and other essays*, Jonathan Cape, 1974, p. 15.
7 See Hirsch, *The Social Limits to Growth*, op cit. Hirsch's account is crucial because it stresses the endemic nature of scarcity not

because of the supposed exhaustion of natural resources but because the positional nature of some goods means that the more they are consumed the less they are 'goods'. When all stand on tiptoe none may see; many social goods are like this. They have an intrinsic positional dimension, not everyone can consume them, whatever the rate of growth. Because of this, it is of vital importance that those who do consume positional goods do so legitimately in the eyes of those who do not. Social scarcity of this sort is going to give rise to problems about social justice and equality however much the standard of living generally increases. Hirsch's subtle argument puts into doubt some of the optimism of the final pages of *The Future of Socialism*. (See also chapter 10, note 1.)

8 *Socialism Now, op cit*, p. 15.
9 Steven Lukes, *Essays in Social Theory*, Macmillan, 1977. See particularly the essay 'Socialism and Equality'.
10 *The Future of Socialism, op cit*, p. 150.
11 C. Jencks, *Inequality*, Penguin, 1974, p. 25.
12 Frank Parkin, *Class, Inequality and Political Order*, Palladin, 1971, p. 183.
13 *The Future of Socialism, op cit*, p. 168; see also p. 144, 'It seems unjust and unwise to penalise people to quite such a prodigious extent for inherited characteristics.'
14 *Socialism Now, op cit*, p. 15.
15 *The Future of Socialism, op cit*, p. 145.
16 Lukes, *op cit*, p. 140.
17 Ian Gilmour, *Inside Right*, Quartet Books, 1977.
18 W. G. Runciman, *Relative Deprivation and Social Justice*, Penguin, 1972.
19 Colin Welch in 'Crosland Reconsidered', *Encounter*, January 1979.
20 *Socialism Now, op cit*, p. 249.
21 John Goldthorpe, 'Social Inequality and Social Integration', in Wedderburn (ed.), *Poverty, Inequality and Class Structure*, Cambridge University Press, 1974, p. 228.
22 Irving Kristol, 'When Virtue Loses All Her Loveliness', in I. Kristol and D. Bell (ed.), *Capitalism Today*, Humanities Press, New York, 1971.
23 *The Future of Socialism, op cit*, p. 140.
24 John Vaizey in *Encounter*, August 1977, 'Remembering Anthony Crosland', p. 87. Vaizey sees this feature of Crosland's work as indebted to the analysis of moral judgment developed by A. J. Ayer, in *Language, Truth and Logic*, Gollancz, 1946.

25 *Socialism Now, passim.*
26 Stuart Hampshire, 'A New Philosophy for the Just Society', *New York Review of Books*, 24 February 1972.
27 See Vaizey and Bell in 'Anthony Crosland and Socialism', *Encounter*, August 1977.
28 Samuel Brittan, *The Economic Consequences of Democracy*, Temple Smith, 1977, p. 272.
29 John Goldthorpe, 'Social Inequality and Social Integration', in Wedderburn (ed.), *op cit*, p. 231.
30 John Rawls, *A Theory of Justice*, The Clarendon Press, 1972, p. 105. I have tried to discuss these themes in 'Community: Concept, Conception and Ideology', in *Politics and Society*, Volume 8, number 1, 1978, and in *Political Philosophy and Social Welfare*, Routledge and Kegan Paul, 1980.

10 The Place of Public Expenditure in Socialist Thought
Colin Crouch

1 A sophisticated version of this argument can be derived from Fred Hirsch's thesis of positional goods (*The Social Limits to Growth*, Routledge and Kegan Paul, 1976). He argues that there are many goods which can by their nature be enjoyed only by a minority, and that no improvements in the general standard of living can do anything to change this. To give just one example, not everyone can have a house overlooking the sea. Some of these situations are incapable of any remedy – no amount of educational reform will lead to everyone's child being top of the class – but others can be alleviated if there is communal provision of some of the goods in question, rather than private ownership. Thus, it is far more intolerable for those of us without houses overlooking the sea if the whole coast is pre-empted by private building plots and much better if stretches of it are left open to public access. In many cases only publicly financed provision can provide this kind of access.
2 Not all public spending has this effect; for example, taking an industry into public ownership involves public (capital) spending, but does not necessarily have any effect on demand.
3 This is not entirely true: the extent to which demand is boosted will depend on the marginal propensity to consume of the initial recipients of the spending; but this is largely a technical question not immediately related to political principle.
4 M. Kalecki, 'Political aspects of full employment', *Political Quarterly*, number 14, 1943.

5 B. Semmel, *Imperialism and Social Reform*, Allen and Unwin, 1960.
6 I. Gough, *The Political Economy of the Welfare State*, Macmillan, 1979.
7 In many ways this reluctance to accept a large state role was peculiar to countries industrialising in the Anglo-Saxon pattern, with a long period of economic liberalism. In France, Scandinavia and countries within the German political tradition, the state was more active in industrial development from the outset. As a result, public spending of various kinds was possible at an early stage; the legacy of this can still be seen in the high spending levels of governments in these countries, irrespective of contemporary political complexion. See, for example, Colin Crouch's 'The conditions for trade union wage restraint', in L. N. Lindberg and C. S. Maier (ed.), *The Politics and Sociology of Global Inflation and Recession*, The Brookings Institution, Washington DC, forthcoming.
8 T. H. Marshall, *Citizenship and Social Class*, Cambridge University Press, 1950.
9 J. Harris, *William Beveridge: a Biography*, Oxford University Press, 1977; D. E. Moggridge, *Keynes*, Macmillan and Fontana, 1976; M. Stewart, *Keynes and After*, Penguin, 1967.
10 When government assistance to industry is taken into account, private enterprises in Britain have in fact been net *gainers* from the balance between taxation and public spending for many years. However, businessmen may still claim to respond to the effect of taxation on their personal incomes.
11 D. Howell, *British Social Democracy*, Croom Helm, 1976.
12 C. A. R. Crosland, *The Future of Socialism*, Jonathan Cape, 1956.
13 J. K. Galbraith, *The Affluent Society*, Hamish Hamilton, 1958.
14 David Butler and Donald Stokes, *Political Change in Britain*, Macmillan, second edition, 1974, pp. 296–300.
15 It is not always clear whether the central concern of recent reactionary writers is with individual freedom and natural rights – an essentially moral commitment – or with the technical criterion of efficiency. The two are not necessarily compatible. This issue really needs sustained philosophical analysis. For present purposes, comment will be restricted to a small number of critical observations, some of which are directed to the moral, others to the technical, versions of the doctrine.
16 Anthony Downs, *An Economic Theory of Democracy*, Harper and Row, 1957.

17 J. Buchanan and R. Wagner, *Democracy in Deficit: the Political Legacy of Lord Keynes*, Academic Press, New York, 1977; also, S. Brittan, 'The Economic Contradictions of Democracy', *British Journal of Political Science*, 1975.

18 For a good discussion on these lines, see B. Barry, 'The Inflation of Political Economy: a Study of the Political Theory of Some Economists', in Lindberg and Maier (ed.), *op cit*.

19 Downs's arguments apply most clearly to economies in the Anglo-American tradition. As pointed out in note 7 above, other political traditions have experienced less difficulty in achieving high levels of public expenditure – and have also found it easier to levy the taxation to pay for them.

20 By 'internal' rationality I mean the clarity, objectivity and rule-governed nature of the process, and recognise implicitly that the substantive outcomes of the market are often irrational.

21 W. D. Nordhaus, 'The Political Business Cycle', *Review of Economic Studies*, number 42, 1975.

22 R. W. Bacon and W. A. Eltis, *Britain's Economic Problem: Too Few Producers*, Macmillan, 1976. The thesis of this was refuted by B. Moore and J. Rhodes, 'The Relative Decline of the UK Manufacturing Sector', *Economic Policy Review*, number 2, 1976; and by Nick Bosanquet, *Economic Strategy: a New Social Contract*, Fabian Society, 1977.

23 See S. Blank, 'Britain: the Politics of Foreign Economic Policy, the Domestic Economy and the Problem of Pluralist Stagnation', *International Organisation*, 1977, Volume 31, number 4; F. Longstretch, 'The City, Industry and Economic Planning', in Colin Crouch (ed.), *State and Economy in Contemporary Capitalism*, Croom Helm, 1979; S. Strange, *Sterling and British Policy*, Oxford University Press, 1971.

24 J. M. Keynes, *The General Theory of Employment, Interest and Money*, Macmillan, 1936; see also A. Martin, 'The Dynamics of Change in a Keynesian Political Economy: the Swedish Case and its Implications', in Colin Crouch (ed.), *op cit*.

25 Alan Budd, *The Politics of Economic Planning*, Fontana, 1978; and J. Leruez, *Economic Planning and Politics in Britain*, Martin Robertson, 1976.

26 This has not been true of the most recent contributions to Labour Left economic policy, especially the work of Stuart Holland. See, for example, *The Socialist Challenge*, Quartet Books, 1975.

27 A. Martin, *op cit*.

28 *Ibid.*
29 France is, however, a country of high public spending levels.
30 A. H. Halsey, *Change in British Society: based on the Reith Lectures*, Oxford University Press, 1978.
31 R. H. S. Crossman, 'The Role of the Volunteer in a Modern Social Service', in A. H. Halsey (ed.), *Traditions of Social Policy*, Blackwell, 1976.
32 A. H. Halsey, *op cit*, p. 85.
33 Norman Dennis, *People and Planning: the Sociology of Housing in Sunderland*, Faber and Faber, 1970; and *Public Participation and Planners' Blight*, Faber and Faber, 1972.
34 R. H. Titmuss, *The Gift Relationship*, Allen and Unwin, 1970.
35 Fred Hirsch, *op cit*.
36 See, for example, A Fabian Group, *Can Tenants Run Housing ?*, Fabian Society, 1980.
37 Evan Luard, *Socialism without the State*, Macmillan, 1979, and *Socialism at the Grass Roots*, Fabian Society, 1980; Giles Radice, *Community Socialism*, Fabian Society, 1979.
38 For some studies of the possibilities and limitations, see: C. Clarke, 'Community Councils: Power to the People?', in Colin Crouch (ed.), *British Political Sociology Yearbook*, Volume III: *Participation in Politics*, Croom Helm, 1977; G. Smith, R. Lees and P. Topping, 'Participation and the Home Office Community Development Project', in Colin Crouch (ed.), *ibid*; Stephen Hatch and Howard Glennerster (ed.), *Positive Discrimination and Inequality*, Fabian Society, 1974, especially G. Green's chapter, 'Towards Community Power'; A. Heath, 'Sociology and Community Work: the Problem of Participation', in P. Evans (ed.), *Community Work*, Arc Publications, 1971.
39 C. A. R. Crosland, *Socialism Now and other essays*, Jonathan Cape, 1974, p. 67.
40 *Ibid*, p. 90.
41 Stemming from the work of A. O. Hirschman, in his study of problems of state owned enterprises in Latin America, there has recently been considerable interest among political scientists in the difference between the alternative modes of 'exit' (the market and analogous processes, where one expresses preference by 'taking or leaving' an offered service) and 'voice' (where one participates in decision making within a service which one is incapable of 'leaving'). Only too often public services eliminate the chances of 'exit' without providing scope for 'voice'. See A. O. Hirschman, *Exit, Voice and Loyalty*, Harvard University Press, 1970.

11 Liberty and the Left Professor Maurice Peston

1 C. A. R. Crosland, *The Future of Socialism*, Jonathan Cape, 1956, p. 104.
2 *Ibid*, pp. 247–8.
3 Clement Attlee, *The Labour Party in Perspective*, Gollancz, 1937, pp. 139–44.
4 Sydney Hook, *Commentary*, Volume 65, 1977.
5 Professor Arrow, *Commentary*, Volume 65, 1977.
6 Professor Glazer, *Commentary*, Volume 65, 1977.
7 Adam Ferguson, *Principles of Moral and Political Science*, 1792.

12 Democratic Socialism and Education Tyrrell Burgess

1 C. A. R. Crosland, *The Future of Socialism*, Jonathan Cape, 1956, p. 258.
2 John Raven, *Education, Values and Society*, H. K. Lewis, 1977.
3 *Ibid.*
4 R. H. Tawney, *The Radical Tradition*, Allen and Unwin, 1964, p. 168.
5 R. Held and A. Heim, 'Movement produced stimulation in the development of visually guided behaviour', *Journal of Comparative and Physiological Psychology*, Volume 56, pp. 872–6.
6 T. Burgess and E. Adams (ed.), *Outcomes of Education*, Macmillan Education, 1980.

The Authors

Tyrrell Burgess is Reader in the Philosophy of Social Institutions at the North East London Polytechnic. An ex-Director of the Advisory Centre for Education, he has worked for both *The Times Educational Supplement* and *New Society*. His books include *A Guide to English Schools* (1964), *Home and School* (1973), *Education After School* (1977) and (with Tony Travers) *Ten Billion Pounds* (1980). He was the Labour Candidate for Croydon South in the 1964 General Election.

Colin Crouch is Reader in sociology at LSE. He is the author of *The Student Revolt* (1970), *Class Conflict and the Industrial Relations Crisis* (1977) and *The Politics of Industrial Relations* (1979). A member of the Fabian Executive Committee 1969–78, he was Chairman of the Society in 1976.

Lord Donaldson was Minister for the Arts 1976–79, having previously served as Parliamentary Under Secretary in the Northern Ireland Office 1974–76. He is a former Director of the Royal Opera House, and Chairman of the National Association for the Care and Resettlement of Offenders.

Dick Leonard has been an assistant editor of *The Economist* since 1974 and is now based in Brussels, responsible for its coverage of the EEC. He was Labour MP for Romford 1970–74, when he acted as Anthony Crosland's PPS and edited his last book, *Socialism Now and other essays* (1974). He is the author or part-author of several books, including *Elections in Britain* (1968), *The Backbencher and Parliament* (1972), *Paying for Party Politics* (1973) and *The BBC Guide to Parliament* (1979). He is a former Assistant General Secretary and past Chairman of the Fabian Society.

David Lipsey is on the political staff of the *Sunday Times*. He was Political Adviser to Anthony Crosland from 1972 until his death and then served on the Prime Minister's staff until the May 1979 Election. He is a member of the Fabian Society's Executive Committee and Chairman of the General and Municipal Workers' Central London Branch.

I. M. D. Little is an international economist, serving most recently as Special Adviser to the International Bank for Reconstruction and Development. He succeeded Anthony Crosland as a Fellow of Trinity College, Oxford, in 1950, moved to Nuffield College in 1952 and was Deputy Director of the Economic Section of theTreasury from 1953-55. He became President of the OECD Development Centre from 1965-67 and Professor of the Economics of Underdeveloped Countries at Oxford from 1971-76. His publications include *A Critique of Welfare Economics* (1950) and *Project Analysis and Planning* (1974).

William McCarthy is a Fellow of Nuffield College, Oxford, and university lecturer in Industrial Relations. He was Research Director to the Donovan Commission, an adviser to the 1964-70 Labour Governments, and has served on many industrial arbitrations and committees of inquiry. His works include *The Closed Shop in Britain* (1964) and *Wage Inflation and Wage Leadership* (1975). He was made a Life Peer in 1975.

Professor James Meade, winner of the Nobel Prize for Economics in 1977, is a Fellow of Christ's College, Cambridge. His works include *The Economic Basis of a Durable Peace* (1940), *The Theory of International Economic Policy*, two vols (1951-55), *The Principles of Political Economy*, four vols (1965-76) and *The Intelligent Radical's Guide to Economic Policy* (1975). He recently chaired the Institute of Fiscal Studies' Inquiry into the UK Tax Structure.

Professor Maurice Peston is Professor of Economics at Queen Mary College, London. He was a member of the SSRC and chaired its economics committee 1976-79. He was Special Adviser to the Secretary of State for Education and Science 1974-75 and to the Secretary of State for Prices and Consumer Protection 1976-79. He is a former member of the Executive Committee of the Fabian Society.

Professor Raymond Plant is Professor of Politics at the University of Southampton, having been Senior Lecturer in Philosophy at the University of Manchester. His works include *Hegel* (1973), *Community and Ideology* (1974) and *Political Philosophy and Social Welfare* (1980). He is a member of the Grimsby Constituency Labour Party.

Giles Radice is Labour MP for Chester-le-Street and Chairman of the PLP Employment Group. He was formerly Head of Research at the General and Municipal Workers' Union. His publications, in addition to a number of Fabian pamphlets, include *Democratic Socialism* (1965), *More Power to the People* (1968) and *The Industrial Democrats* (1978). He is a member and past Chairman of the Executive Committee of the Fabian Society.

Index

Adams, E., 216
Advisory, Conciliation and Arbitration Service (ACAS), 130
aerospace industry, nationalisation of, 51
airports, third London airport, 13
Andersen, Kristi, 45
arbitration, wage rates, 101–3, 105–6
Argentina, 70
armed forces, *see* defence
Arrow, Kenneth, 190
Attlee, Clement, *The Labour Party in Perspective*, 187–9, 193–4
Austria, 52–3, 54, 125, 175

Bacon, R. W., 33, 34, 169
Bad Godesberg, 53
balance of payments, 22, 23, 32, 66–7, 69–70
banks, nationalisation of, 51
bargaining, *see* incomes
BBC, 158
Beckerman, Wilfred, 32
Bell, Daniel, *quoted*, 135
Benn, Tony, 21, 23
Bernstein, Edward, 137
Bevan, Aneurin, 31
Beveridge, Lord, 163, 164
Birnbaum, Norman, 138
Bismarck, Otto von, 161
Blatchford, Robert, 109
Boer War, 161
Bolshevik revolution, 159
Bosanquet, Nicholas, 170
Boyson, Rhodes, 185

Brazil, 66
Brecht, Bertolt, 59
Bretton Woods agreement, 67, 68
British Election Study, 47–8
British Empire, 161, 174
British Leyland, 76
Brittan, Samuel, 150
Bukharin, Nikolai, 35
Bullock Committee, 130
bureaucracy, 35–6, 56–7, 178–85
Burgess, Tyrrell, 2, 201–17
Butler, David, *Political Change in Britain*, 46, 47, 50
Butskellism, 165

Callaghan, James, 13; Crosland as possible successor to, 9; as Foreign Secretary, 14; and incomes policy, 113, 115; influence of voters on, 45; nationalisation, 51; opposition to *In Place of Strife*, 32–3; rejects freedom of information Bill, 58
Cambridge group, 66–7, 128
Can Labour Win?, 44
capital, labour co-operatives and, 96–8
Capital Gains Tax, 128
Capital Transfer Tax, 128
capitalism, 204–5; and democracy, 197–9; and individual liberty, 191, 192–3, 197–200; and inflation, 70; and public expenditure, 161–2, 164, 170–4; and scarcity, 108–9; and social democracy, 37; 64
Castle, Barbara, 32–3
Charity Organisation Society, 180

235

growth: and balance of payments, 23; control by monetary policies, 84; decline of, 22, 26–7; and equality, 10–11, 27, 37–8; and inflation, 29; means of achieving, 28–32; and nationalisation, 52; and public expenditure, 27, 34; and public ownership, 29, 30–1; rate of, 27–8
Guardian, 121

Halsey, A. H., 179, 180–1
Hampshire, Stuart, 148
Hayek, Friedrich August von, 136, 146, 147, 151, 197
Healey, Denis, 12
health care, 39, 160–1
Heath, Edward, 31, 53, 114, 119, 177
Heim, A., 215
Held, R., 215
higher education, 216–17
Hirsch, Fred, 136, 181
Holland, 52, 175, 189, 190
Hook, Sydney, 189
House of Lords, 188
housing, 35; council housing, 23, 176; sale of council houses, 49, 57–8, 169; tenants' rights, 36
Housing Finance Act (1972), 14, 41, 123
human rights, 55–8
Hume, David, 146, 147
Hungary, 190

Iceland, 14
import controls, 32, 66–7, 74, 111, 112, 115, 128
In Place of Strife, 33, 121
incentives, 142–3
incomes: arbitration, 101–3, 105–6; collective bargaining, 76–81, 129; comparability, 88–90; competition in the labour market, 92–5; corporate approach to fixing earnings, 99–100; decentralised settlements, 85–7; differentials, 83, 114, 128–9, 152–3; 'going rate' of increase, 112–13, 114; labour co-operatives, 95–9; low pay, 91–2, 114–15, 129; methods of fixing rates of pay, 75–106; and money supply, 68–9; productivity and wage fixing, 90–1; redistribution of, 27; social wage, 34, 111; unearned, 79–80, 128

incomes policy, 100; Crosland's view of, 38–9, 71–2, 121; and equality, 77–8, 146; for growth, 85; and import controls, 32; and inflation, 32, 75; Labour party and, 75, 107, 110–12, 115, 124, 126–7; and low pay, 23; sanctions, 103–5; and socialism, 107–16
Independent Commission into the Co-operative Movement, 38, 118
India, 160
individual liberty, 55–8, 63, 186–200, 204–5
industrial democracy, 35–6, 119–20, 129–30
Industrial Relations Act, 55, 123
industry: co-operatives, 37, 38–9; government intervention, 127–8; and inflation, 70; management, 10, 30; productivity and wage fixing, 90–1; staff status, 130–1; work sharing, 128; *see also* nationalisation
inflation, 22; cost-push, 68, 69, 70; and economic growth, 29; incomes policies and, 32, 75; and public expenditure, 70, 166, 167–8, 173; trade unions and, 123; and unemployment, 72–3, 82, 85; wage-push, 66–7, 72–3, 81–2, 83; wage rates, 27, 30; and world recession, 65–74
Institute of Economic Affairs, 43
Institute of Personnel Management (IPM), 112
insurance companies, nationalisation of, 51
International Monetary Fund (IMF), 23–4, 32
investment: and inflation, 72–3; public expenditure and, 169–74
Ireland, 190
Italy, 73, 74, 158, 169

Jackson, Tom, 77
Japan, 13, 174
Jay, Douglas, 148
Jenkins, Peter, 121–2
Jenkins, Roy, 13, 25, 121–2
job creation, 127, 158, 159
job evaluation, 89–90
Johnson, Lyndon B., 167
Jones, Jack, 25
Joseph, Keith, 180
justice, social, *see* equality